Book Two

A New Scottish History

Eric Melvin
MA, MEd
Assistant Head Teacher
Tynecastle High School
Edinburgh

Ian Gould
MA
formerly Principal
Teacher of History
Broxburn High School

John Thompson
MA, PhD
formerly Rector
Madras College
St Andrews

John Murray

Printed in Hong Kong by
Wing King Tong Co Ltd

British Library Cataloguing in Publication Data

Melvin, Eric
  A new Scottish history.
  Book 2
  1. Scotland—History
  I. Title   II. Thompson, John
  III. Gould, Ian
  941.1   DA760

  ISBN 0-7195-3639-1

Foreword

A New Scottish History is the successor to *A Scottish History for Today*.
The change of title is indicative of the extensive revision that has been made.

There can be few teachers of history working in Scotland today who
have not been influenced by the original series—either as teachers or
pupils! The strengths of the books have clearly stood the test of time and
provide the foundations for the new series. The authors, Ian Gould and
John Thompson—themselves practising teachers—sought to produce
history books which presented Scotland's story against a wider background of international events. Each book was well illustrated with
photographs and with line drawings which dovetailed neatly with the
text. The text itself was clear and straightforward, and on occasions the
narrative was reinforced with extracts from poems and contemporary
sources. Indeed, the readability of the books was confirmed by the recent
Bulletin 4 of the Scottish Central Committee for the Social Subjects.

Since the publication of the original series, however, there have been
many developments—both in historical scholarship and in teaching
methodology. There have been changes, too, in school organisation with
the advent of comprehensive schools, a two-year common course and
mixed ability teaching—however defined!

Teachers have responded to these challenges with a variety of approaches
which has enabled history to grow and flourish in these changing climates.
Publishers, too, have responded with a range of topic and source books
to service the new methods. The authors of *A New Scottish History* are convinced, however, that a need exists for a chronological account of Scotland's story which represents both the best traditions of history teaching
and the developments which have taken place since the original books
were published. Such an approach is in keeping with the aims of history
teaching established in Curriculum Paper 15 of the Consultative Committee on the Curriculum.

A New Scottish History has been written in two volumes, each correspond-
ing to one year's work. Book One deals with the question of what history
is and how historians work before looking at events up to the reign of
Mary Queen of Scots. Book Two progresses from the reign of James
VI and I and concludes with an examination of the historical origins of
particular contemporary problems.

The original concept of placing Scottish events in a wider historical
context has been maintained. So, too, has the extensive use of illustrations
linked closely to the text. Now, however, photographs have almost
completely replaced line drawings and it is hoped that Jim Proudfoot's

evocative reconstructions will all the more dramatically help to fire the imagination of pupils. The increasing use of contemporary sources in S1 and S2 is reflected both in the text and in the assignments at the end of the major chapters.

Through their reading, writing and oral work pupils are encouraged to develop the important skills of inquiry, interpretation and reconstruction. Equally important, however, are the unique contributions which history can make to the development of empathy in pupils and to a growing awareness of the richness of their cultural heritage.

It is in this spirit that *A New Scottish History* has been written.

Eric Melvin

Acknowledgements

Without the perspective provided by the passage of time, any attempt to explain our recent past in historical terms is fraught with difficulty. The authors are therefore particularly grateful for advice and criticism from many quarters: in particular they record their thanks to Mary Bryden, Alistair Docherty, Jack Hamilton, Frank McGrail, Lynda Melvin, Gavin Sprott, Ann Stone and Don Winford for their help and encouragement. The responsibility for what is written, however, remains with the authors.

Alongside the problems of teaching modern history there are advantages: not least the background and insight it affords to an understanding of our contemporary world. For those teachers prepared to undertake the challenge, there are two valuable assets to be utilised.

First, there is the wealth of photographic evidence available for study. This visual reinforcement of the spoken and written word develops skills and challenges the emotions. Any selection of photographs is inevitably personal and subjective, but the authors have included some well-known illustrations in the belief that—just as there are historic events which merit study—young readers should be able to examine how the camera has recorded particular moments in these events.

The identification, selection and collection of the illustrations throughout the book has been a major task and expert help has been greatly valued. In particular the authors express their gratitude to Mr Stuart Maxwell and Miss Mary Bryden of the National Museum of Antiquities of Scotland; Mrs Bishop of the National Library of Scotland; Miss Sheena McDougall of the Edinburgh Room, Edinburgh District Council Central Library; Mr Nick Jones of the BBC Hulton Picture Library; Miss Sheila Gill of the Scottish National Portrait Gallery and Miss Isbister of the Royal Commission on Ancient and Historic Monuments of Scotland.

The second asset for the teacher of modern history is the ready availability of first-hand historical evidence. Most teachers are aware of eyewitness accounts for some events which may be gleaned from family, friends, colleagues and the families of pupils themselves. Locating, recording and working with these accounts is a particularly rewarding teaching experience.

The source extracts at the end of some later chapters have been collected in this way and the authors express their indebtedness to the late Magnus McIntyre Hood, the late Ian Melvin, Eric Melvin senior, Jim Pearson and Mrs Lynda Melvin (née Napier) for individual contributions.

The authors have attached considerable importance to the inclusion of a reliable and helpful glossary. The definitions on pages 264 to 267 are based on entries in dictionaries published by Chambers of Edinburgh. To them the authors express their thanks: in particular to Chambers' Chief Dictionaries Editor, Mrs E. M. Kirkpatrick, for her help and advice.

Finally, the authors are anxious to record their debt of gratitude to Mr Kenneth Pinnock of John Murray. His professional help and friendship have now extended over twenty-five years: from the conception of the original series to this, its successor.

The authors express their thanks to the following who have kindly permitted the reproduction of copyright photographs:

Aberdeen City Libraries (p. 71); Aerofilms Ltd (p. 148 (top)); Society of Antiquaries of London (p. 14); Ashmolean Museum, Oxford (pp. 26, 27, 29); BBC Hulton Picture Library (pp. 57 (top), 65, 69, 81, 87, 88, 93, 94 (top), 95, 96, 101, 115, 118, 124 (bottom), 127 (top), 130, 132, 142, 144, 145, 148 (bottom), 149, 153, 154, 159 (top), 162, 164, 165, 170, 171, 173, 174, 175, 176, 178, 179, 182, 183, 184, 185, 186, 187, 188 (top), 199, 200 (bottom), 201, 205, 206, 207 (bottom), 209, 210, 211 (bottom), 212, 213, 217 (bottom), 218, 219, 220, 225, 237, 239, 245, 246 (bottom)); Barnaby's Picture Library (p. 215); British Library (pp. 17, 28, 30 (top), 38, 42 (bottom), 49, 77 (top), 103); The Syndics of Cambridge University Library (p. 168); Camera Press Ltd (pp. 247, 248, 249, 250, 252, 261); The Master and Fellows of Corpus Christi College, Cambridge (p. 7); The Chief Librarian, Edinburgh District Council (pp. 61, 100 (top), 107, 167); Edinburgh University Library (p. 63); Mary Evans Picture Library (pp. 13, 43, 98, 102, 146, 166, 196); City of Glasgow District Council (the Mitchell Library) (pp. 105, 106, 172); Glasgow University Library (p. 10 (top)); Imperial War Museum (pp. 155, 188 (bottom), 189, 190, 191, 193, 223, 224, 226, 227 (top), 228 (top), 231, 233); Keeper of the Records of Scotland (p. 4 (top)); Keystone Press Agency (pp. 157, 197, 217 (top), 229, 236, 240 (bottom), 241, 242, 254, 257, 260, 262); Museum of London (p. 156 (photo— John Freeman)); Clerk of the Records, House of Lords (p. 48); Mansell Collection (pp. 3, 10 (bottom), 12, 23, 25, 34, 36, 70, 79, 126, 131, 150, 151, 152, 159 (bottom), 203, 204, 207 (top)); Eric Melvin (pp. 70, 180); Metropolitan Museum of Art, New York (p. 129); National Museum of Antiquities of Scotland (pp. 4 (bottom), 42 (top), 64, 72, 73, 78, 98 (top)); National Army Museum (pp. 121, 137); National Coal Board (p. 92); Trustees of the National Library of Scotland (pp. 22, 32, 41 (bottom), 76, 77 (bottom), 100 (bottom), 110); National Maritime Museum, London (pp. 40, 135); National Portrait Gallery (pp. 11, 19, 20, 21, 30, 37, 94 (bottom), 99, 114, 119, 124 (top), 129); National Trust for Scotland (p. 2 (bottom)); Novosti Press Agency (pp. 198, 227 (bottom), 228 (bottom), 230, 235); Popperfoto (pp. 200 (top), 202, 211 (top), 216, 221, 238, 240 (top), 244, 246 (top), 251, 256, 258, 259, 263); The Press Association (pp. 5, 15); By Gracious Permission of Her Majesty the Queen (pp. 18, 59, 120, 122); University of Reading, Institute of Agricultural History and Museum of Folk Life (p. 74); Royal Commission on the Ancient and Historical Monuments of Scotland (pp. 111, 113); Scottish National Portrait Gallery (title-page, pp. 1, 8, 9, 41 (top), 44, 45, 46 (top), 50, 52, 55, 57, 58 (by kind permission of the Duke of Atholl), 68, 84, 112, 127 (bottom), 133, 143, 161, 169); Victoria and Albert Museum (pp. 117, 139, 141); The Commanding Officer, H.M.S. Victory (p. 85); Reece Winstone (p. 54); Verlag Tradition Wilhelm Kolk, Berlin (p. 214); NASA/Woodmansterne Publications Ltd. (p. 177).

Contents

Part one
The making of one kingdom

1	Using historical evidence	2
2	The Union of the Crowns	8
3	The beginnings of Parliament	15
4	King Charles the First	20
5	Commonwealth, Covenant and Crown	28
6	The colonies of the New World	37
7	Union or War?	44
8	The Jacobite Rebellions	52
9	The Highlands after the '45	62
10	Work in the country	72

Part two
The Workshop of the World

11	The Industrial Revolution	80
12	Life in factory and mine	88
13	Roads and canals, railways and steamships	96
14	A tale of two cities	105
15	The struggle between Britain and France	114
16	The USA is born	123
17	The French Revolution	130
18	Britain in 1815	140
19	Votes for the people!	147
20	'Unity is strength'	157
21	The health of the people	166

Part three
War and Peace

22	The gathering storm	178
23	The First World War	187
24	Russia—the road to revolution	197

25	The Roaring Twenties	205
26	The Troubled Thirties	214
27	The Second World War	223
28	Problems of peace	235
29	The rise of Communist China	245
30	Today's headlines are tomorrow's history	253
	Our global village	262
	Glossary	264
	Index	268

Note to Readers

You will find a number of important words in this book which have been printed in *italics* the first time they are used. The exact meaning of these words is explained in the Glossary at the end of the book, between pages 264 and 267.

PART ONE
The making of one kingdom

James VI and Anne

1 Using historical evidence

History is about everyday life, not just great events

You may remember that early in Book One we asked the question 'How do we know about what happened in the past?' We found that the answer 'By reading history books' is not a very good one. For how did writers know what to put in history books?

We found that a historian works very much like a police detective. He makes inquires and collects his evidence. Then he interprets all the evidence he has collected and tries to reconstruct what happened in the past. So the work of the historian, like that of the detective, can be compared with looking for all the pieces of a jigsaw and then trying to put them together.

Do you remember some of the different pieces of the historical jigsaw we read about—the different types of historical evidence?

There are buildings—from grand castles to humble cottages and doocots. There are documents, pieces of writing such as an Act of Parliament or a letter by Mary Queen of Scots. There are illustrations—from Stone Age cave paintings to recent photographs. There are

2

everyday articles—from Stone Age handaxes to old cars and aircraft or the first computers. And of course there are eyewitness accounts such as the diaries of Andrew Melville and Samuel Pepys.

But there are special problems in dealing with this historical evidence.

The first great problem with the historical jigsaw is that there is always something missing.

Why are there pieces missing? And why are there so many pieces missing for some events in history?

The police detective can be fairly sure that he has traced all the witnesses of an event and taken their statements. But most of our eyewitnesses of historical events are dead: there are living eyewitnesses only for very recent happenings. There have not been many people such as Samuel Pepys who actually wrote down their evidence, what they saw and heard.

Again, the detective can also be fairly sure that he has noted all the clues at the scene of the crime. But a lot of historical evidence has been lost. Have you ever left a metal object or a book outside for a week or two by mistake? What were they like when you found them? As time passes, things made of metal, cloth, wood and paper rot away. So a lot of historical evidence has been lost.

Luckily, sometimes someone realised how important a piece of evidence was and so it was saved. The Bayeux Tapestry contains the only *contemporary* illustrations of the Norman Conquest: you will remember that we can see how both sides fought, what clothing they wore and what weapons they used. But all this was very nearly lost. Nearly two hundred years ago it was going to be cut up and used to make sacks!

Unfortunately, a lot of documents have been lost. In 1661 many of our Scottish national records were being returned from London

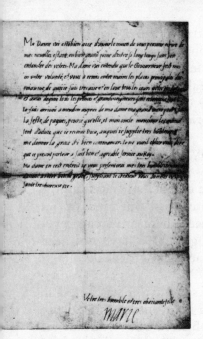

Letter written by Mary
Queen of Scots when she
was twelve

Ogham letters

to Edinburgh and were lost for ever when the ship carrying them
was wrecked.

So you can see that, as the years and centuries have passed, historical evidence such as buildings, tools, weapons, clothing, jewellery,
books and pictures has been lost or destroyed. For some periods of
history we have very few pieces of the jigsaw—which makes it
even more interesting when new pieces of evidence are discovered,
(A simple rule to remember is that we usually have more historical
evidence for a recent event than for an event a long time ago.)

The second problem with historical evidence is that we often
have to translate the evidence we have.

You have probably tried to translate a foreign language, such as
French or German, into English. The historian has this problem too,
for obviously not everyone speaks or writes English and foreign
writings have to be translated.

A lot of the evidence for Scottish history has to be translated,
for many of the older documents are written in Latin or French.
Look again at Queen Mary's letter on this page. Can you see what
language she used? The historian has a double problem: translating
the document from one language to another while trying to make
out Mary's handwriting! How good is your handwriting and
spelling? Perhaps you should improve—in case someone is using
something you have written as historical evidence four hundred
years from now!

Indeed, as you have already seen, old documents written in English
(or the English which people spoke in Lowland Scotland) can also
be difficult to read and 'translate' into the English we use.

Some old writings still cannot be translated by historians. Do
you remember the Ogham letters, carved by Picts living in Scotland
about 1600 years ago? We are still not sure what they mean.

It is strange to think that Egyptian *hieroglyphics*, used about
4000 years ago, were equally puzzling until less than 200 years ago.
Then the Rosetta Stone was discovered. It had an inscription in
hieroglyphic writing and in Greek, and Jean-François Champollion
realised that the inscription carried the same message in the two
languages. By comparing the Greek letters with the hieroglyphic
pictures, he was able to work out what the hieroglyphics meant.
Using this knowledge, historians were then able to translate other
hieroglyphic inscriptions and learn much more about the way of
life of the people of Ancient Egypt.

In all translations, of course, the historian must take great care to
be accurate—otherwise he may mislead many people.

The third problem in dealing with historical evidence is what
we call bias. What is 'bias'?

4

Imagine that your best friend comes to stay with you for the weekend. You decide to go to a football match on Saturday afternoon. Your team is playing at home and you expect them to win easily. Your friend supports the other side.

The scores are level at 2-2 with the referee already looking at his watch to blow for full-time. Suddenly, the opposition's centre-forward collides with your goalie in the penalty area. The crowd roars. The whistle blows. What's the ref's decision? To your horror he points to the penalty spot. The kick is taken and it is now 3-2 for the opposition. The whistle blows for full-time.

Would you and your friend agree about the final result? Almost certainly, no. You would probably argue all the way home! You would claim that it was a foul on the goalie, that the centre-forward 'took a dive' or that the ref was blind. Your friend would say that it was perfectly fair, that the ref had been quick to spot the obvious foul.

If you and your friend were both asked to write a report of the match, would your reports be the same? Again, no. You would agree about the result, 3-2. That would be a fact. But your descriptions of the match, particularly of the penalty incident, would be very different.

All of us see things differently. What is attractive to one person is perhaps ugly to another. It all depends on our point of view. Our own point of view depends on what we like and what we dislike, on what we feel strongly about. Do you and your parents agree about pop music or clothes? Again, probably not—because you have different points of view. You are seeing things as a teenager today. Your parents are seeing things as adults, as people who were teenagers twenty to thirty years ago—when things were different.

Your point of view gives you a bias towards one thing or another;

towards one side or the other. In that penalty incident your sympathies would be with your own team and your bias would be seen in your written report of the game. Anybody reading your report and wanting to know what actually happened would have to remember your bias towards your own side.

And so in interpreting historical evidence we have to try to identify any possible bias towards one side or another. Here is an obvious example. It is a historical fact that a battle was fought at Bannockburn on June 24th 1314 between Scottish and English armies, and that this battle was won by the Scots. Obviously Scottish people saw this as a great victory; English people saw it as a disaster. So if we read a report on the battle we have to ask ourselves whether it is written by an Englishman or a Scot. It makes a lot of difference!

These, then, are just some of the problems that a historian has to tackle when he is trying to reconstruct the past. He can be misled because some evidence is missing. He may have to translate old or foreign languages or depend on the translations of other experts. And he must realise when a piece of evidence is biased. So the evidence that we have is always asking questions of us, just as we should always be asking questions about the evidence.

THINGS TO DO

1 Explain in your own words why there are always pieces missing from the 'historical jigsaw'.

2 Why do you think it is easier for a historian to reconstruct recent events compared with events that happened many years ago? Is there anything about the evidence for recent events that would make the historian's job harder?

3 Here is an extract from a Scottish document known as the Statutes of Iona. It was an agreement in 1609 between King James VI of Scotland (and I of England) and the *clan chiefs* of the Western Isles.

It is inactit that everie gentilman ... within the said Ilandis ... haveing childreine maill or famell, and being in goodis worth thriescore ky, sall put at the leist their eldest sone, or haveing no childreine maill thair eldest dochter, to the scuillis on the Lawland ... and bring tham up thair quhill thay may be found able sufficientlie to spaik, reid, and wryte Inglische.

In your history notebook write a heading 'The Statutes of Iona 1609—an example of translation' then copy the extract carefully. Now translate this passage into modern English.

4 Here is a short contemporary report on the battle of Bannockburn.

> However as the King of England with his army had marched from the town of Berwick-upon-Tweed to the castle of Stirling, which is distant from about sixty miles and which is set on the Water of Forth ... distant from Edinburgh twenty-three miles to the west, and which was beseiged by the Scots, there was fought between them a horrible battle, and alas for woe! the Scots prevailed [won], and killed Gilbert of Clare Earl of Gloucester ... and many other noble knights, and hardly did the King of England escape from Berwick by water.

If a historian used this source and said that this was how everybody at the time—Scots and English—felt about the battle, he would be interpreting the source wrongly. He would not have allowed for the writer's bias.

In your notebook write the heading 'Identification of bias' and answer the following questions:

(a) Give three facts which the writer reports.

(b) From the way the writer describes the battle, do you think he was English or Scottish? Give reasons for your answer.

2 The Union of the Crowns

It was Saturday evening—March 26th 1603—and the courtyard of Holyrood Palace in Edinburgh was peaceful. Suddenly the sound of galloping hooves broke the silence and a breathless horseman clattered in. He was a royal messenger, Sir Robert Carey, and he had just ridden the 640 kilometres from London in three days.

He was hurried into the royal apartments. There he told the King, James VI of Scotland, the news he had been expecting for several years. His aged cousin, Queen Elizabeth of England, had died. She had no children, so James—the son of Mary, Queen of Scots and the heir of Robert Bruce—was to be crowned King of England.

In great excitement James prepared to make the journey south; in April he and his party left for England. On that long journey to London James must have had much to think about.

Perhaps he thought back to the dangerous years of his childhood. Remember, he had been only one year old when his mother had been forced to *abdicate*. Later, of course, she had fled to England. His father, Lord Darnley, had been murdered earlier that same year: 1567. James, a royal child without the protection of his parents, was very much at the mercy of greedy, ambitious men.

One after the other, four of the great families of Scotland tried to govern the country. In 1570 James's uncle, the *Regent* Moray, was shot and killed in Linlithgow by a member of the rival Hamilton family. The next Regent was the young king's grandfather, the Earl of Lennox. He was killed in 1571 when a group of Mary's supporters tried to kidnap the young king. The third Regent, the Earl of Mar, died in 1572 and his successor, the Earl of Morton, was executed in 1581.

So poor James had a most unhappy time. Things were not made easier for him by his tutor George Buchanan. He made the lad spend many long hours trying to master subjects such as Greek, Latin, arithmetic and astronomy. To make matters worse, Buchanan hated Mary and did his best to turn the boy against his mother, now imprisoned in England. Even as a teenager, James was not out

John Knox

of danger. In 1582 he was seized by the Ruthven family and kept a prisoner for nearly a year.

In June 1583, when he was seventeen, he took over control as king—but even then his troubles were far from over.

With the help of *Parliament* he tried to restore law and order. For example, he divided Scotland into four districts, and for each district he appointed two royal judges who had to go round their districts twice a year and *try* all the criminals brought before them by the *sheriffs*. Of course the judges were not very successful in the far-away Highlands or in the Borders where local chiefs were still too strong, but in the Lowlands they did much good.

There were problems with religion, too. You will remember that in 1560 Scotland had broken away from the Roman Catholic Church. A *Presbyterian* Church had been established by *reformers* such as John Knox. These men believed that each separate church should be run by *kirk sessions* of elders chosen by the congregation. The services should be much simpler, with psalm-singing and sermons instead of the ceremony of the Catholic Church. In place of *archbishops* and *bishops*, this Church of Scotland should be run by a General Assembly made up of ministers and elders.

James, however, had different ideas. He was not a Catholic but he took the Church of England as his example. There, the monarch was the head of the Church. His cousin Elizabeth chose her own bishops and archbishops. James believed very strongly that he was responsible to God for the way he governed the country—and for the way he controlled the Church. James called this idea 'the Divine Right of Kings': meaning that, as he believed he was chosen by God; he could not be told what to do by a General Assembly or by a Parliament. We shall see later how this idea was to cause problems for James (and, even more so, for his son Charles).

The Presbyterians were so strong that at first James had to agree to their demands. John Knox had died in 1572 but their new leader, Andrew Melville, wanted churches—without bishops and without royal interference—to be set up all over Scotland. Melville had a furious argument with James at Falkland Palace. Melville's nephew James described in his diary how his uncle stormed up to the king, seized him by the sleeve and called him 'God's sillie vassal'! (He meant that James was as much a humble servant of God as anyone else in Scotland.)

This was too much for James. For a while Melville was *exiled* from Scotland. Gradually James gained more control over the Church. By 1602—shortly before he left for London—he was able to appoint bishops again and allowed them to sit in the Scottish Parliament.

In fact, James had such clear ideas about how a king should govern that he wrote down these ideas in a book called 'Basilikon

Doron' in 1598. This book was a do-it-yourself handbook for his eldest son Henry on how to be a good king. As well as explaining the Divine Right of Kings, James advised Henry not to eat or drink too much, to avoid violent games such as football and to read history books! Unfortunately Henry died before he could put all this into practice. (Indeed, five of James's seven children died when they were children or teenagers.)

James wrote on other subjects too : in fact, he was the first monarch to realise the importance of the printing press. He also arranged for the Bible to be printed in everyday English. He himself said that 'it becometh a King to purifie and make famous his owne language'. He wrote many books, including collections of poetry and a book on the bad effects of smoking tobacco. Other Scots, too, were writing books about their ideas. Among them was John Napier of Merchiston who invented logarithms.

James was deeply superstitious—like so many others of his time. If someone fell ill, or if an animal died, or a crop failed, people did not look for scientific reasons for these misfortunes. Instead, they put the blame on witches and their spells. During these years,

hundreds of men, women and even children were arrested, tortured and executed for witchcraft. (In 1612, for example, Alison Devise —only eleven years old—was put to death in Lanarkshire.) Often these poor, simple, folk were picked on by their neighbours and, under the pain of torture, made to confess to ridiculous crimes. James actually wrote a book about witchcraft.

On that long journey to London, then, we can imagine that

A Prospect of LONDON as before the Fire.

THAMESIS FLVVIVS.   South worke.

James thought about all these things and about his life as King of Scotland. At the same time he must have been excited at the thought of ruling this bigger, richer, country. About four and a half million people had now become his subjects. A land made wealthy by farming and trade was his to control. As King of Scotland James had not enough money to pay his servants or keep an army. (On one occasion, we are told, he had to borrow a clean pair of socks to greet the Spanish *ambassador*!) Now he would have money to spend on things such as clothes, jewellery and entertainment.

And so James arrived in London.

Many Scots followed the king south, hoping to make their fortunes. Among them was an Edinburgh man, George Heriot. He had owned a shop, a *luckenbooth*, in the High Street and his skill as a jeweller attracted the attention of James's Danish wife Queen Ann. Soon Heriot was appointed Court jeweller. He became very wealthy and in his will left his money to found a school in Edinburgh for the 'puir faitherless bairns' of his native city.

The Scots coming to London must have been struck by the size of the city. About 300 000 people lived there, compared with perhaps 30 000 then living in Edinburgh. London was full of life. Merchants and tradesmen mingled with Members of Parliament and courtiers. Down at the docks merchant ships, trading with far-off lands such as India and America, unloaded their cargoes. The river Thames itself was alive with small boats ferrying passengers to and fro, for only one bridge—the famous London Bridge—crossed the river.

For entertainment, you could watch bear-baiting, street entertainers such as jugglers, or perhaps a public execution. For a newer kind of entertainment you could visit one of London's theatres—perhaps the famous Globe Theatre. Here you could see the latest play by William Shakespeare (who wrote many of his most famous plays during the reign of King James).

London was also a dangerous place, however. With no proper police force, robberies and riots were a constant threat. Here is part of a contemporary description of a riot which took place in March 1617. It describes what happened when a gang of *apprentices* took to the streets.

> They fell to great disorders in pulling down of houses and beating the guards that were set to keep rule, especially at a new playhouse in Drury Lane where the Queen's players used to play. Though the fellows defended themselves as well as they could and slew three of them and hurt divers [several], yet they entered the house and defaced it, cutting the players' apparel [costumes] in pieces and all their furniture, and burned their playbooks and did what other mischief they could.

Shakespeare

11

James enjoyed his new wealth and power, especially his new power to rule Scotland.

Notice carefully what had happened. Both countries had the same king but they were still separate countries. Scotland still kept her own army, her own navy, her own Parliament. No laws made by the English Parliament applied to Scotland. When James went to London, he ruled Scotland through his Privy Council, a number of nobles and bishops appointed by the king. They could make rules which had to be obeyed as if they were Acts of Parliament. James boasted about it: 'Here I sit and govern by my pen. I write and it is done, and by a clerk of the Council I govern Scotland now which others could not do by the sword.'

But James inherited problems too. Let us look at three of them.

First, there was a problem with religion. As King of England, James found himself head of the English Church. Not everyone, however, agreed with the ways of this Church. There were extreme Protestants who, like the Presbyterians in Scotland, wanted a simple church controlled by its congregations. They were known as Puritans.

They thought that James, as a Scot, would help them—but they were wrong. At a meeting with their leaders in 1604, called the Hampton Court Conference, James made it very plain that the Church of England was to keep its bishops and its prayer-book. The Puritans did not like this. A few left England for Holland, where they could worship freely. Later some Puritans sailed to America to start their own colony. We shall read about their adventures later. But the great majority stayed in England—and later made a great deal of trouble for James's son.

Secondly, the Catholics, too, objected to the ways of the Church of England and to the laws which made their lives very difficult. In 1605 a small group of them, including Guy Fawkes, tried to blow up Parliament on the fifth of November 1605. However, the plot was discovered and the plotters were arrested. After being cruelly tortured, Fawkes and his companions were hanged, drawn and quartered. Here you can see their execution. The cellars of

Parliament are still searched and of course we have our own way of remembering the day of 'gunpowder, treason and plot'.

Thirdly, James had trouble abroad, too. Under Elizabeth, England had begun a war against the power of Spain. At first all had gone well. English seamen such as Sir Francis Drake made successful attacks on Spanish colonies in America and on the Spanish treasure ships. The huge fleet which the Spaniards sent to carry soldiers into England in 1588—the Great Armada—was smashed by English ships. Finally it was scattered by a storm which blew the Spanish ships northwards. (One of them, trying to return to Spain round the north of Scotland, was sunk in Tobermory Bay.) After 1588 the English attacks on Spain and on Spanish ships were not so successful.

To make matters worse, in Ireland there had been a rising against the English and Elizabeth had sent troops there. So James found that as King of England he was at war with Spain and had a rebellion in Ireland to put down. So what did he do? At once he made peace with Spain and was soon able to crush the Irish rebellion. Later he sent many Protestant Scots to settle in Northern Ireland, in Ulster.

The wars and the rebellion had cost a great deal of money. James found that the English Parliament would not give him the necessary money very readily. In fact, he found that in England Parliament wanted to have more power. To James, who had learned in Scotland that only a strong king could make a peaceful country, the power of the English Parliament seemed much too great. He was to have many quarrels with his parliaments and in the next chapter we shall look at some of the reasons for these quarrels.

A new war with Spain and fresh arguments with the English Parliament tired James out and he died on March 27th 1625, aged fifty-eight. Remember that for fifty-seven of those years he had been a king, first of Scotland and then of Great Britain.

THINGS TO DO

1 Make a list of the problems that faced James in Scotland and England.

2 Imagine that you are George Heriot. Write a letter home to Edinburgh, describing your first impressions of London.

3 As you have read already, James wrote about many subjects. Here is what he thought about tobacco-smoking. Read it carefully and then answer the questions below.

> Is it not both great vanity and uncleanness, that at table, a place of respect, of cleanliness, of modesty, men should not be ashamed, to sit tossing of tobacco pipes and puffing of the smoke of tobacco one to another, to inhale athwart [over] the dishes and infect the air, when very often men that abhor [hate] it are at their repast [meal]? Surely smoke becomes a kitchen far better than a dining chamber, and yet it makes a kitchen also oftentimes in the inward parts of man, soiling and infecting them with an unctuous [greasy] and oily kind of soot, as hath been found in some great tobacco takers, that after their death were opened. It is a custom loathsome to the eye, hateful to the nose, harmful to the brain, dangerous to the lungs and in the black stinking fume thereof, nearest resembling the horrible smoke of the pit that is bottomless [hell].

(a) Do you think James approves or disapproves of smoking?

(b) What does he think about smoking at table?

(c) What evidence is there in this passage that *post mortem* operations were carried out in James's day?

(d) James lists the effects of smoking on a person's health. Remembering how little was known about medicine in his day, how accurate is he?

14

3 The beginnings of Parliament

Perhaps you recognise this photograph. It shows Parliament—or, to be more accurate, the House of Commons—at work. You probably realise already just how important Parliament is from what you have seen on television and read in the newspapers. It is Parliament that makes our laws and it is Parliament that takes the important decisions about how our country is to be run.

How much tax should people have to pay? How much money should we spend building hospitals and schools? In what ways should unemployed people be helped? What should our relations be with other countries? How fast should motorists be allowed to drive? At what age should young people be allowed to leave school, to vote, to marry? These are just a few of the questions that Parliament has to consider.

The House of Commons is the most important part of Parliament. You must not forget, however, that the approval of both the House of Lords and the Queen is needed before a decision of the House of Commons can become an Act of Parliament and so a law of the land.

There are 635 members of the House of Commons today. They are known as Members of Parliament, or MPs for short. We elect our MPs at what is known as a General Election. It is a law of Parliament that this must happen at least once every five years. MPs belong to different political parties—that is, groups of people who believe that Britain should be governed in certain ways. Do you know the names of the main political parties?

After a General Election the party which has most MPs has the job of governing the country. The party leaders become the Ministers of Her Majesty's Government. The most important one, of course, is the Prime Minister, but there are many others. We must remember that whatever the government decides is best for the country still has to be approved by Parliament.

Parliament has not always been like this, however. To take one example, at the beginning of this century women were not allowed to vote nor could they be elected as MPs. (Later in this book we shall be looking at their struggle to win these rights.)

How did it all start?

At first chiefs or kings usually decided what was right and what was wrong. In other words, they made the laws. A king's laws and orders were carried out by his officials and his soldiers. By the time of the Ancient Egyptians, about 5000 years ago, the king— called a pharoah—had hundreds of these people working for him.

Kings divided some of their lands among the most important nobles. Often these powerful men kept 'the King's peace' by catching lawbreakers and collecting the king's taxes. Kings turned to these men for advice or 'counsel', to use an old-fashioned word. (Even today, some of the Queen's most important ministers and advisers are called Privy Councillors.) Opposite you see an Anglo-Saxon king surrounded by his councillors, known as the Witan— while in the background one of the royal servants is carrying out an execution!

16

Kings were always in need of money. Royal castles and palaces had to be built, soldiers and servants had to be paid. How was this money to be raised? Some came from the rents from royal estates but the rest had to come from *tolls* and taxes.

Few people (especially the powerful nobles) liked having to pay money to the king's greedy tax collectors. So when King John of England quarrelled with his nobles in 1215, they forced him to make a long list of promises. The barons, as they were called, collected all these promises in a document called Magna Carta—or 'Great Charter'. One of these promises said that 'No scutage (tax) shall be imposed unless by common council of our Kingdom'. This meant that the king was supposed to get the agreement of his councillors, the barons, before taxing the people—but later this was often ignored.

You will remember that by the thirteenth century many burghs had grown up in both Scotland and England. Many of the towns-folk of these burghs grew rich by trading and kings in need of money invited representatives of these *burgesses* to 'parler' in his Council. (Now do you see where the word 'Parliament' comes from?) Edward I of England may have been the first king to do this—perhaps to help to pay for his wars with Scotland!

This drawing shows the coronation Parliament of Edward I, held in 1274. If you look closely you can see King Alexander III of Scotland seated beside him. We are not sure whether Alexander was actually present—perhaps as a guest at the coronation. This may have been a piece of *propaganda* by Edward to support his later claim to the Scottish throne.

In Scotland, burgesses were probably first invited to the Scottish Parliament in 1326 to help to raise money for King Robert Bruce. They were certainly present at the Parliament of 1364. This Parliament was called to raise money to pay the ransom of the unfortunate son of Robert Bruce, King David II, who had been captured by the English. He had been released after eleven years, but some of the ransom money had not been paid.

This Parliament of 1364 was made up of nobles, churchmen and men from the burghs and the counties. It was called 'The Three Estates', meaning the meeting of the three most important groups of men in Scotland after the king. The Three Estates continued to meet together whereas in England the *Commons* began to meet separately from the *Lords*.

Gradually the English House of Commons, as it came to be called, began to demand more powers from the king. In return for advising him and for agreeing to his laws and his taxes, they wanted more control over their own affairs. Parliament could not yet make laws but they wanted the right to discuss 'affairs of state': that is, things concerned with the government of the country. By the time of Queen Elizabeth (1558–1603) the House of Commons felt that it ought to be able to talk about such things as *foreign policy*. They even told Elizabeth she ought to get married! She was furious with them.

Then MPs demanded that they should be able to talk about anything without fear of being punished by the queen. This was too much for Elizabeth and several MPs were imprisoned in the Tower of London for daring to suggest this. Eventually, however, the MPs got their way. Elizabeth needed money for the war against Spain and most of that had to be approved by Parliament.

So the English Parliament that greeted James in 1603 was much stronger than the Scottish Three Estates. James, with his belief in the Divine Right of Kings, found this hard to understand and ruled for several years without Parliament. Once again, however, the desperate need for money to fight another war with Spain forced him to call a Parliament. Like Elizabeth before him, he had enough good sense to come to terms with Parliament. But his son Charles chose to challenge Parliament—with fatal results for himself, as we shall see.

Elizabeth

THINGS TO DO

1 Find out the names of as many Government Ministers as you can.

2 Write a short paragraph to explain in your own words why burgesses came to be invited to 'parler' with the king.

3 Why do you think the English House of Commons did not like King James's ideas about the Divine Right of Kings?

4 King Charles the First

In 1625 James VI and I died and his son Charles became King of Scotland and England. With the kingdoms he also took over all his father's troubles. Like James, he believed firmly in the idea of the Divine Right of Kings. During his reign he quarrelled with the Churches in both countries, with Parliament in England and with the Three Estates in Scotland. Unlike his father, however, he was often petty and weak-willed in his actions. As we shall see, he lost the support of many people and damaged the strength of the Crown. In the end, after a bitter *civil war*, he was defeated and executed by his opponents.

Let us look first at his troubles in England.

When Charles became king, England was fighting with Spain and soon Charles was at war with France, too. We need not concern ourselves with what happened in these wars, but the English forces were not successful. The important thing to notice is that these wars, like all wars, cost a lot of money. Charles could get money lawfully only by asking the English Parliament for it—but Parliament was not very willing to agree to more taxes. For, as we have already seen, MPs felt that they ought to have more say in the running of the country. They were prepared to challenge the king in return for giving him more money.

The MPs insisted that Charles should agree to certain demands called the 'Petition of Right'. The king was not to impose taxes unless Parliament agreed, nor imprison anyone without a proper trial. Reluctantly, Charles agreed to this in 1628 but still Parliament was not willing to give him enough money. Finally Charles decided to dissolve Parliament—that is, to dismiss it—and rule without it. This was a mistake as it turned many MPs against him.

So how was Charles to rule now—and, in particular, how was he to raise money? In trying to solve these problems, he was helped by his close advisers William Laud, Archbishop of Canterbury, and Thomas Wentworth, Earl of Strafford. Charles decided to revive long-forgotten laws which had allowed the king to raise money without having to get Parliament's agreement. For example, he began to fine heavily all those who at any time had added parts of the royal forests to their land. Again, in earlier times, coastal towns and ports had had to pay money for the upkeep of the navy. Now Charles made everybody pay this tax, known as Ship Money. Many objected to this. One man, John Hampden—who had been an MP—refused to pay and was arrested. Another, William Prynne, criticised what the king had done and had his ears cut off. This heavy-handed way of ruling the country shocked and angered people.

Charles lost even more support by the way he treated the Puritans. Like the Scottish Presbyterians, remember, they believed in a simple church service of psalms, sermons and prayers in a plain, undecorated, church building. The ministers were chosen by their congregations and were responsible to them—not to a bishop or a king.

Archbishop Laud

Encouraged by Archbishop Laud, Charles now tried to restore many of the things that had been lost at the Reformation. Churches were brightened with stained-glass windows; simple communion tables were replaced with richly-decorated altars; organs (regarded by Puritans as instruments of the devil) were introduced and the ministers were ordered to wear costly robes. The bishops were allowed to fine those people who preferred the Puritan way.

The Puritans suspected—quite wrongly—that Charles and Laud were trying to make the Church Roman Catholic again. Many of them were rich landowners and merchants in close touch with MPs. Once again the king had made mistakes by trying to force his ideas on others. Now more and more people who had been loyal subjects of his father were turning against Charles. From 1629 to 1640, however, he managed to rule without Parliament. But in the end troubles in Scotland forced him to turn to Parliament for help.

Charles had been born in Dunfermline but had spent so little time in Scotland that he knew very little about the people and their problems. You will remember the troubles that James had as the young King of Scotland. His experience in those early years taught him at lot about the difficulties of ruling Scotland. But Charles had no such experience yet he tried to govern Scotland, as his father had done, through a Council in London.

We can see his lack of understanding about Scotland from his first actions as king. Usually, the king had the support of the nobles and lairds—but Charles quickly lost all this. What happened?

After the Reformation of 1560 in Scotland, much of the land that had been owned by the Catholic Church was taken over by the nobles and lairds for their own use. This left the Presbyterian Church very poor, so Charles proposed that this land should be

21

taken back and used to help the new Church. An Act of Parliament —the Act of Revocation—was drawn up in 1625, but there was such an outcry that Charles had to give way. He allowed the nobles and lairds to keep the land in return for small payments of money. So Charles had failed to help the Church and enraged most of the powerful nobles and lairds.

Charles made more trouble for himself at his coronation as King of Scotland, held in Edinburgh in 1633. The Presbyterians—nobles, lairds and common folk alike—were shocked when they realised the service was a Church of England one. It seemed that Charles was determined to make the Presbyterian Church of Scotland like the Church of England. In 1637 he ordered that an English Prayer

Book was to be used in the Scottish kirks. When it was first used in St Giles' Kirk in Edinburgh there was a riot. 'Dost thou say Mass in my lug?' was the cry, and seats were thrown at the Bishop of Edinburgh. More riots followed as the people protested against what they thought was a return to Roman Catholic ways.

Charles failed to see how serious the situation was for him. The country was in an uproar and worse was to follow. In February 1638 a group of men signed a statement in the graveyard of the Greyfriars Kirk in Edinburgh. This National Covenant, as it came to be called, stated that the men would resist to the end any attempt to make Scotland Roman Catholic again. Soon copies of the Covenant were being signed in many parts of Scotland.

Here is part of the National Covenant:

We promise, and sweare by the Great Name of the Lord our God, to continue in the Profession and Obedience of the Foresaid Religion [Presbyterianism]. That we shall defend the same, and resist all these contrary errours according to the uttermost of that power that God hath put in our hands, all the dayes of our life. And in like manner with the same heart, we declare before God and Men, that we have no intention nor desire to attempt any thing that may turne to the dishonour of God, or to the diminution of the King's greatness and authority. But on the contrary, we promise and sweare, that we shall, to the uttermost of our power, with our meanes and lives, stand to the defence of our dread Soveraigne, the Kings Majesty.

Notice that the Covenanters, as they called themselves, still promised to be loyal to 'the King's Majesty'. It seems to have been an odd sort of promise because the Covenanters began to prepare for war. Scottish *mercenaries* who had been fighting abroad were called home. Among them was General Alexander Leslie, a veteran of thirty years' service, who had learned his soldiering in the Swedish army.

Charles tried to raise an army, too, but he found this very difficult. (Can you think why?) His army was made up of untrained, unwilling, soldiers. Sooner than risk a defeat, he came to terms with the Scots. Then, to pay his men, he was forced to recall the English Parliament. The MPs were in no mood to help the king, so after three weeks of argument this 'Short Parliament' was dismissed by Charles. Next year, 1640, there was more trouble for the king when he tried to crush Scotland. This time the Scots defeated his army and occupied Newcastle. To pay for these 'Bishops' Wars', Charles was forced to recall his English Parliament.

The MPs of this 'Long Parliament'—it was to last for twelve

Long Parliament

years—were in no mood to bargain with Charles. They presented him with a whole series of demands which would have meant that Parliament would control the army, the Church and, indeed, the whole government of the country. For a monarch who believed in the Divine Right of Kings this was clearly unacceptable. By 1642 it was plain to both sides that either King or Parliament must rule. Both sides prepared for the war that we call 'The Civil War'.

The forces of the king—the Royalists or Cavaliers—at first had the better of the fighting. After all, the forces of Parliament (nick-named the Roundheads because many had short haircuts) needed time to prepare. Here is how one writer in 1641 saw the Round-heads. (Do you think he was a supporter of Parliament or of the King?)

> What creature's this with his short hairs
> His little band and huge long ears
> That this new faith hath founded?
> The Puritans were never such,
> The Saints themselves had ne'er so much
> Oh, such a knave's a Roundhead!

Whatever some people thought of them, however, the Round-heads gradually beat back the Royalists and defeated them. Three things gave the advantage to Parliament. Firstly, an alliance was made with the Scots in 1643. This 'Solemn League and Covenant' meant that twenty thousand well-trained Scottish soldiers would now fight for Parliament. In return, Parliament promised to make England Presbyterian—although this promise was never kept. These Scots helped to win the important battle of Marston Moor. Secondly, Parliament had control of London—which gave them a tremendous advantage in money and men over the Royalists. Thirdly, after their early defeats, Parliament organised the training of a new army. One of the leaders of this New Model Army was Oliver Cromwell, an East Anglian farmer. The Ironsides, as they came to be called, were well-equipped, well-disciplined and well-led. They swept all before them and soon became the most powerful force in the land.

For a short time events in Scotland gave Charles a ray of hope. In 1644 James Graham, the Marquis of Montrose, raised an army of Highland and Irish soldiers to fight for the king. Many of these men were Catholics and had no love for the Puritan Parliament. Montrose had signed the National Covenant, but he felt bound by his promise to fight for the king. Although he was heavily outnumbered, Montrose won a series of startling victories. At Tippermuir near Perth, at Inverlochy near Inverary and at Kilsyth, outside Glasgow, he outmanoeuvred and outfought his enemies.

24

It seemed for a time that he would win control of all Scotland for Charles. As he moved south, however, many of his Highlanders deserted and returned with their plunder to the safety of their glens. What remained of his army was destroyed by the Covenanters' army at Philiphaugh, outside Selkirk. No prisoners were taken and even camp followers were put to the sword. Montrose only just managed to escape.

There was no escape for Charles, however. In 1646 he surrendered to the Scots, who handed him over to Parliament in return for £400 000. The Army under Cromwell was quite clear about his fate: he was to be tried for treason. The Army forced Parliament to agree to this drastic step by expelling all those MPs who did not agree.

This 'Rump Parliament' prepared to try the king. Charles might have made many mistakes and many enemies in the past but at his trial he defended himself with great skill and courage. His sentence had already been decided, however. In January 1649 the Court gave this verdict: 'That he, the said Charles Stuart, as tyrant, traitor, murderer and public enemy to the good people of

The trial of
Charles I

this nation, shall be put to death by the severing of his head from his body.' The sentence was to be carried out four days later.

On a cold winter's morning Charles Stuart stepped onto the scaffold erected outside his banqueting hall at Whitehall Palace. He had asked for two shirts to wear in case people in the crowd thought he was shivering from fear. He made a brief speech, then knelt at the block. And so, barely sixty years after the execution of his grandmother, another Stuart died by the executioner's axe.

THINGS TO DO

1 Make a list of the mistakes that you think Charles I made. Try to say why each was so important.

2 What part did Scotland play in the Civil War? Write a paragraph about this, using the information on pages 23 to 25.

3 Why do you think Parliament eventually won the Civil War? List as many reasons as you can.

4 On page 25 you have some details of Charles's trial. Prepare a class trial of Charles, using the information in this chapter. You will need someone to conduct the prosecution, someone else for the defence, judges and jury—as well as someone to represent Charles himself.

26

5 Here is part of an entry for January 1649 in a diary kept by a man named John Evelyn.

> The villany of the rebels proceeding now so far as to try, condemn, and murder our excellent King on the 30th of this month, struck me with such horror, that I kept the day of his martyrdom a fast, and could not be present at that execrable wickedness, receiving the sad account of it from my brother George.

(*a*) John Evelyn was a Royalist. Can you select three pieces of evidence from this extract to show this?

(*b*) Did John Evelyn actually witness the execution?

(*c*) What did John Evelyn actually do on January 30th?

(*d*) How did he hear details of the execution?

6 This illustration shows a broadsheet. This was a kind of newspaper that people had in those days. As you see, it has text and pictures. Prepare your own broadsheet about the events of the Civil War. You can write either as a Royalist supporter or as a Roundhead.

5 Commonwealth, Covenant and Crown

The execution of Charles I did not end the Civil War. Many people were horrified by what they saw as the murder of the king. The Scots, the Covenanters in particular, were furious. Although they had supported Parliament against Charles, they could not accept that an English Parliament had the right to put to death the King of Scotland. The Scots now declared his son Charles II as king and they invited him to return from his exile in Holland.

Charles sent the gallant Montrose over first. He was not welcome to the Covenanters, however, and in April 1650 they defeated his small army at Carbisdale in Rosshire. Montrose was captured and executed in Edinburgh. Once again the Covenanters approached Charles. They promised to fight for him if he in turn promised to support the Presbyterian ideas of the National Covenant. This

contemporary cartoon shows 'Jocky' and a Presbyterian minister forcing the young king's nose to the grindstone of the National Covenant. Charles agreed—reluctantly—and returned to Scotland.

Meantime Cromwell had gone to Ireland to crush the Royalist supporters there. Once again his Ironsides were completely victorious. Cromwell showed no mercy to his beaten opponents, many of whom were Catholics. His cruelties left bitter memories which still linger today.

Battle of Dunbar

The news from Scotland brought Cromwell hurrying back to prepare for an invasion. He marched north with 16 000 men and was faced by the Scottish army led by General David Leslie. With great skill they trapped Cromwell at Dunbar and defeat for the Ironsides seemed certain. Foolishly, however, the ministers with the Scots urged the army to move down from their strong position in the hills. Cromwell took his chance and the Scots were heavily defeated. He then advanced northwards and captured Edinburgh.

The Scots were not finished yet. Charles was crowned at Scone and a new army was gathered. In 1651 they invaded England but on September 3rd, the anniversary of the battle of Dunbar, they were again beaten at Worcester. After many adventures Charles escaped to France.

How was Britain to be governed without a king?

Parliament did away with the House of Lords and divided the country into districts, each controlled by a Major-General of the New Model Army. A 'Commonwealth' of England, Scotland and Ireland was declared, with Cromwell as 'Lord Protector'. (Here you see the seal of the Commonwealth, showing Parliament in session.)

For Scotland, this meant occupation by English troops. There were some benefits, however. The years of peace were particularly welcome after the savagery of the Civil War. Scottish merchants could now trade freely with England and her colonies. But people resented the attempts by the new government to stamp out much of the fun in their lives. Church-going was made compulsory; drinking, gambling, theatre-going and games such as football were discouraged. Even holidays, including Christmas, were banned. To the Puritan way of thinking, such holidays reminded people of Roman Catholicism, so they had to be stopped.

Cromwell proved himself to be a strong ruler, both at home and abroad. His Ironside troops and sailors won victories over the Dutch and captured the West Indian island of Jamaica from the Spanish. Like Charles before him, however, Cromwell had quarrels with his Parliament. When he did not get his way he was quite ruthless. Parliament was dismissed and he replaced the MPs by his own supporters.

The question was: How long would people put up with this? Then, in 1658, Cromwell died. His son Richard was more interested in a quiet life with his family than in running the country. Secret *negotiations* were begun to restore Charles II to the throne. General Monck marched his army from Scotland into England and later declared his support for Charles. So, in 1660, Charles II returned from his years of exile. The king had 'come into his own again'.

Cromwell

The Restoration was hailed with great rejoicing. In Edinburgh and other burghs the fountains ran with wine. The Commonwealth was ended and in Scotland the Three Estates was recalled. It passed the Rescissory Act which *repealed* all laws made since 1633. Among other things this meant that the laws abolishing *episcopacy* were ended. The Church of Scotland again became a Church governed by bishops. Although Charles had the good sense not to try to force an English Prayer Book on the Scottish Church, many people were deeply suspicious of his intentions.

Trouble first broke out in the south-west of Scotland. Altogether about three hundred ministers in the Lowlands refused to accept the authority of bishops. Many left their churches and held open-air services in the hills, known as 'conventicles'. The government decided to crack down on these new Covenanters. Patrols of cavalry-men scoured the hills to break up the conventicles and fine the

Charles II

30

worshippers. Some Covenanters decided to resist. In November 1666 they marched on Edinburgh but were defeated at Rullion Green in the Pentland Hills by General Tam Dalyell, a Scot who had served in the Russian army. Many prisoners were taken—and treated most cruelly. Some were tortured by 'the boot' or by thumbscrews; some were *transported* to the West Indies; others were hanged.

For the next thirteen years there was an uneasy peace. The Covenanters continued to meet and the government continued to fine those that were caught. For a time Highland clansmen were brought in to 'police' the troubled south-west part of Scotland. In 1679, however, matters came to a head. The Archbishop of St Andrews, James Sharp, had been particularly harsh towards Covenanters. His coach was stopped on Magus Muir outside St Andrews by a band of twelve Covenanters and the Archbishop was dragged out and murdered in front of his terrified daughter.

This was taken as the signal for rebellion by some Covenanters. At Drumclog in Ayrshire they beat off an attack by troops under John Graham of Claverhouse. They were caught at Bothwell Brig, however, and scattered by the cavalry of the Duke of Monmouth. About twelve hundred prisoners were taken to Edinburgh and herded into Greyfriars kirkyard. They were shown no mercy and suffered the same fate as the survivors of Rullion Green.

Now the Covenanters were hunted. This became known as the 'Killing Time'. At their conventicles in the hills, armed men guarded the congregation. One of the ministers, or 'field-preachers', formed his own bodyguard. His name was Richard Cameron and his men became known as the Cameronians. Later, the Cameronians became a famous regiment in the British Army and the only regiment allowed to carry their rifles into church services. (Can you think why?)

32

the dangers of war with Scotland, was certain to accept. But what about Scotland? When the terms of the Treaty were announced, the country was in an uproar. To many Scots it seemed that Scotland's independence was being given away. This petition from the people of Dunfermline was typical of many sent to the Scottish Parliament. 'We humbly beseech the Honourable Estates and do confidently expect that you will not allow of any such Union; but that you will support and preserve entire the Sovereignty and Independence of this Crown and Kingdom, and the Rights and Privilages of Parliament, which have been so valiantly maintained by our heroick ancestors for near two thousand years; that the same may be transmitted to succeeding generations as they have been conveyed to us.'

From September 1706 to January 1707, the Scottish Parliament debated the Treaty. Many of the members were against it. Men such as Andrew Fletcher of Saltoun argued that Scotland would always be at the mercy of the English. Others such as Lord Belhaven regretted the loss of Scotland's ancient independence.

Amongst those who anxiously watched events in Scotland was the author Daniel Defoe. He had been sent to Edinburgh as a spy to report on the progress of the Treaty. He must have worried his masters in London with his reports of riots and disorders. He passed on rumours about armies of Highlanders or Glasgow men marching on Edinburgh to defeat the Treaty.

Parliament Hall, Edinburgh

There is no doubt though that the Treaty was very unpopular. Defoe describes an attack by the Edinburgh mob on the home of one of the Treaty's supporters:

The rabble attended at the door; and by shouting and noise, having increased their numbers to several thousands they began with Sir Patrick Johnston who was one of the treaters and the year before had been Lord Provost. First they assaulted his lodgings with stones and sticks, and curses not a few; but his windows being too high, they came up the stairs to his door, and fell to work at it with great hammers, and had they broke it open in their first fury, he had, without doubt, been torn in pieces without mercy; and this only because he was a treater in the Commission to England [that is, one of the thirty-one Commissioners] for before that no man was so well beloved as he over the whole city.

Luckily Sir Patrick was saved by the arrival of the Town Guard.

Fortunately, however, sense prevailed. Other members of the Parliament spoke strongly in favour of the Treaty. Men such as the Duke of Argyll pointed out the trading advantages that Scotland would have and the terrible dangers of war. In the end these arguments won the day. It is true that some Scotsmen were paid bribes by England to support the Treaty but this made little difference to the final result. The majority of members saw continued poverty and perhaps war with England if the Treaty was not signed. The voting was 110 for the Treaty and 67 against.

The Scottish Parliament met for the last time in April 1707. As he closed the proceedings, the Lord Chancellor, The Earl of Seafield, remarked 'Now there's ane end of ane auld sang.'

THINGS TO DO

1 Give as many reasons as you can why there was such bad feeling between Scotland and England in the years before 1707.

2 Why do you think the Treaty of Union was so important for Scotland and England?

3 From the evidence in this chapter, organise a class debate on the Treaty of Union. You could debate the Treaty as members of the last Scottish Parliament or you could debate the importance of the Union today for young people living in Scotland.

4 Imagine you are a survivor of the Glencoe Massacre. In 1695 the Scottish Parliament held an enquiry into the events at Glencoe. What evidence would you give to this committee? The information on pages 45–6 and the recreative drawing on page 47 will help you with your story.

5 Here is an account of the Highland charge at the Battle of Killiecrankie, 1689. Read it carefully then answer the questions below in sentences:

> Led by their chiefs they came at the cry of 'Claymore!' throwing off their plaids and running half-naked, with heads down behind their targes, dirks in their left hands, broadswords in their right. Within range of Mackay's volleys they halted, discharged what fire-arms they had, threw the pieces away and then ran on to a hacking, stabbing slaughter before the redcoats could screw the bayonets into the muzzles of their muskets. Mackay's men broke.

(*a*) 'Led by their Chiefs'. Who were these 'Chiefs' and how important were they to the Highlanders?

(*b*) From the evidence in this passage what weapons were carried by the Highlanders?

(*c*) Who was the leader of the Highland Jacobites and what happened to him?

(*d*) Who was in charge of the government soldiers?

(*e*) Give the meaning of the following words as they are used in the passage: volleys, redcoats and bayonets.

(*f*) From the evidence in the passage why do you think the Jacobites won the battle?

(*g*) State briefly what happened to the Jacobites after the battle of Killiecrankie.

8 The Jacobite Rebellions

The Old Pretender

The Union of the two Parliaments in 1707 had not been popular in Scotland and the first years of the new United Kingdom made it even more unpopular. Perhaps people expected too much too soon but certainly there was no help for Scottish trade. Scottish industry and agriculture now had to face competition from their richer, more powerful, English neighbours. Grumbles were heard.

In 1714 the Union was put to its first real test. Queen Anne died and, as you know, none of her children was left alive to succeed her. Under the terms of the Act of Union, the new king was George, the Elector of Hanover—a German prince. (His mother Sophia had died earlier that year.) He did not speak much English and much preferred to live in Hanover. Many who had supported Queen Anne, because she was the daughter of King James VII and II did not want this foreigner as king.

The Jacobites nicknamed George 'the wee German lairdie'. To them the time was ripe for a rebellion to restore a Stuart to his rightful throne. They looked to the son of James VII (who had died in 1701) to win back his crown. The Jacobites called him James VIII; his enemies called him 'The Old Pretender'.

In Scotland the Earl of Mar had been a Secretary of State for Scotland and one of the most powerful supporters of the Union. Now, in 1715, he went to London—expecting some reward from the new king. George, however, ignored him. In a temper, Mar returned to Scotland and became the leader of the rebellion. He invited some important Highland chiefs to a hunting party on the Braes of Mar. When they were all gathered together, Mar raised the standard of King James. He urged the clan chiefs to follow him and restore their king.

With an army of about six thousand men, Mar marched south. They captured Perth easily and the way to the Lowlands seemed open to them. Most of the British army were in Flanders fighting the French. Only the Duke of Argyll, nicknamed 'Red Colin of the Battles', with an army of three thousand men stood between the Jacobites and control of Scotland.

Part of the Jacobite army—under Mackintosh of Borlum—

moved into Fife, crossed the Forth in fishing boats and almost seized Edinburgh. At the last moment they were driven off by Argyll's men. Mackintosh now moved into the Border country. At Kelso he joined forces with another Jacobite army led by Viscount Kenmure and the Earl of Derwentwater. Together they invaded England. They had expected a lot of support but few recruits joined them. Why? It seemed that people had become used to the years of peace that followed the events of 1688. They did not want a Catholic Stuart king—particularly if his chief supporters were wild Highlanders, helped and encouraged by the French.

At Preston in Lancashire, this Jacobite army was surrounded by government troops. After fierce hand-to-hand fighting, the surviving Jacobites surrendered on November 14th. On that same day, Mar's army was preparing to do battle with the Duke of Argyll. At Sheriffmuir in the Ochils the two armies met. The right wing of each army broke the left wing of the other.

It seemed to be a drawn battle, but in fact Mar had lost. Argyll held his ground while Mar retreated slowly northwards, burning the corn and driving off the cattle to stop Argyll's men having them.

In December 1715 James landed at Peterhead—but without the French soldiers he was expected to bring with him. He was too late to rally his supporters and it was clear that the rebellion had failed. So in February 1716 James and Mar set sail for France. The Highlanders scattered to the safety of the hills.

There was another small rebellion in 1719. This time James received help from Catholic Spain and some three hundred Spanish troops landed at Loch Alsh. The local Jacobites joined the invaders but they were easily beaten at the battle of Glenshiel.

These two rebellions made the government see that something had to be done to control the Highlands.

In 1725 a Disarming Act was passed to make the clansmen hand in their weapons of war. They handed in useless muskets and rusty swords; the good ones were hidden in the thatch of their cottages to wait for another day. Highlanders loyal to the government were recruited as soldiers. They acted as a Watch or armed police force. Later these soldiers were to form one of the most famous Highland regiments: the Black Watch, so called from their dark tartan kilts issued by the government.

Above all the government tried to keep the Highlands quiet by building forts and roads along which troops, artillery and supply wagons could move. The chief forts were Fort George and Fort Augustus. These, with Fort William, were meant to guard the Great Glen which divides the Highlands.

The man given the job of building the roads was General Wade. Throughout the summer months Wade's soldiers dug, levelled and

Black Watch soldier

laid the foundations for the new roads. Altogether, Wade and his 'highwaymen', as he called them, built 400 kilometres of road. Wade chose his routes very carefully: so carefully, in fact, that some of our main roads today still follow his military roads. Wade also had to build many bridges to carry his roads across the innumerable Highland streams and rivers. This Wade bridge at Aberfeldy, built in 1733, still carries traffic over the river Tay.

So the glens of the Central Highlands were opened up and, for the first time, travellers and soldiers could move easily from township to township. As one grateful road user put it:

> If you had seen these roads before they were made
> You'd have lifted your hands and blessed General Wade.

Not everybody blessed General Wade, however. The poorer Highlanders found the road surface too hard for their bare feet. Cattle *drovers*, bringing their animals south to the great *trysts* at Crieff and Falkirk, had to shoe their beasts. The roads were soon to have another use, however.

In 1745 Britain was again at war with France. Once more most of the British army was abroad, fighting in Flanders. The French government saw that a Jacobite rebellion in Scotland could force Britain to withdraw her troops. So the French allowed Prince Charles Edward Stuart, the elder son of The Old Pretender, to sail for Scotland with two French warships.

The Young Pretender, 'Bonnie Prince Charlie', was very different from his father. He was a brave, energetic, leader with a real sense of adventure. These qualities were soon tested.

54

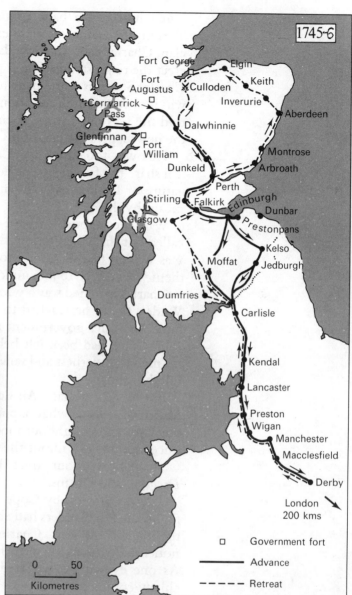

Prince Charles
Edward Stuart

The rebellion got off to a bad start. The French warship carrying the weapons and supplies was stopped by a British *man o' war*. After a fierce fight, the French ship was forced to turn back. Despite this loss, Charles was determined to press on. He landed on the little island of Eriskay in the Outer Hebrides on July 23rd 1745. From there he made his way to Moidart on the mainland to raise his standard at Glenfinnan.

Charles had expected a flood of recruits to his army, but at first few Highlanders were keen to support him. It is easy to see why. Instead of coming with a large French army, Charles had arrived without any supplies and with only seven men! The local chiefs urged him to go back to France, but Charles was determined. Turning to Cameron of Lochiel, chief of the powerful Cameron clan, Charles said, 'In a few days, with the few friends I have, I will erect the royal standard, and proclaim to the people of Britain that Charles Stuart is come over to claim the crown of his ancestors, to win it or to perish in the attempt. Lochiel, who my father has often told me was our firmest friend, may stay at home and learn from the newspapers the fate of his prince.'

This was too much for Cameron of Lochiel. 'No,' he replied, 'I'll share the fate of my prince and so shall every man over whom nature or fortune have given me power.' (What do you think he meant by this?)

With the support of about eight hundred Camerons, other chiefs called out their men to join the Jacobite cause. Not every clansman was willing to risk his life for a Stuart. We are told that many of them were forced to join under threat of having their homes burned.

Charles marched south with an army of 2500 men. Using General Wade's roads, he reached the Lowlands before anyone could stop him. The only government army in Scotland, led by General Sir John Cope, had been left behind in the Highlands. Cope marched his men to Inverness and sailed his army south in an attempt to save Edinburgh.

But he was too late. An Edinburgh newspaper, 'The Caledonian Mercury', tells us what happened. 'September 18th 1745. Affairs in this City and Neighbourhood have taken the most surprising turn since yesterday, without the least bloodshed or opposition, so that we have now in our streets Highlanders and Bag pipes in place of *Dragoons* and Drums.'

The cavalry left by Cope to defend Edinburgh had fled. Late at night, the Highlanders had slipped into the city by one of the gates, the Netherbow Port. Charles made a triumphant entry but it was noticeable that there were few men to cheer the Jacobite leader. As one eyewitness reported, 'These demonstrations of joy were chiefly confined to one sex: few gentlemen were to be seen on the streets or in the windows.' Why was this, do you think?

Charles now held court at Holyrood Palace and had his father proclaimed king at the Mercat Cross. Then news reached him that General Cope had landed at Dunbar and was advancing towards Edinburgh. Cope halted at Prestonpans in a strong position, with the flank of his army protected by a marsh. A local guide led the Highlanders through the marsh during the night and when the morning mist cleared they were on firm ground ready to attack. In one fierce charge Cope's army was scattered and the prince was master of Scotland. The Jacobite song 'Hey Johnnie Cope', which is still the *reveille* of the Highland regiments today, reminds us of this victory.

56

Jacobite camp at Edinburgh

Cumberland

After Prestonpans, Charles waited in Edinburgh for six weeks, gathering supplies and recruits for the march on London. This was precious time lost. During those weeks, the government was hurriedly calling back soldiers from Flanders and General Wade was sent to hold Newcastle with a large army.

On November 1st the Jacobite army left Edinburgh and invaded England by the western road through Carlisle. Carlisle was captured and the army pressed steadily southwards through Preston and Manchester to Derby. London lay only 200 kilometres away.

The Jacobite leaders were faced with real problems, however. Ahead of them, London was guarded by a large army under the command of the Duke of Cumberland, a son of George II. To the east was the army of General Wade, who could cut them off from Scotland and safety. Few recruits had joined the Jacobites on their way south.

The Jacobite army was in bad shape, too. This is how a Derby man described the Highlanders: 'They had several bag-pipers who played as they marched along. They were in general a crew of shabby, lousy, pitiful-look'd fellows, mixed up with old men and boys dressed in dirty plaids and as dirty shoes, without breeches, some without shoes or next to none. They appeared more like a parcel of chimney-sweepers than soldiers.'

To make matters even worse, many of the Highlanders were deserting and making their own way home. On December 5th

57

Charles agreed, reluctantly, to a retreat. In very bad weather the Highlanders made their way northwards, hotly pursued by government soldiers.

On December 20th they crossed the river Esk back into Scotland. One of the Jacobite leaders, Lord George Murray, described the scene: 'We were a hundred men abreast and it was a very fine show: the water was big and took most of the men breast-high. When I was near cross the river, I believe there were two thousand men in the water at once. The pipes began to play so soon as we passed and all the men danced reels, which in a moment dried them.'

On Christmas Day 1745 the ragged army reached Glasgow and the townfolk were forced to give clothes for the weary soldiers. The long retreat continued. On January 17th the Jacobites defeated General Hawley's pursuing army at Falkirk. This was the last victory for Charles. Now many more men deserted as the Jacobites entered the Highlands.

Behind them came the Duke of Cumberland, leading an army of experienced soldiers. Here is a verse from one of the songs they sang as they marched. Can you guess the tune?

> God grant that Marshal Wade
> May by Thy mighty aid
>   Victory bring!
> May he sedition hush
> And like a torrent rush
> Rebellious Scots to crush
>   God save the King!

On the morning of April 16th the Jacobite army, still some five thousand strong, waited on Culloden Moor outside Inverness. A night raid on Cumberland's camp at Nairn had failed. The men were cold, wet, tired and hungry. Marching towards them, with drums beating, were nine thousand British soldiers. These soldiers were not all Englishmen: several Scottish regiments fought on the government side, including the regiments we now call The Royal Scots and The King's Own Scottish Borderers.

Lord George Murray

The Battle of Culloden was lost before it was fought. The Jacobites were heavily outnumbered and in no condition to fight. The government soldiers were well-trained, well-armed and supported by artillery. For once, Charles had ignored the advice of his best officer, Lord George Murray. Murray felt that Culloden Moor, being flat and without cover, would help Cumberland's men. Unfortunately for the Jacobites, Murray was right.

For about twenty minutes Cumberland's cannon tore great gaps in the ranks of the Highlanders. Charles still would not give the order to charge. The clansmen lost patience and hurled themselves at the government soldiers. They were mown down by the accurate

volleys of Cumberland's men. The few that reached the front ranks were bayoneted to death.

This painting of the battle was done shortly afterwards. You can see quite clearly how the redcoats beat back the charge of the Highlanders. (The artist probably used Jacobite prisoners as models.)

The Highlanders turned and ran. Cumberland's cavalry galloped after the survivors, who desperately sought shelter in the heather and the hills. Cumberland ordered his soldiers to kill the wounded Jacobites and this act of cruelty earned him the nickname 'Butcher'.

Altogether, about a thousand Jacobites were killed at Culloden. During the rebellion, 3470 Jacobite prisoners were taken. Of these, one hundred and twenty were executed and nearly a thousand more transported to the American colonies. The Highlanders paid a heavy price for supporting Charles.

And what of Charles himself? For five months he was hunted by government soldiers. Although there was a price of £30 000 on his head, the Highlanders did not betray their prince. Some of those who sheltered him, such as Flora Macdonald on Skye, were put in prison for what they had done. At last, in September 1746, Charles took ship for France.

The battle of Culloden ended for ever the hopes of the Jacobites. It also ended the clan system and over the next hundred years the old Highland way of life was swept aside.

59

THINGS TO DO

1 What did the government do to try to keep the peace in the Highlands after the 1715 Rebellion?

2 Apart from the Highland clansmen, there were few recruits for the Jacobite armies.

(a) Why do you think the Highland clansmen fought for the Jacobite cause?

(b) Why do you think so few other people supported the Jacobites?

3 On page 58 you read 'The battle of Culloden was lost before it was fought'. Say in your own words why it was.

4 Imagine that you are a clansman of Cameron of Lochiel. You join the prince at Glenfinnan and are in the Jacobite army throughout the Rebellion, finally escaping from Culloden. If you had kept a diary during those months what entries would you have made?

5 Here is part of a report of the battle of Culloden printed in the 'Caledonian Mercury' on May 1st 1746. Read it carefully then answer the questions below in sentences.
(Regiments then were named after their commanding officers, for example Barrel's and Sempil's.)

> The rebels began firing their cannon, which was extremely ill-served and ill-pointed: ours immediately answered them, which began their confusion. They then came running on in their wild manner, and upon the Right where his Royal Highness had placed himself, imagining the greatest push would be there.
> General Hawley had, by the help of our Highlanders, beat down two little stone walls and come in upon the Right Flank of their second line.
> As their whole first line came down to attack at once, their Right somewhat out-flanked Barrel's Regiment and the greatest part of the little loss we sustained was there, but Bligh's and Sempil's giving a Fire upon those who had out-flanked Barrel's soon repulsed them, and Barrel's Regiment fairly beat them with their Bayonets. There was scarce a soldier of Barrel's who did not kill one or two men each with their Bayonets.
> Lord Ancrum was ordered to pursue with the Horse as far as he could and did so with so good effect that a very considerable number was killed in the Pursuit.

(a) Who were 'the rebels'?

(b) What evidence is there in the passage to show that the government soldiers had the better artillery?

(c) How does the writer describe the Highland charge?

(d) Who was 'His Royal Highness'?

(e) Why do you think General Hawley might have been particularly keen to beat 'the rebels'?

(*f*) What evidence is there in the passage to show that there were Scottish soldiers in the government army?

(*g*) Which regiment in the government army had to do most of the fighting?

(*h*) Before the battle, the government soldiers were given special bayonet practice. They were trained to attack the man to their right, not the man directly in front of them. This meant that the Highlander could not use his targe to defend himself. If you look at the picture on page 59 you can see what actually happened. From the evidence in this passage was this tactic successful?

(*i*) What part did the government cavalry play in the battle?

(*j*) Give three pieces of evidence from the passage to show that the writer was part of the government army.

The Caledonian Mercury.

Edinburgh, Thursday, May 1, 1746.

From the London Gazette, April 26.

Whitehall, April 26, 1746.
This Afternoon a Messenger arrived from the Duke of Cumberland, with the following Particulars of the Victory obtained by his Royal Highness over the Rebels, on Wednesday the 16th instant near Culloden.

Inverness, April 18.

ON Tuesday the 15th the Rebels burnt Fort Augustus, which convinced us of their Resolution to stand an Engagement with the King's Troops. We gave our Men a Day's Halt at Nairn, and on the 16th marched from thence, between 4 and 5, in four Columns. The three Lines of Foot (reckoning the Reserve for one) were broken into three from the Right, which made the three Columns equal, and each of five Battalions. The Artillery and Baggage followed the first Column upon the Right, and the Cavalry made the 4th Column on the Left.

After we had marched about 8 Miles, our advanced Guard, composed of about 40 of Kingston's, and the Highlanders led by the Quarter-Master-General, perceived the Rebels at some Distance making a Motion towards us on the Left, upon which we immediately formed; but, finding the Rebels were still a good Way from us, and that the whole Body did not come forward, we put ourselves again upon our March in our former Posture, and continued it to within a Mile of them, where we again formed in the same Order as before. After reconnoitring their Situation, we found them posted behind some old Walls and Huts, in a Line with Culloden House. As we thought our Right entirely secure, Gen. Hawley and Gen. Bland went to the Left with the two Regiments of Dragoons, to endeavour to fall upon the right Flank of the Rebels, and Kingston's Horse were ordered to the Reserve. The ten Pieces of Cannon were disposed, two in each of the Intervals of the first Line, and all our Highlanders (except about 140 which were upon the Left with Gen. Hawley, and who behaved extremely well) were left to guard the Baggage.

When we were advanced within 500 Yards of the Rebels, we found the Morass upon our Right was ended, which left our right Flank quite uncovered to them; his R. Highness thereupon immediately ordered Kingston's Horse from the Reserve, and a little Squadron of about 60 of Cobham's which had been patrolling, to cover our Flank; and Pulteney's Regiment was ordered from the Reserve to the Right of the Royals.

We spent above half an Hour after that, trying which should gain the Flank of the other; and his R. Highness having sent Lord Bury forward within 100 Yards of the Rebels, to reconnoitre somewhat that appeared like a Battery to us, they thereupon began firing their Cannon, which was extremely ill serv'd and ill pointed: Ours immediately answer'd them, which began their Confusion. They then came running on in their wild Manner; and

upon the Right, where his R. Highness had placed himself, imagining the greatest Push would be there, they came down three several Times within 100 Yards of our Men, firing their Pistols and brandishing their Swords; but the Royals and Pulteney's hardly took their Firelocks from their Shoulders, so that after those faint Attempts they made off; and the little Squadrons on our Right were sent to pursue them. Gen. Hawley had, by the Help of our Highlanders, beat down two little Stone-walls, and came in upon the right Flank of their second Line.

As their whole first Line came down to attack at once, their Right somewhat out-flanked Barrel's Regiment, which was our Left, and the greatest Part of the little Loss we sustained was there; but Bligh's and Sempil's giving a Fire upon those who had out-flanked Barrel's, soon repulsed them, and Barrel's Regiment and the Left of Monro's fairly beat them with their Bayonets: There was scarce a Soldier or Officer of Barrel's, and of that Part of Monro's which engaged, who did not kill one or two Men each with their Bayonets and Spontoons.

The Cavalry, which had charged from the Right and Left, met in the Center, except two Squadrons of Dragoons, which we missed, and they were gone in Pursuit of the Runaways: Lord Ancram was order'd to pursue with the Horse as far as he could; and did it with so good Effect, that a very considerable Number was killed in the Pursuit.

As we were in our March to Inverness, and were near arrived there, Major Gen. Bland sent the annexed Papers, which he received from the French Officers and Soldiers surrendring themselves Prisoners to his R. Highness. Major Gen. Bland had also made great Slaughter, and took about 50 French Officers and Soldiers Prisoners in his Pursuit.

By the best Calculation that can be made, 'tis thought the Rebels lost 2000 Men upon the Field of Battle, and in the Pursuit. We have here 222 French, and 326 Rebel Prisoners, as will appear by Lists hereunto annexed. Lieut. Col. Howard killed an Officer, who appeared to be Lord Strathallan, by the Seal, and different Commissions from the Pretender found in his Pocket.

'Tis said Lord Perth, Lord Nairn, Lochiel, Keppoch, and Appin Stuart are also killed. All their Artillery and Ammunition, of which a List is also annexed, were taken, as well as the Pretender's and all their Baggage. There were also 13 Colours taken.

All the Generals, Officers and Soldiers, did their utmost in his Majesty's Service, and shewed the greatest Zeal and Bravery on this Occasion.

The Pretender's Son, it is said, lay at L. Lovat's House at Aird, the Night after the Action. Brigadier Mordaunt is detached with 900 Volunteers this Morning into the Fraser's Country, to attack all the Rebels he may find there. Lord Sutherland's and Lord Rae's People continue to exert themselves, and have taken upwards of 100 Rebels, who are sent for; and there is great Reason to believe Lord Cromerty and his Son are also taken. The

9 The Highlands after the '45

The defeat at Culloden marked the end of Prince Charles's attempt to regain the throne for the Stuarts. He managed to escape to France, but many of his Jacobite supporters were not so lucky. As we have read, nearly a thousand were killed on the battlefield; others were transported to the colonies or left to rot in prison.

Most of the Prince's followers had been Highlanders, called out to fight by their clan chiefs. The government in London decided to make severe laws to ensure that there would be no more rebellion in the Highlands. The clan system must be destroyed.

Before we see what laws were passed, let us remind ourselves what the clan system was. Captain Edward Burt, who we think was one of General Wade's officers, has left us this description:

> The Highlanders live by hunting and fishing; by raising herds of sheep and cattle and by cultivating the soil. The land is divided up in different ways in different parts of the country but generally a part is kept by the chief for his own use and the remainder is rented out to tacksmen who are sometimes related to the chief. They are the fighting men of the clan and they usually sublet most of their land to other tenants who pay them rent and who fight when required. Crops of oats and barley are grown; large herds of cattle and sheep are raised and thousands of animals are herded down the drove-roads to the cattle fairs or trysts at Crieff and Falkirk.
>
> The houses of the people are very primitive with turf or stone walls and a thatched or turfed roof. People and animals share the one room and furniture is seldom found. Your eyes are always running from the open peat fires. When the hut has been built for some time it is covered with weeds and grass and I assure you I have seen sheep that had got up from the foot of an adjoining hill feeding upon the top of the house!

You can see from this drawing, done shortly after Culloden, how uncomfortable and overcrowded these houses were. How many members of this family are sharing the one room?

People such as Captain Burt felt sorry for the ordinary Highlanders. Bad weather, thin soil, poor harvests, skinny animals, wretched housing, ragged clothing—all these were part and parcel of life for the clan folk. Their lives were very hard indeed compared

to the comfortable ways of the south. Despite these hardships, however, the Highlanders were fiercely proud of their clan and of the chief.

But this way of life was already changing before Culloden. Since the Union of 1707 there had been more contact with the outside world, for Wade's roads made travelling much easier. Captain Burt and others noticed that some clan chiefs were more interested in spending money in Edinburgh than in spending time looking after members of their clan. Several chiefs had run up large debts which they tried to repay by raising the rents from their lands. The old loyalties of the ordinary clan folk were being put to the test. Perhaps this is why many clansmen had to be forced to join the Jacobite army.

What was left of the clan system was ended for ever after Culloden. The government took away all the powers of the clan chiefs and their word was no longer law. Many of those who had survived the battle were forced into exile while the government *confiscated* their lands. Highlanders were forbidden to carry weapons on pain of death. In addition the traditional Highland dress was outlawed:

> And it is further enacted. That from and after the 1st of August 1747 no man or boy within Scotland, other than such as shall be employed as officers and soldiers in the King's forces, shall on any pretence whatever wear or put on the cloaths commonly called highland cloaths. Every such person so offending, being convicted shall suffer imprisonment, without bail, during six months and being convicted of a second offence shall be liable to be transported to any of His Majesty's plantations beyond the sea, for seven years.

Here is an extract from the report of a military patrol in 1751:

> The party at Strathglass apprehended Archibald Chisholm of Glencarrick in Strathglass, wearing the philabeg [kilt] and he is at my instance committed to Inverness Gaol for six months. The day following a young fellow in full plaid was pursued by the said party on their patrol and to avoid them attempted swimming a loch and was drowned.

It was not until 1782 that Highlanders were allowed to wear tartan again. The government also encouraged the building of schools in the Highlands to teach the children English. Any child heard speaking Gaelic could be punished.

All these laws were heavy burdens for the Highlanders to bear. They were used to looking to their chiefs for help in times of hardship, but those chiefs who were left could do little to help. Many of them were already deeply in debt; some chiefs were forced to sell their estates to meet these debts. Other estates that had been confiscated by the government were now sold off to new lairds. These men were not interested in the old ways. They did not keep men on their estates to fight their battles for them. These lands were now to be farmed for profit and the old ways would have to change.

New ways of farming were introduced—new crops such as turnips and potatoes, new breeds of animals and new farming machinery to replace the age-old hand tools of the Highlands. In some places land was *enclosed* with dykes and the crops protected from the wind by shelter-belts of trees.

These new ways were already being used in the Lowlands. (We shall look at changes in farming there in the next chapter.) All these changes, however, cost money. The new lairds raised the rents and those who could not afford to pay were *evicted*. So, too, were those who got in the way of changes—those folk who were not needed on the new improved estates.

All this was very strange to the Highlanders used to the caring protection of their chiefs. Soon some of them were drifting to the farms and towns of the Lowlands looking for work. Others gave up everything and left their native land to seek their fortune across the water in North America.

A snuff box of the time

64

The emigrants'
farewell

What had started as a trickle in the years after Culloden soon became a flood. By the early years of the nineteenth century, thousands of Highlanders were leaving their homes. Some went willingly, glad to escape from the poverty of their *crofts*. Others were forced to go, cleared from the land to be replaced by sheep.

Numerous flocks of large and heavy sheep now graze almost the whole year round on these mountains and wilds where before were to be found, and only for the summer months, a few light sheep and goats, small hill horses and some herds of Black Cattle. There may be about 20 000 sheep in the parish.

So wrote the minister of Glenorchy in the 1790s. The 'large and heavy sheep' were not the sheep normally kept by the Highlanders. The traditional 'light sheep' had been small, scraggy creatures no bigger than collie dogs. They had been kept for their milk and their wool, which was so thin that they were often plucked by hand. These new sheep came from the Border country—brought north by shepherds looking for new grazing pastures, or sheep-walks as they were called. Two breeds of sheep were introduced: the Blackface Lintons and the Cheviots. From 1760 onwards they were brought to the Highlands in ever-increasing numbers. Why?

Firstly, it was found that these sheep could survive all but the worst weather out in the fields. They could graze on the high mountain pastures for most of the year. As the minister of Glenorchy tells us, these 'shielings' (as they were called) had been used by the Highlanders only in the summer months. Secondly, sheep required very few men to look after them and high prices were paid for their wool and mutton. So the men who owned the flocks of sheep could afford to pay much higher rents than the Highland crofter struggling to make ends meet with his poor crops and few black cattle.

The flocks of sheep spread further and further north, soon reaching the islands as well. In the 1840s the minister of Kilninian parish on the Isle of Mull wrote 'The Cheviot breed of sheep were some years ago introduced by Mr Cameron and they are thriving beyond all expectation.'

The Highlanders were turned off the land to make way for the sheep. In Glengarry, Easter Ross, the Isle of Skye, the Isle of Mull, people were cleared out from their houses. It has been estimated that between 1771 and 1806 about thirty thousand people were made homeless. In Sutherland, the 'clearances' left particularly bitter memories.

Like many other Highland estate owners, the Countess of Sutherland wanted to improve her lands. Huge flocks of sheep were brought to Sutherland and the people were told to move out from their crofts. Unfortunately, the man given the task of clearing the

townships did it with great cruelty. People were dragged from their homes, their furniture was smashed and their buildings set on fire. At least one person died from this rough handling; many others, particularly the old and the sick, never recovered.

This is how Donald Macleod described a clearance in Strathnaver on the Sutherland estate in 1814:

> When they had overthrown the houses they set fire to the wreck, so that timber, furniture and every other article that could not be instantly removed was consumed by the fire. I was present at the pulling down and burning of the house of William Chisholm, in which was lying his wife's mother, an old bed-ridden woman of near 100 years of age. Fire was immediately set to the house, and the blankets in which she was carried were in flames before she could be got out. She was placed in a little shed; she died within five days. Many deaths ensued from alarm, from fatigue, and cold; the people being instantly deprived of shelter and left to the mercy of the weather. To these scenes I was an eyewitness.

Patrick Sellar, the man responsible for this cruelty, was put on trial in Inverness but was found not guilty.

Other clearances followed: in all about ten thousand people were moved between 1807 and 1821. There was nothing *illegal* in this: after all, the land was owned by the Countess. To be fair, she did try to help by encouraging fishing and weaving in townships on the coast. But it was not the same: these folk were used to farming and their old ways. The new ventures did not succeed.

Thousands more boarded the *emigrant* ships. While the population of Scotland increased by about 30 per cent between 1801 and 1821, the population of Sutherland grew from 23 114 to only 23 840, a rise of only 3 per cent.

The government was very worried about the distress of the Highlanders and about the large numbers emigrating. Attempts were made to encourage the Highlanders to take up fishing and harbours were built at Ullapool, Stornoway and Tobermory. Yet very few Highlanders became fishermen: as we have already seen, they were farmers and not many wished to risk their lives at sea. For there were other dangers apart from drowning. Between the years 1793 and 1815 Britain was again at war with France. Fishermen risked capture by French *privateers* or by *press gangs* always on the lookout for sailors for the Royal Navy.

Many young men, of course, joined the British Army. What else could the Highlanders do?

During the years of the French war there was money to be made from the kelp industry. The Highlanders collected and burned seaweed and the ash produced, known as kelp, was used in the making of soap and glass. The price at one time was as high as £20 for a ton and a whole family, working throughout the summer, could produce three or four tons.

After 1815, however, the industry collapsed. Potash, the chemical in kelp, was imported from abroad and also made more cheaply in England from salt. On Mull the minister reported: 'Kelp used to be manufactured on the different properties in the parish which contributed considerably to the support of the population; but of late years this source has entirely failed, as no kelp is now made.'

By the 1840s the Highlanders were becoming desperate. Despite the clearances, the population was still increasing. In 1750 about 337000 people were living in the Highlands; by 1841 this had risen to 472000. Unlike the Lowlands, there was very little fertile land and there were no new industries to provide jobs for the Highlanders. Over the years, the crofts became smaller and smaller as parts of them were given to married sons and daughters. What kept many families alive was the growing of potatoes: in fact, some people had little else to eat.

This is how the minister of Portree on the Isle of Skye described the poverty of the crofters in 1845: 'The poor tenants are almost invariably under the necessity of having their cattle under the same roof with themselves without partition, without division, and without a chimney, their houses therefore are smoky and filthy in the extreme; and having little either of night or day clothing, and their children nearly approaching to absolute nakedness; they are fully as much without cleanliness in their persons as they are in their houses. No people on earth live on more simple or scanty diet than those in this parish. The greater number subsist on potatoes of the worst kind, sometimes with, but oftener without fish.'

Look again at the picture on page 63. Has there been much change?

During these years the Highlands were faced with a new invasion. This time it was a peaceful invasion—of tourists who flocked to the mountains and the glens. They came to enjoy the magnificent scenery—and the hunting. They were helped northwards by the new network of roads and bridges built by Thomas Telford. (We shall find out more about this famous Scottish engineer in a later chapter.) The interest of these tourists in the Highlands may have been aroused by the poetry of Robert Burns or the stories of Sir Walter Scott. It become fashionable to wear tartan and Scott even managed to persuade King George IV to wear the kilt on his famous visit to Edinburgh in 1822. But, as this cartoon shows, not everyone thought it such a good idea!

What did the new tourists think of the Highlands? Here is part of a diary entry for 1842. Can you guess who wrote it?

Taymouth, Thursday September 8th.
Albert went off at half-past nine o'clock to shoot with Lord Breadalbane. I walked out with the Duchess of Norfolk along a path overlooking the Tay, which is very clear and ripples and foams along over the

stones, the high mountains forming such a rich background, and there is a very pretty view of Loch Tay. Albert returned at half past three. He had had excellent sport and the trophies of it were spread before the house—nineteen roe deer, several hares and pheasants and three brace [three pairs] of grouse. Albert had been near Aberfeldy and had to shoot and walk the whole way back. Lord Breadalbane himself beating and three hundred Highlanders out.

This was, of course, written by the young Queen Victoria. Her interest in the Highlands led to her buying Balmoral Castle where our present Royal Family still enjoy a Highland holiday.

Tourism and shooting did little to help the Highlanders, however. Although a Crofters' Commission was set up in 1886 to improve their conditions, the emigration continued. And the drift from the Highlands continues to this day. At the last *census*, the population of the Highland Region was only 175 000. Despite the efforts of the Highlands and Islands Development Board, the Forestry Commission and the Hydro-Electric Board, jobs are still scarce. Modern tourism and work for the North Sea oil industry have helped—but the problems remain.

This picture shows Crackaig, a deserted township on the Isle of Mull. In 1841, thirty-three crofters and fishermen lived there. In the census of 1881 only five people, including a shepherd, were left. By 1891, everyone had gone, perhaps to join the thousands of Scots whose descendants now live abroad. There are hundreds of such deserted townships in the Highlands: sad reminders of a way of life that has now passed for ever.

THINGS TO DO

1 What things did the government do after 1745 to end the clan system?

2 'Numerous flocks of large and heavy sheep' (page 65)

(*a*) What were the names of these two new breeds of sheep?
(*b*) What part of Scotland had they come from?
(*c*) Why did they do so well in the Highlands?

3 'The poverty of the crofters' (page 68)
Why was life so hard for Highlanders in the nineteenth century?

4 Imagine that you were a crofter in Strathnaver. You were cleared from your home and are now living in Canada. Your grandchildren ask you what life was like 'in the old days' and why you had to leave Scotland. What would you tell them? The information on pages 64–7 and the recreative drawing on page 66 will help you.

70

5 Here you can see a photograph of crofters taken about 1880. As you can see, their way of life has changed little over the years. Look at the picture carefully then answer the questions below in sentences.

(*a*) How have the cottages been built?

(*b*) Why do you think there are ropes with stones on them on the roof?

(*c*) What job do you think the woman is doing?

(*d*) What job do you think the man is doing?

(*e*) 'Their way of life has changed little.'
What evidence in the photo would show this?

(*f*) 'The poverty of the Highlander'
What evidence is there in the photo to show this?

6 Organise a class discussion on the problems facing the Highlands today.

10 Work in the country

In the last chapter we saw how the introduction of new breeds of sheep into the Highlands helped to end the old clan system. These Blackface Lintons and Cheviots were bigger and stronger than the native sheep: they had been specially *bred* to give more wool and more meat. This improvement in the farm animals was just one of many changes that took place in Scottish farming during the eighteenth century.

At the beginning of that century visitors to Scotland had found Scottish farming very backward. Most of the people still lived in *ferm touns*. The old, wasteful, ways—sometimes hundreds of years old—were still followed.

Much of the land was bare hill, rough moorland or squelchy marsh. The marshy land was really the most fertile but, as it had not been drained, the higher land was ploughed for growing crops. This ploughed land still lay in unfenced patches as had been the custom for hundreds of years. The infield was given most attention and was cropped every year without a rest. The outfield patches were ploughed for a few years and then rested. They were very rarely manured, for folk believed that

> If land be three years out and three years in
> It will keep in good heart till the de'il grows blin.

The infield and outfield were still divided into ridges or 'rigs' which changed hands every year or so. This, of course, is one reason why there was so little change. It was not worth a man's time and trouble to improve the land if it was to be given to somebody else to farm in a year or two. Each man looked after his own rigs but at ploughing, sowing and harvest they all worked together.

Rigs outside Arbroath

The old heavy wooden ploughs were still in use, 'more fit to raise laughter than raise soil', one Scots laird said. We can get an idea of how *inefficient* these old ploughs were from this description of the old ways: 'In some districts, from their great weight, eight, ten and sometimes twelve oxen, were yoked to one plough. While in others, from the smallness and weakness of the cattle, four men and seven horses were sometimes employed to turn up the same furrow.'

Some of the other farming methods were no better. Do you remember the story told by Jesus about the sower and the seed? Seventeen hundred years later that way of sowing broadcast—that is, taking handfuls of seed and scattering them to the right and to the left—was the only way known. Once grown, the grain was harvested with sickles or scythes. The seeds were knocked from the stalks with wooden flails, then thrown up into the air to be *winnowed* by the wind.

The return for all this hard work was pitiful. Often they reaped only three seeds for each one sown. Then they had 'ane tae saw, ane tae gnaw, and ane tae pay the laird witha''—because rents were still paid in food and service and not in money.

The same crops were still grown: oats, barley and, in some districts, flax for linen.

The cattle and sheep were small and scraggy. As there were no dykes or fences to protect the crops on the rigs, the animals often wandered over them searching for food. You will probably have noticed that the farmers did not grow a crop such as turnips to feed these animals in winter. Beasts had to be killed in the autumn or sold to drovers; the others were fed on hay in their owners' houses until the spring. By then they were often so weak that they had to be carried out to the grass. This was called 'the lifting time'.

The houses of the ordinary folk were built much as they had been for centuries: stone walls, heather-thatch roofs, no glass windows to let the light in or proper chimneys to let the peat reek out. We would think them terribly dirty but, they used to say, 'the clartier, the cosier'.

Their clothes, too, were very simple. The women wore dresses of undyed woollen cloth spun at home. The men wore rough shirts of wool or a coarse linen called 'harn', and cloth breeches. On Sundays they dressed for the kirk in their best clothes and painfully put on shoes and stockings. Then the women wore a kind of headscarf of harn, called a 'toy', and a coloured plaid over head and shoulders. The men wore suits of homespun cloth and blue bonnets.

Everything for their meals, Sunday and weekday alike, was provided by their land or their beasts. They had porridge, broth made with kail, peas and beans, bannocks and oatcakes with milk and ale. They did not eat much meat, but sometimes salmon from the nearby river or herring if they were near the sea, or salted fish.

In most years, then, Scotland's soil, rivers and sea provided enough food for her folk to live in their simple way. But years of bad harvests were years of tragedy. As we read in Chapter 6, there were seven bad harvests in a row at the end of the seventeenth century. Then hundreds of people died of starvation; thousands more became beggars, scouring the countryside for whatever food they could find.

Quite clearly, the old ways of farming were wasteful—but, after all the years they had been used, what could be done to change them?

We have already read about the Act of Union and how many years passed before Scotland enjoyed the real benefits of the Treaty. Soon after 1707, however, Scottish landowners began to see how much better-off the English landowners were. They visited English estates and it was obvious to them that the English ways of farming were very much better.

In 1723 a group of landowners formed 'The Society of Improvers in the Knowledge of Agriculture in Scotland to spread the new Ideas.' Some of these 'Improvers' were lairds such as Sir Archibald Grant of Monymusk in Aberdeenshire and Adam Cockburn of Ormiston in East Lothian. (Cockburn had seen the advantages of the new English ways of farming on his long journeys to and from London as one of the Scottish MPs in the new Parliament.) Nobles such as the Earl of Haddington and the Duke of Atholl joined the ranks of the Improvers and encouraged the new methods on their estates.

So what were these new methods?

In England Robert Bakewell had shown how bigger and better cattle and sheep could be bred. Jethro Tull had invented a seed drill which saved seed by sowing it in straight rows, thus making weeding easier. Lord Townshend had lived in Holland and discovered there what a useful crop turnips were. Like clover, they provided winter feed for the animals and gave the land a rest from growing grain.

Other lessons were learned, too. Marshes were drained and ditches were dug. Low-lying land which before had been water-

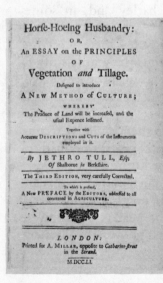

74

logged and useless was now ready for the plough. Trees were planted to protect crops from the wind as well as to provide precious timber. Farmers discovered the usefulness of lime to keep the soil sweet and of ground bones to fertilise it.

Much money was spent carting manure from the growing towns to the neighbouring farms. By 1790 a hundred thousand cartloads of manure were carried each year from Edinburgh to Cramond. The manure cost a shilling (5p) a load but the farmers had to pay another shilling and sixpence (7½p) to get it to their fields because the roads were so bad.

New machines were introduced. From Holland, James Meikle brought the idea of a mill for grinding barley. Previously, barley had been ground by hand. James's son Andrew, who lived in Dunbar, invented a threshing-mill to take the place of the old flails. A mill cost about £45 to build and soon hundreds were to be found on Scottish farms.

Later—after 1800—the minister of Carmyllie, Patrick Bell, invented the first reaping machine. Perhaps the best-known invention at this time, however, was the metal plough designed by James Small. As the minister of Borthwick parish reported: 'At the village of Ford lives James Small, the best ploughmaker in Scotland. He makes 300, 400 and sometimes 500 ploughs in a year.' This iron plough was so popular not only because it ploughed better than the old wooden one but also because it needed only one man and two horses to work it.

At first, however, these changes and new ideas did not catch on easily. To begin with, many were suspicious of the new crops and machines. They were used to the old ways of their fathers and grandfathers before them.

Secondly, it cost money to improve a farm and few people could afford the new methods. Thirdly, a man could not use the new methods if his land was split up in different rigs which could change hands each year.

So what was to be done? Here is how a contemporary writer described what happened: 'About the year 1751, the proprietor

An 'improved farm'
(High Cross, Ayrshire)

[landowner] the late Earl of Abercorn, began to subdivide his estate into commodious [large] farms, to build convenient farmhouses upon each and to enclose them with ditches and hedges.'

As you can see, it was once again the landowners who set the pace. They 'enclosed' their land with dykes or hedges, ploughed the rigs flat, built new farmhouses to replace the squalid cottages and rented out the new larger farms for a number of years. The landowners made sure that the tenant farmers used the new methods and often helped with loans of money. In return they charged much higher rents, sometimes ten or twelve times what they had received before. The farmers in turn produced heavier crops and got much higher prices for their produce—for (as we shall see) Scotland's population was growing and had to be fed.

These 'enclosed' farms, then, produced better crops and better animals. The farmers and their families lived in smart new farmhouses. The farmworkers could earn good wages compared to the old days. A ploughman was paid about £18 (a year!); a labourer about 6p a day (for working from 6 a.m. to 6 p.m.) while his wife and children could earn about 2½p a day at harvest-time. This does not seem much to us but in those days it did allow the farmworkers to eat quite well and even to have a penny or so for luxuries such as soap.

Perhaps they did not spend all their money wisely, however. The minister of Dalmeny reported: 'Their food consists of oat-meal porridge, oat-cakes and pease bannocks, barley broth with greens, potatoes, butter-milk and water. Some begin now to use wheaten bread and small beer but seldom eat any butcher meat. The luxuries in which they indulge, are tea, and what is worse whisky.'

76

And so in the space of about forty to fifty years the face of Scotland's countryside was changed. The vast open fields of rigs gave way to the neat enclosed fields that we see today. This map of the time shows clearly the changeover from individual rigs to enclosed fields.

Not everyone benefited, however. As you have read, few men could afford the cost of improvement or the new high rents. The new methods did not need so many men to work the land. As in the Highlands, then, hundreds of people had to leave the land to look for work. For most of them that work was to be found in the new factories of the growing towns.

THINGS TO DO

1 Explain the following old Scots sayings:

(*a*) 'If land be three years out and three years in
It will keep in good heart till the de'il grows blin'.'
(*b*) 'Ane tae saw, ane tae gnaw
And ane tae pay the laird witha'.'

2 Say in your own words what was wrong with the old farming methods.

3 What part did the landowners play in improving farming in Scotland?

4 Perhaps you have noticed in the last two chapters how much we have relied on the evidence of parish ministers for what life was like then. The reason for this is that in 1790 one of the most famous Improvers, Sir John Sinclair, had the idea of writing to each parish minister in Scotland in order to find out more information about the country. You must remember that there were no government departments collecting *statistics* as we have today. People knew very little about what was happening outside their own communities. Sinclair drew up a long questionnaire asking for information about such things as population, industry, agriculture, wages and prices. Can you guess why he decided to ask the parish ministers to do this job?

With over nine hundred parishes in Scotland, Sinclair had taken on a mammoth task. He published the information for others to see. In all the operation took until 1799. The information, known as the 'Statistical Account', was published in twenty-one volumes. You should find the information about your parish in your local library. You should look at this to see what life was like in your district at the end of the eighteenth century. In the 1840s, the exercise was repeated and published as the 'New Statistical Account'. This too should be available in your local library.

5 The 'Statistical Account' is a mine of information. For example, the minister of Inveresk described how the Newhaven fishwives played football each Shrove Tuesday! The minister of Domock in Dunbartonshire wrote down what the yearly expenses of a farm worker, his wife and four children were. Read the extract carefully, then answer the questions below.

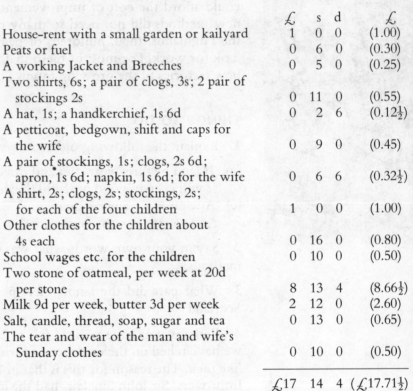

	£	s	d	£
House-rent with a small garden or kailyard	1	0	0	(1.00)
Peats or fuel	0	6	0	(0.30)
A working Jacket and Breeches	0	5	0	(0.25)
Two shirts, 6s; a pair of clogs, 3s; 2 pair of stockings 2s	0	11	0	(0.55)
A hat, 1s; a handkerchief, 1s 6d	0	2	6	(0.12½)
A petticoat, bedgown, shift and caps for the wife	0	9	0	(0.45)
A pair of stockings, 1s; clogs, 2s 6d; apron, 1s 6d; napkin, 1s 6d; for the wife	0	6	6	(0.32½)
A shirt, 2s; clogs, 2s; stockings, 2s; for each of the four children	1	0	0	(1.00)
Other clothes for the children about 4s each	0	16	0	(0.80)
School wages etc. for the children	0	10	0	(0.50)
Two stone of oatmeal, per week at 20d per stone	8	13	4	(8.66½)
Milk 9d per week, butter 3d per week	2	12	0	(2.60)
Salt, candle, thread, soap, sugar and tea	0	13	0	(0.65)
The tear and wear of the man and wife's Sunday clothes	0	10	0	(0.50)
	£17	14	4	(£17.71½)

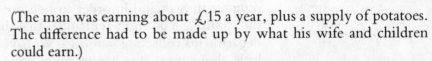

(The man was earning about £15 a year, plus a supply of potatoes. The difference had to be made up by what his wife and children could earn.)

(*a*) What is the cost of renting and heating the family home?

(*b*) From the information given what comments would you make on the clothes of the members of the family?

(*c*) Apart from food and clothing, what else do the parents spend money on for their children?

(*d*) From the information given, what are the main items of the family diet? How much variety is there in what they eat? How does it compare with your diet?

(*e*) What luxuries does the family spend money on?

(*f*) What evidence is there to suggest that the family are religious?

(*g*) What sorts of things does the family not spend money on that your family spends money on? Can you give reasons for each thing?

18th century farm worker's clothing

PART TWO
The Workshop of the World

A collier, 1814

11 The Industrial Revolution

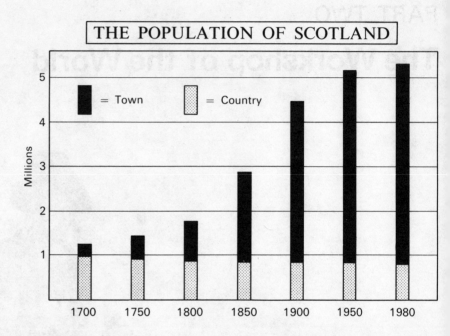

THE POPULATION OF SCOTLAND

■ = Town   ▦ = Country

Millions

Look at the diagram on this page. It shows two very interesting things. First, the population of Scotland has grown from about one and a quarter million people in 1700 to over five million today. Next, look where most people lived in 1700: four out of every five were farmers and country-dwellers. Today five out of every six of us live in towns. To put it another way, the number of country folk today is about the same as it was in 1700—but there are twenty times as many people living in towns. Obviously there must be much more work in towns than there used to be. How did this come about?

In the early eighteenth century, as we know, most folk still earned their living from the land. They lived in small, self-sufficient communities producing most of what they needed. This is how Sir John Sinclair described their way of life:

> The men build their houses, tan the leather, fabricate the shoes, make the implements of husbandry [farm tools] and cultivate the land; while the women spin the wool, dye it, weave cloth and make up the garments of the family. They thus provide, by their own efforts, every article required.

80

Linen-making

For centuries women had spun woollen and linen thread to be woven into cloth for their own dresses and shawls and for the shirts and suits of their menfolk. After 1707, however, many Scots preferred the cheaper and better English woollen cloth.

But linen-making flourished, especially in Fife, Forfar and Perthshire. Flax was difficult to grow and preparing it for spinning was a messy business. So some merchants sent packmen round the countryside with linen yarn for the women to spin at home. The packmen later collected the thread and took it to towns where men weavers wove it into cloth. The weavers (who were often known as 'websters' in Scotland) passed the cloth on to men known as fullers or 'waulkers', who then cleaned it before sending it to the tailors to make up into clothing. (How many of you spotted your own surname in the last sentence? Many of our surnames remind us of the jobs once done by members of our families.)

The government encouraged the linen industry and weavers from France and Holland were brought over to show Scots weavers how to make finer cloth. Some settled outside Edinburgh in the district still called Picardy Place.

Remember that most people worked at home—but not always at spinning and weaving. In places such as Aberdeenshire whole families were expert knitters of socks and gloves. Others made spoons and combs from bone and horn. The work was hard, the hours were long and the wages very small. But at least people could take time off when they wanted to relax, to go for walks or dig their gardens. Sinclair tells us that it was common for weavers to go out for a stroll after their suppers, to smoke a pipe in the gloaming before working until 10 p.m.

We call this way of working at home the Domestic System—from the Latin word 'domus', meaning a house. Some people were employed as colliers, at the ironworks or the saltpans—but most worked on the land or in their homes.

In the last chapter we read about the changes in farming that we call the Agricultural Revolution. From about 1760 onwards there were important changes in industry, too, and the Domestic System was replaced. Large factories, employing hundreds of workers, took the place of the cottages where families worked. Machines powered by water and steam replaced the hand-operated spinning wheels and looms. Thousands of people had to leave their homes in the countryside and move to the towns to look for work. Why did this Industrial Revolution take place in both England and Scotland?

There were many reasons. One was the rapid growth in population during the eighteenth and nineteenth centuries. Look at these figures showing Scotland's population:

1755	1 265 000
1811	1 806 000
1821	2 091 000

As you can see, after centuries of very little increase, Scotland's population nearly doubled in about seventy years.

Thanks to the Agricultural Revolution, the dreaded years of famine were now over. More and better food could be bought at the markets. There had been improvements in medicine, too. More doctors were being trained and hospitals were being built in the cities. Treatment was still very primitive, but (as we shall see in Chapter 21) improvements in medical care were being made. One important development was the introduction of *vaccination* against smallpox by an Englishman, Dr Edward Jenner. Smallpox had been a killer disease, claiming the lives of thousands, but now it was brought under control.

There were other reasons for the increase in population. The Industrial Revolution meant that there were more jobs to be had. Young couples could afford to marry earlier and to have large families, as even children of four or five years old could earn money in the new factories. These same factories produced cheap cotton clothes which were easier to clean than the heavier woollen ones.

All these additional people had to be fed, housed and clothed. They needed tools to work with and furniture for their homes. The

82

old Domestic System could not produce enough to meet these increased needs. New ways had to be found to increase the production of goods of all kinds.

Trading in tobacco

Britain's colonies overseas played an important part. They provided cheap *raw materials* such as cotton, timber and tobacco. The same colonies were markets for goods made in Britain. You will remember that the 1707 Treaty of Union had given Scotland the chance to share in this trade. Many people made a lot of money from this, particularly the merchants of Glasgow.

Between 1700 and 1770 Glasgow grew quickly. Her merchants built up huge fortunes trading in tobacco and sugar. Several Glasgow street names—Virginia Street, Jamaica Street and Tobago Street—

remind us of this trade with the west. But when the American War of Independence broke out in 1776, the tobacco trade was cut off for a time, and the rich 'tobacco lords' looked for some other way to invest their money. And so their money helped to pay for the Industrial Revolution.

The question was where the money should be invested? There seemed to be little profit to be made in the old linen and woollen industries. The cotton industry looked much more promising.

Cotton-making

For some years cotton had been spun and woven in Lancashire in England, and so it was in Lancashire that the first important inventions were made to increase production.

83

In 1767 James Hargreaves of Blackburn made his 'spinning jenny' which spun eight reels of thread at a time. Then in 1769 Richard Arkwright, from Preston, invented a machine which spun very strong twisted thread—so that a cloth could be made of cotton alone instead of a mixture of cotton and linen.

This machine was called a 'waterframe' because it was driven by water power. These waterframes were too large and too expensive to be placed in cottages so they were housed in factories, or mills as they were called. These mills, of course, had to be built beside rivers so that the waterwheels could be turned.

The next invention made use of a new source of power—steam. Steam engines had been used since the beginning of the eighteenth century to pump water out of mines. James Watt of Greenock worked for many years to try to produce an improved steam engine. By 1781 he had produced a steam engine which could drive wheels and this was put to work in the textile factories.

During the American War of Independence (1775–1783) Glasgow merchants realised that in Lanarkshire and Renfrewshire the climate was suitable for spinning cotton—and that the raw cotton from America could be brought very easily into the Clyde. The first cotton mill was built at Rothesay in 1779, but the best known one was built at New Lanark by David Dale of Glasgow, helped by his friend Arkwright. Later on, Dale was joined by Robert Owen, whose work we will read about in the next chapter.

After that the cotton industry grew and grew until by 1800 it was by far the biggest industry in Scotland. In 1775 only about 52 000 kilos of cotton were being imported into Glasgow. By 1812 this had increased to 5 million kilos. In all about 154 000 men, women and children were employed in the cotton industry—compared with 24 800 in the woollen industry, 76 600 in the linen industry and only 2400 in the iron industry. In Glasgow alone there were fifty-two cotton mills and it is little wonder that people talked of 'the reign of King Cotton'.

James Watt

Smelting and using iron

The growth of the cotton industry, with its factories and machines, sparked off a growth in two other industries—iron-making and coal-mining.

Iron had been mined in small quantities in the south of Scotland since very early times, but there were no real iron-works until after the Union of 1707. In England, the supply of wood for charcoal to smelt the iron was running short. So English ironmasters began to set up furnaces in, of all places, the Scottish Highlands. There, there was plenty of timber and the heavy iron could be taken by boat up rivers and lochs. The first works were at Invergarry in

Inverness-shire and others were soon built beside the lochs of the West Highlands.

But not long after the Union an Englishman, Abraham Darby, showed how to smelt iron with coke—made from coal—instead of with charcoal. Now it was known that Scotland had plenty of coal and that there were deposits of iron ore round about Bo'ness. So in 1759 a large iron-works was set up at Carron near the River Forth. Soon it became famous for the making of a naval gun called the carronade.

A carronade on board HMS 'Victory'

The iron-works grew quickly, but there were two drawbacks. The local iron ore was not very good and so most of the ore used had to be imported. Secondly, Scots coal was not very suitable for making coke. Why, then, did the iron industry in Scotland grow so quickly between 1825 and 1850? And why did it grow up in the west of Scotland when it had really started on the Forth?

There were three main reasons for this. First, very rich iron ore was found in the parish of Old Monkland. In 1825 it was a farming district with a few hundred people. Twenty years later, eight thousand people lived in the new town of Coatbridge, most of the men working in the iron furnaces. Secondly, James Neilson found that Scots coal could be used for smelting, in place of coke—if instead of cold air you blew in very hot air into the furnace.

The third reason for the huge growth of the iron industry was that, as time went on, more and more iron was needed—for the new machines in cotton mills and for many other things. About 1840 (as we shall see) the railway-building age began and just at this time Scots iron-works began to use the inventions of Henry Cort, which allowed better iron to be made more cheaply. In 1856 Henry Bessemer showed how some of the impurities could be taken out of iron quite easily so that steel (which had always been very scarce and dear) now became far more plentiful and cheap.

All this meant that more and more coal was needed to smelt the iron and feed the steam engines. Until about 1800 the only big mines were on the east coast—nearly all in Fife. When the new iron-works in Lanarkshire needed much more coal, mining began there and in Ayrshire. There was a major problem, however. Few people were prepared to work underground because the working conditions in the mines were so terrible. We shall look at these conditions in the next chapter.

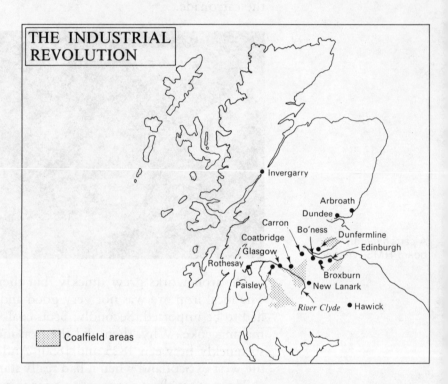

THE INDUSTRIAL REVOLUTION

Invergarry

Arbroath
Dundee
Carron
Bo'ness
Coatbridge
Dunfermline
Glasgow
Edinburgh
Rothesay
Broxburn
Paisley
New Lanark
River Clyde
Hawick

Coalfield areas

By 1825—the time that Sir John Sinclair was writing—the Industrial Revolution had had far-reaching effects on Scotland. Notice from the map, however, that most changes were taking place in central Scotland, particularly in the west. Why was this? Clearly, there were the deposits of coal and iron. There were also streams to turn factory wheels. There was the money of the Glasgow tobacco lords and the skill of engineers such as James Watt. There were plenty of skilled textile workers eager for jobs in the factories.

Notice, too, that the raw cotton being landed at Glasgow and the finished products from the factories did not have far to travel. This was important, because the roads were very poor. We shall read about these poor roads and transport problems in Chapter 13.

The Industrial Revolution, then, brought great changes to Scotland. Over much of the country factory chimneys were springing up, small villages were mushrooming into towns and the towns themselves were rapidly becoming overcrowded. Many people made their fortunes at this time. As we have read, there were real benefits—cheaper clothes, for example. But not everyone gained. The cottage weavers with their handlooms could not compete with the power-driven machinery of the mills. Their wages fell from £1 per week to only eight shillings (40p). They could no longer enjoy the holidays and the walks in the gloaming as they struggled to make a living. Many could not find work and joined the hundreds of other families from all over Scotland who moved to the factory towns to look for jobs there.

THINGS TO DO

1 Give as many reasons as you can to explain why the Industrial Revolution took place in Britain.

2 Why did the iron and coal industries benefit from the developments in the textile industry?

3 Why do you think so much industry came to be located in the West of Scotland?

4 It is 1821 and you are a reporter for a local newspaper. You have been interviewing an old handloom weaver, Mr John Duncan. You have been trying to find out what life was like working in the Domestic System and how the new inventions have changed things. Write out an account of your interview with him.

5 Here are some population figures for Scotland collected by Sir John Sinclair. Study them then answer the questions below in sentences.

	1755	1811	1821
Edinburgh	57 000	81 600	138 000
Glasgow	31 000	83 700	147 000
Lanarkshire	81 700	191 800	244 400
Sutherland	20 800	23 600	23 800

(a) Which city was the largest in 1755?

(b) Which city was the largest in 1821?

(c) Which city had grown the fastest by 1821?

(d) What reasons would you give for this?

(e) What do you think the county of Lanarkshire had grown so rapidly?

(f) Why do you think the increase in population in the county of Sutherland was so small?

(g) From the information given what was happening to Scotland's population between 1755 and 1821?

87

12 Life in factory and mine

In the last chapter we looked at some of the reasons for the growth of factories in Britain. We saw how this Industrial Revolution meant that more coal was needed to provide the heat and the power for industry. For the owners of the factories and the mines there was the chance to make a lot of money. Sadly, in their drive for profits, many owners *exploited* their workers. As we shall see, the conditions in the factories and mines during the early years of the Industrial Revolution were dreadful.

When you start work yourself, you will find that your employer has to satisfy many rules and regulations. These cover such things as how many hours you are allowed to work and the kind of safety training you should have. There are factory inspectors appointed by the government to make sure that these rules and regulations are being obeyed. In the eighteenth century, however, there were no laws like these to protect the workers. There were no government departments with the job of making sure that hours of work were not too long and that the work was not too dangerous. Each worker was at the mercy of his or her employer.

If you could have visited one of these new factories you would have been horrified by the conditions.

The new machines were housed in large barrack-like factories and sometimes as many as a thousand workers toiled together under one roof. The factories themselves were normally dirty, smelly, hot and noisy. There were no proper facilities for the workers:

Mills at New Lanark

often the only toilets were buckets on the floor. The machines themselves smelt of oil and grease; the noise of the machinery was deafening and the workers could scarcely hear themselves speak. You may remember that cotton needs a warm temperature to prevent the threads snapping. So workers in cotton mills were forbidden to open windows and the temperature was often over 20°C. To make things worse, the warm air was thick with fibres which made it difficult for the workers to breathe. What effect do you think all this would have on the health of the workers?

These conditions were bad enough for men and women but you would have been even more shocked to see that many of the workers were children—some only about seven years old. Why was this?

For one thing, the machines had replaced the skilled adult workers and much of the work could now be done by children. Many were employed in cotton mills as 'piecers'. They stood by the machines and when a thread snapped they had to tie the broken ends together. Often this meant crawling under the moving machinery. With no proper protection, accidents were common and hundreds of children were killed or injured at work.

This is how the father of one of these child-workers described such an accident: 'My eldest daughter when she first went there—the cog caught her forefinger nail and screwed it off below the knuckle. She was five weeks in Leeds Infirmary. As soon as the accident happened her wages were totally stopped.'

It is no wonder that there were so many accidents when you consider the number of hours worked in the factories. This is how one factory owner, Mr Lee, described what he demanded from his employees in 1832 (although he seems to have got his arithmetic wrong). 'From 6 a.m. to 8 p.m., allowing 40 minutes for dinner, 20 minutes for coming in, making 12 hours' work for 5 days and 11 hours for Saturday—in all 76 hours per week.' Remember this was for all the workers—including the children. How does it compare with your school working day or the working week of members of your family?

In return for all these hours in such horrible conditions what sort of wages were paid? Adults were paid from fifteen shillings (75p) to £1 per week, while children were paid from two shillings and sixpence to five shillings ($12\frac{1}{2}$p to 25p). Here, of course, is another reason why so many children were employed. They were cheap labour for the factory owner.

Moreover, in some factories part of the weekly wage was paid in tokens which could be exchanged only at the factory owner's shop. Often the prices there were much higher than in other shops so this 'truck system', as it was called, was hated by the workers. In addition to this, many employees operated a system of fines for a wide range of 'mistakes'. In one factory, any worker who opened

a window, who arrived late at work or who was heard whistling, could be fined a shilling (5p). These fines would be taken off the weekly wage.

Some factory owners used an even harsher discipline to keep their workers in order. The foremen and overseers were ordered to keep a strict control. Beatings with straps were quite common. Some overseers delighted in growing their thumbnails long and pinching the ears of children who fell asleep at work. Shocked visitors reported that they saw blood flowing down the necks of these unfortunate youngsters. One lad claimed that it was common in his factory for children to be nailed to their workbenches by the ear if they fell asleep.

Such cruelty was found in other places of work, too. This is how fourteen year-old Frederick Hopkins described his work at Camelon Park to a group of visitors in 1843. 'I do not know my proper age as my mother has been dead four or five years. She died of fever while father and she were stopping in the Grassmarket [in Edinburgh]. After her death I was picked up by someone and taken to the *Workhouse*. I stayed there two years and then I was sent here. I make 1500 sixpenny (2½p) nails daily except Saturday and Monday when I am allowed to make 1000. We start at six in the morning and lay by at half past ten at night. It is some work. I like it fine.'

When the visitors questioned him again, Frederick said that his master had told him to say that he 'liked it fine'. He went on: 'I never change myself as I have no other clothes. I wash sometimes on Sundays. I don't really care about the work and I've run away twice but they caught me and beat me and brought me back.'

You may well wonder why the workers put up with all this. For one thing, there were very few *trade unions* to protect them. Indeed, as we shall see later, for many years trade unions were illegal. In addition, there was no help for a worker who got the sack. There was no money given by the government to someone who was unemployed. So workers were forced to accept these conditions rather than risk losing their jobs. Those who had no work had either to beg, steal or hope for some help from their church.

If factories were like this, what were conditions in the coal mines?

We have seen that more and more coal was needed after about 1760 to smelt iron and drive steam engines. Coal had been used in Scotland for many centuries before this: the monks of Newbattle Abbey were digging for it five hundred years before. But the early diggings were like quarries, not pits, and the amount of coal found was very small.

So when more coal was needed, men dug tunnels into the earth from these open quarries. This was dangerous work, because the earth was always falling into the tunnel. Later they dug deeper and this brought greater difficulties and greater danger. Water seeped

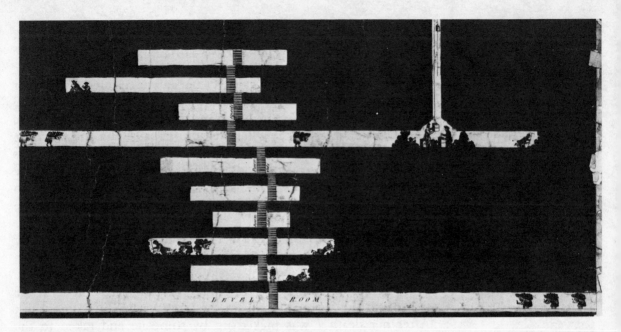

Gilmerton colliery
near Edinburgh

into the bottom of the pits, poisonous and explosive gases collected, and taking the coal to the surface was hard work.

Slowly the dangers were overcome. Miners became more skilful at supporting the roofs of the tunnels and engineers began to use steam engines to pump the water out. They lit fires at the bottom of pit shafts to drive out foul air and Sir Humphry Davy invented a lamp which would not set fire to explosive gases. But although some improvements were made, the mines were still terrible places to work in.

Moreover, until 1799 the miner folk were serfs. If they ran away, they could be brought back and forced to work again. Few men were prepared to lose their freedom and face the hardships of life underground.

As in the factories, the whole family had jobs to do. The men who 'won' the coal were known as 'colliers'. The hauling of coal to the surface was done by 'bearers', women and boys and girls—some of them quite young.

Where the tunnels were high enough, women and girls carried the coal in creels on their backs. It was bad enough to have to stumble along the filthy floor of the tunnel, but it was worse to climb slimy, slippery ladders to the top of the shaft. Some of the women, it was said, carried 200 kilos of coal at a time and it took two men to lift the loads on their backs. One visitor to a mine found a girl carrying 25 kilos of coal. On each journey to the top, she climbed as many steps as there are to the top of St Paul's Cathedral and she made fourteen journeys a day. She was six years of age. (It is, of course, hard to imagine that the weights described are accurate. What do you think?)

92

Here is a description of the work of these bearers, written in 1825:

The collier women of this village [Niddrie, near Edinburgh]—poor, overtoiled creatures, who carried up all the coal from underground on their backs by a long, turnpike stair inserted in one of the shafts—continued to bear more of the marks of serfdom then even the men. It has been estimated that one of their ordinary day's work was equal to the carrying of a hundredweight [50 kilos] from the level of the sea to the top of Ben Lomond. I have seen these collier women crying like children when toiling under their load along the upper rounds of the wooden stair, and then returning scarce a minute after with the empty creel, singing with glee.

Worst of all were some of the pits in the east of Scotland. These women and children were harnessed to little trucks or 'hurleys' and crawled painfully on hands and knees along tunnels less than a metre high.

Even the youngest children of four or five were employed. They worked as 'trappers', opening and shutting the trap doors in the tunnels to let the trucks through. It is hard to imagine what it must have been like for those wee souls, sitting alone for hours on end in the darkness of the pit.

These, then, were the terrible working conditions for thousands of folk during the early years of the Industrial Revolution. Not many employers bothered about the life and health of their workers. They could always find another if one fell ill or was injured at work.

There were some exceptional employers, however. One of these was Robert Owen, who took over the New Lanark cotton mill

from his father-in-law David Dale in 1799. He took care that his workers were properly housed and worked in decent conditions. No children under ten were allowed to work in his mill: instead, they had to go to school. Here you see visitors to the school being entertained by the children. Owen also opened a nursery for the very youngest ones so that they did not have to go to the mill with their mothers. He also set up a shop where workers could buy goods at reasonable prices and a night school to help them after the day's work.

Some mine-owners also tried to make life better for their workers. The Earl of Dalhousie set an example by building pleasant cottages for the colliers and by looking after them and their families when they needed help.

But there were few employers like these. Something had to be done to force all employers to shorten hours and to stop putting women and children on hard, back-breaking, work. The only way this could be done was by passing Acts in Parliament.

The man who did more than anyone else to persuade Parliament was Lord Shaftesbury. He was a landowner who need not have bothered at all about poor folk in factories and mines. But he made it his life's work to improve their lot. He visited factories to see for himself what conditions were like. He even went underground to see what life was like for the colliers and their families. He then tried to convince others that there must be changes.

At first things were very difficult for men such as Shaftesbury. Few people could vote in elections for Parliament: they and their MPs did not care much about folk less fortunate than themselves. But a change began in 1832: Parliament passed an Act which gave more men the vote, and MPs began to listen more to those who wanted to improve things at home and abroad.

So in the very next year, 1833, Parliament passed a new Factory Act. This said that children under nine were not to work at all, and that working hours for women and young folk were to be

Shaftesbury

94

shortened. This was now the law of the land and, if a factory inspector found an employer breaking the law, the employer would be prosecuted and punished.

Shaftesbury had a longer struggle to persuade Parliament to stop women and children working underground. First he persuaded Parliament to investigate what conditions underground were really like. So a Commission was set up and the members asked collier folk to describe their work.

Here is the evidence they heard from Isabella Reid, a twelve year-old coal bearer at the Edmonstone colliery in East Lothian:

It is very sore work. I make about 30 or 35 journeys from the pit's bottom to the wall's face. The distance varies from 100 to 250 fathoms [nearly 200 to 500 metres]. I have to carry about a hundred-weight and a quarter [65 kilos] on my back. I have to stoop much and creep through water which often comes up to the calves of my legs. When first down I often fell asleep from heat and fatigue. When the weather is warm, there is difficulty in breathing and frequently the candles go out. I do not like the work, nor do the other lassies but they are made to like it.

Now people could read for themselves just how bad things were. But to make sure that the real horror of life underground was understood, the Commission included drawings, such as this one, in its Report. And so Parliament passed the Mines Act in 1842.

These Acts were, of course, only the first of many. Gradually Parliament and the employers came to realise the importance of good working conditions. Sadly, however, much of the wealth made during the Industrial Revolution was earned at the expense of the workers.

THINGS TO DO

1 Why were children employed in the first factories and mines?

2 On page 89 we read that the girl injured at work had her wages 'totally stopped'. What do you think this meant? Find out what happens today to a person who is off work through illness or injury.

3 Describe in your own words the dangers which faced miners in the first pits.

4 Read again the last sentence of this chapter. Give as many reasons as you can to show that the factory owners and mine owners did make money 'at the expense of the workers'.

5 On page 94 we read that Lord Shaftesbury went to see for himself what conditions were like in the mines. Imagine that you are Lord Shaftesbury. Write a report for Parliament—remembering that you are trying to persuade MPs to stop women and children working underground.

13 Roads and canals, railways and steamships

Travelling is something that we accept as part and parcel of our lives. Whether it is travelling to school or to work, travelling to a new home in a different part of the country or travelling for a holiday, we all spend a good deal of time travelling. Indeed, in the course of our lives we will probably travel countless thousands of kilometres by bike, bus, car, train, boat or plane.

Many of these journeys will be made at speeds which would have been considered impossible not so many years ago. Yet we take it for granted that we can travel in a car at more than 100 km an hour, in a train at more than 200 km an hour or in a plane at more than 1000 km an hour. Some of you may even be lucky enough to fly in Concorde which can cross the Atlantic from Europe to America in just over three hours. In 1492 Christopher Columbus took more than ten weeks to do this!

There is another way of travelling, too. In the last few years men have begun the exciting exploration of space. In 1969 an American, Neil Armstrong, walked on the surface of the Moon after a journey of four days. Since then space probes have travelled hundreds of thousands of kilometres to send our scientists information about neighbouring planets. As you read this, dozens of satellites are circling the Earth doing such things as sending information for weather forecasting and beaming TV pictures from one continent to another.

And yet it is not much more than seventy-five years since the first aeroplane flight. Here is Orville Wright's 'Kittyhawk' during its twelve-second flight in 1903. It is little more than a hundred years since the first motor cars were seen on our roads and only about a hundred and fifty years since the first railways were built. Quite clearly there has been tremendous progress in ways of travel in recent times.

Roads

Two hundred years ago there were few properly made, hard surface, roads in Britain. Apart from General Wade's military roads, the last good roads had been built by the Romans more than thirteen hundred years before! Travellers, goods and messages were carried on horseback—and long, uncomfortable, journeys they were. It took days for goods from Edinburgh to reach Selkirk. It took a day and a half to travel between Glasgow and Edinburgh, and about a fortnight to reach London.

What were called roads were what we would call rough farm tracks: dusty in summer, flooded in spring and autumn and frozen in winter. This is how a traveller described the roads in Forfarshire: 'They are almost impassable except in dry weather or during hard frost. During wet weather, horses sink to their bellies, and carts to their axles.'

So it is not surprising that few people risked getting trapped in mud or snow, being drowned when trying to ford a swollen river or being attacked by one of the many robbers who swarmed around the highways of the countryside. Nor is it surprising that few farmers or manufacturers wanted to send their produce any distance to market. The costs were too high and the risk of loss or damage too great.

Why was nothing done to improve the roads?

For one thing, few people needed to travel. They lived and worked in their own villages and towns. There were no package holidays as we know them, so folk had little reason to travel. Also, there was no government department or *local authority* responsible for building and repairing roads. A Scottish Act of Parliament in 1669 had required each man to work six days a year on the roads of his parish. They were not paid for this, however, so you can imagine how much work was actually done.

During the later eighteenth century, however, something was done at last. In different parts of the country groups of local men formed what were known as Turnpike Trusts. A Turnpike Trust obtained the permission of Parliament to improve a stretch of

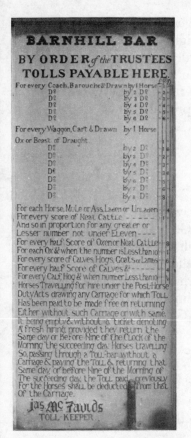

road. They paid the costs of the work and kept the new road in good repair. In return they were allowed to charge a toll from the road users. A toll house was built and a barrier placed across the road. A sign giving details of the charges was displayed and a man was employed to collect the money. Those of you who have driven across the Forth or Tay road bridges will recognise this system of paying for the use of a transport improvement. Before these bridges were built, travellers had to pay to cross by ferry boat.

The Turnpike Trusts obviously wanted to build a good, long-lasting road surface. They were helped by the work of two Scottish engineers—John Macadam of Ayr and Thomas Telford from Westerkirk in Dumfriesshire. Both men went back to the ideas of the Roman road-builders. Proper foundations were dug and layers of stones were rammed down. Then a camber was put on the surface so that rainwater ran to either side and proper drains were laid to carry this water away. Macadam's method was cheaper because he did not insist, as Telford did, on a foundation of large stones. His ideas are still used in road-making today and road surfaces made of small stones bound together with tar are called 'tarmacadam' or 'tarmac'.

By 1833 hundreds of kilometres of good roads had been built in Scotland. Thousands of passengers were being carried great distances in the new stagecoaches and mailcoaches. A few years earlier it had taken several days to reach London; now the journey from Edinburgh had been cut to forty-five hours. Travellers between Glasgow and Edinburgh could make the trip in about four and a half hours. Travelling was still expensive, however: passengers travelling on the outside of a coach paid about 1p a km while those sheltering inside paid as much as 2p a km. How does this

compare with the cost of a journey today? (Remember that a working man's wage was about 75p a week.)

Each day about sixty coaches left Edinburgh to journey to all parts of Britain, even to the remote Highlands where before 1760 a wheeled carriage was unknown. Travel to and from the north was now much easier—thanks to Thomas Telford.

Telford was born in 1757, the son of a Border shepherd. He became an apprentice stonemason and spent some time helping to build Edinburgh's New Town. Like many Scots, he decided to go to England to make his fortune. There he earned a great reputation as an engineer. He planned the rebuilding of Portsmouth Docks and the construction of the Ellesmere Canal; he designed the famous Menai Bridge in Wales. His fame spread abroad and he was asked to do work in Europe, including the making of the Gota Canal in Sweden. He was admired and honoured by all who knew him. In recognition of his work he was made the first President of the Institute of Civil Engineers. In Scotland, however, he is best remembered for his work in the Highlands.

In Chapter 9 we read that the government was very worried by the movement of people away from the Highlands. In 1801 Telford was given the task of opening up the Highlands to travellers and to trade. For twenty years he laboured at this task and by the time his workmen had finished about 1400 kilometres of roads had been built. The dangerous fords and ferries had been replaced by about a thousand bridges, including the famous Tay Bridge at Dunkeld and the iron bridge over the Spey at Craigellachie. He also planned many new harbours, including those at Peterhead and Tobermory.

Telford

Canals

Perhaps, however, the hardest part of Telford's task was the planning of the Caledonian Canal running through the Great Glen from Inverness to Fort William.

What is a canal? Simply an artificial river, a large man-made ditch filled with water. The first modern canal, the Bridgewater Canal, was built by James Brindley in 1761. It linked the coalfields of Worsley with the growing city of Manchester about 12 km away. Soon other factory-owners and mine-owners realised that a canal was a cheap way of carrying heavy goods quickly and safely —away from the delays and dangers of the roads. More canals were built and by 1800 all the major towns in England were linked by a network of waterways. Hundreds of horse-drawn barges carried the products of the Agricultural and Industrial Revolutions.

In Scotland the Monkland Canal and the Forth and Clyde Canal were both opened in 1790. In 1822 the Union Canal was built from Edinburgh to join the Forth and Clyde Canal near Falkirk. Here

you see a barge on the Union Canal aqueduct at Slateford, then a village outside Edinburgh. These barges took coal and building stone to Edinburgh and carried away much of the city's manure. Passengers, too, were carried on the fourteen-hour trip between Edinburgh and Glasgow for a fare of about 30p.

That same year, 1822, the Caledonian Canal was completed. Yet within a few years this canal, like so many of the others, was not much used. The waterways could not compete with the new steam railways.

Railways

For many years some of the Scottish collieries had used 'waggon-ways', rails along which horses pulled the coal waggons. One of these, at Tranent, was opened in 1745 and soon they became quite common in Ayrshire and Lanarkshire coalfields. So it is not surprising that the first locomotives, or steam-engines on wheels, were used at these collieries where there were already rails and plenty of coal. The first locomotive was made by Richard Trevithick in

Glasgow-Garnkirk railway

1804, but the best known engine-builder was George Stephenson. The first railway in Scotland was opened in 1826 and it carried coal from the Monkland collieries to the Forth and Clyde Canal at Kirkintilloch.

At this time nobody thought of using railways to carry passengers, but in 1831 the first passenger line in Scotland was opened. George Stephenson himself drove the first train along it from Glasgow to Garnkirk in Lanarkshire. But many people distrusted new inventions, and the new railways and engines had many enemies. Among these were the owners of the Forth and Clyde Canal and the Town Council of Linlithgow. The canal owners tried to prevent the building of a railway from Glasgow to Edinburgh—because it would take business away from the canal. At Linlithgow, the Town Council tried to make the railway pay for all the goods it carried through the town: just like the 'dues' that 'foreign' merchants had to pay in earlier times.

But people slowly realised the advantages of railways. They were quicker and cheaper than even the canals. Also, they did not freeze in very cold weather! In 1830 there was only about 50 km of railway in the whole of Britain; by 1870 this had risen to 25 000 km! Railway-building was a very costly business, of course. Track had to be laid, stations built and bridges constructed. There were disastrous accidents, too. In 1879 the railway bridge over the Tay collapsed while a train was crossing to Dundee. All the passengers and crew were killed. The railway boom continued, however, A new bridge was built over the Tay; the Forth was spanned by a huge iron bridge which stands today as a monument to the skill of the railway engineers.

All this work of course provided much-needed jobs. Just think of all the different kinds of work connected with a railway. The actual labouring was done by the 'navigators' or 'navvies'. These men had built the canals; now they toiled to build 'the great iron roads'. They had a bad reputation for fighting and drinking. Here is how the minister of Ratho parish, writing in 1839, described their behaviour:

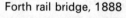
Forth rail bridge, 1888

The cutting of the (Union) Canal had at one time a very injurious effect upon the character of the population, from the scenes of riot and dissipation among the Irish labourers, of which the village was the centre, and after the work was finished, from the number of Irish who took up their residence in it. But time has produced a marked change for the better. Still, however, there is room for improvement with not a few on the score of intemperance [drunkenness] which is the crying evil among the Scottish population.

The arrival of the railways did more than just speed up the movement of goods. Thousands of passengers were carried, too. People could now travel some distance to work and so pleasant suburbs grew up on the outskirts of the bustling towns and cities. Holidays became possible for more and more people as the railway companies offered cheap travel to the new seaside resorts or to the Highlands.

At one time there were about fifty railway companies in Scotland, many of them very small, but by 1900 there were only five big ones. Later these companies were swallowed up by the London, Midland and Scottish (L.M.S.) and the London and North Eastern Railway (L.N.E.R.). Now, as you know, all railways are 'nationalised'; they belong to the State and are known as British Rail.

Steamships

The steam-engine not only brought great changes in land travel. It completely altered sea travel, too. Until the nineteenth century, ships had been made of wood and had used sails, but about 1850 big sailing ships called 'clippers' were built of wood and iron. These ships were very fast and were used to race the new season's tea crop back from China. Many of them were built at Aberdeen and some at Greenock. One very famous clipper, the 'Cutty Sark', was made at Dumbarton. They must have been a wonderful sight as they sped along, crowded with sails, but they were the last of the great sailing ships.

For long before the age of clippers, men were experimenting with steam-engines in ships. Some of these early experiments were made by Scotsmen. In 1800 William Symington built his tug, the 'Charlotte Dundas', at Grangemouth and showed what it could do on the Forth and Clyde Canal. Again, men were afraid of new things: the owners of the canal would not allow it to be used regularly and Symington died penniless. Meanwhile, in America, paddle steamers were being built for use on the lakes and rivers and Henry Bell of Helensburgh used these as models. His ship, the 'Comet,' was launched on the Clyde in 1812 and carried passengers on the Clyde and along the west coast.

One big drawback of these early steamships was that the coal fuel took up a great deal of space that could have been used for cargo. The earliest sea-going steamships like the American 'Savannah', which was the first to cross the Atlantic, carried sails in case they were needed. These coal-burning engines were gradually improved, but the problem of stowage space for fuel was not completely solved until oil-burning engines were introduced.

The 'Charlotte Dundas'

So the steam-engine brought the great changes of railway and steamship travel. Experiments were also made with steam-cars. They had little luck, for they were very heavy and did much damage to the roads. Another problem was that an Act passed by Parliament in 1865 said that they must not travel at more than two miles an hour in towns and five miles an hour in the country. As if that was not enough, each car had to have three men in charge of it, one of whom had to walk in front with a red flag!

In 1884, however, a German named Gottlieb Daimler invented the petrol-burning internal combustion engine. Soon hundreds of cars using this engine were to be seen on the roads. In 1896, Parliament ended the 'Red Flag' Act. The modern motor-car age with all its advantages—and all its problems—had arrived.

THINGS TO DO

1 Describe in your own words, the work done by a Turnpike Trust.

2 It is 1818, Thomas Telford has just been made President of the Institute of Civil Engineers. Write an article describing his career for your local newspaper.

3 Writing in 1845, a famous Scotsman, Lord Cockburn, had this to say about the coming of the railways:

> Britain is at present an island of lunatics, all railway mad. The patients are racing even in the wildest recesses of the Highlands. The world is not half the size it was a few years ago.

(*a*) On page 101 you read first how quickly Britain's railways were built. Give as many reasons as you can why you think people at that time were thought to be 'railway mad'.

(*b*) What do you think Lord Cockburn means when he writes: 'The world is not half the size it was a few years ago'?

4 Read again the last sentence of this chapter. We are all very much a part of the motor-car age. What do you think are the advantages and the disadvantages of the motor-car today?

5 In the last few chapters we have been looking at the great changes that affected our country which we call the Agricultural and Industrial Revolutions. These changes have continued, to the present day, of course. Changes in technology always pose fresh problems, however. In our own time, for example, we enjoy the benefits of computers and silicon chips; on the other hand we have to face problems such as unemployment and *pollution*. Have the benefits of the Agricultural and Industrial Revolutions been worth the cost? Organise a class debate to discuss this question.

14 A tale of two cities

Between 1760 and 1860 a very great change took place in England. Before 1760 most English lived in the fertile lands of the south. When they began to use steam-engines and iron machines the factories had to be built where coal was plentiful—in the Midlands and North England. So folk moved north to find work and out of small villages grew big towns such as Leeds. Factories were built quickly; houses for the working folk were built even more quickly—and often very badly.

In Scotland things were rather different. Some towns did grow up rapidly from little villages. We have mentioned one of these, Coatbridge, which grew up where iron was found. But most of Scotland's big towns have grown out of the small trading burghs of earlier times: Edinburgh, Glasgow, Dundee, Paisley, Perth, Aberdeen. In such burghs the coming of steam power meant that the old industries were carried on in new factories, and other industries were brought in.

The best example of a small trading burgh which has grown into a big modern trading and manufacturing city is Glasgow. At the time of the Union of 1707, Glasgow was a clean and pretty little

town with places and streets that remind us of a Scots burgh in Queen Mary's time. If you arrived from the south of the Clyde, you would cross the bridge by the pleasant district of Gorbells and walk by the Briggate and the Saltmarket to the High Street. You would probably pause at the Cross by the Trongate and the Gallowgate before you climbed up the High Street past the College to the Cathedral on the hill.

Daniel Defoe visited Glasgow in 1726. This is how he described it: 'Glasgow is, indeed, a very fine city; the four principal streets are the fairest for breadth, and the finest built that I have ever seen in one city together. In a word 'tis the cleanest and beautifullest, and best built city in Britain, London excepted.'

In 1707 about 13 000 folk had lived in Glasgow. By the time of Defoe's visit the city had begun to grow rapidly. Why was this? We have already looked at the benefits the Treaty of Union brought to Scotland—and perhaps Glasgow gained most of all.

This is how Defoe explained the rise of the city: 'Glasgow is a city of business: here is the face of trade, as well as foreign and home trade: and I may say 'tis the only city in Scotland at this time that apparently increases and improves in both. The Union has answer'd its end to them more than to any other part of Scotland, for their trade is new form'd by it: and, as the Union open'd the door to the Scots in our American colonies, the Glasgow merchants presently

For **POTOMACK RIVER,**
VIRGINIA & MARYLAND,

THE Ship MINERVA, Captain GIBSON, now in Port-Glasgow, and will be clear to sail early in April.

For freight or paſſage apply to Findlay, Hopkirk, and Co. Glasgow, Mr. John Dunlop or Captain Gibſon, Port-Glaſgow.

March 15th, 1791.   A

For **JAMES RIVER, VIRGINIA,**

THE Ship MARY ANN, John SIMPSON, Maſter, now ready to take on board goods at Greenock, and will be clear to sail by the firſt of next month. For freight or paſſage apply to Mr. James Broun, Glaſgow, or Roger and Robert Stewart, Greenock.

Who have for SALE,

A quantity of beſt James River TOBACCO, of laſt year's importation.

Advertisement from the 'Glasgow Mercury'

fell in with the opportunity, for they have the greatest addition to their trade by it imaginable: for I am assur'd that they send near fifty sail of ships every year to Virginia, New England and other English colonies in America, and are every year increasing.'

The tobacco merchants of Glasgow—the 'tobacco lords'—made their fortunes from this trade. Their money brought work to the city as this trade grew. In 1715 about one million kilos of tobacco was brought to the Clyde; by 1771 this had grown to twenty-one million. The old Broomielaw quay was made bigger, new quays were built, the river was deepened and shipbuilding yards sprang up. Soon the noise of the machinery in the new cotton mills was added to the din of the busy city. By 1801 the population had grown to almost 84 000; by 1830 to about 200 000. Glasgow was on the move.

What was happening in Edinburgh, the capital city?

In 1707 about 40 000 folk lived inside the protection of the walls of what came to be known as the Old Town.

Execution in the Grassmarket

Edinburgh had grown up along the 'Royal Mile', along the ridge from the Castle down to Holyrood. On each side were tall tenements or 'lands', some about ten storeys high. Originally they had enclosed gardens or 'closes' stretching behind them, but during the eighteenth century more houses were built in these, and now we think of a 'close' as a passageway leading to a courtyard surrounded by houses built close together.

Edinburgh in those days was a busy, bustling, place. What would a visitor to the High Street have found?

The air would be filled with a rich variety of sounds. Street traders shouting their wares, the clatter of horses' hooves as soldiers from the Castle passed by; the creaking of carts carrying farm produce; the lowing of animals on their way to the Grassmarket; the laughter of barefooted children scampering to the safety of a dark close after some mischief.

Perhaps these youngsters had been poking fun at one of the Town Guard. Edinburgh, like other towns and cities, had no proper police force. The city relied on a Town Guard made up of old soldiers, many of them Highlanders. As you can imagine, they were not much good at keeping law and order.

In 1736 Edinburgh's Town Guard was commanded by Captain Porteous. When some popular *smugglers* were hanged in the Grassmarket, the crowd got out of control. Porteous panicked and ordered his men to open fire. Twelve citizens were killed and others wounded. People demanded that Porteous be tried for murder, but he was pardoned. Perhaps you know the rest of the story? One night a mob broke into the Tolbooth jail, dragged out the unfortunate Porteous and hanged him. A reward was offered for

the capture of the ringleaders but no-one was ever found out.

At the public wells, the servant girls would be exchanging the latest gossip as they waited their turn. Perhaps they would pause in their chatter to gaze curiously at a rich lady being carried by in her sedan chair.

At the Mercat Cross, the 'caddies' would stand—waiting to carry messages or run errands for the better-off townsfolk. It was said that a visitor could stand at the Cross and, in a few minutes, see some of Scotland's most important men. He might see Adam Smith the famous *economist*, David Hume the philosopher, William Robertson the historian, Henry Raeburn the artist and, for a time, Robert Burns the poet. These and others helped to make Edinburgh one of the most famous cities in Europe.

But there were problems for townsfolk and visitors alike. Edinburgh, like Glasgow, was growing quickly and by 1755 the population had increased to more than 57 000.

About 1760 an English preacher named John Wesley visited Edinburgh and said that 'the chief street stank like a sewer'. This was not really surprising, because no proper arrangements were made for sanitation or for the taking away of rubbish. It was risky to walk in the streets about ten o'clock at night, because that was the time when folk opened their windows and tossed the day's rubbish out on to the cobbled street below or on to the head of any unfortunate passer-by. From the duchess's maid on the top flat to the rag and bone merchant's wife at the bottom, they all cried out 'Gardyloo!' (from the French 'Gardez l'eau!', 'Mind the water!') and then let the water—and the rest—go. If a passer-by could not shout out quickly 'Haud yer han'!' or duck into the nearest doorway, it was just too bad.

Another English visitor, Joseph Taylor, wrote 'In the morning the scent was so offensive that we were forced to hold our noses as we passed the streets, and take care where we trod for fear of disobliging our shoes, and to walk in the middle at night for fear of an accident on our heads.' (You can guess what kind of 'accident' Joseph Taylor means?)

As you can imagine, this made the overcrowded Old Town a very unhealthy place to live in: especially as all the drinking water was drawn from public wells in the middle of the street.

Some of the leading citizens organised a competition for the design of a 'New Town' to the north of the city across the swampy Nor' Loch. In 1766 the entry by James Craig was declared the winner. If you look closely at the map on the next page you can see what Craig's ideas were. Notice the neat parallel streets and the well laid-out squares. Compare these with the jumbled, overcrowded, closes of the Old Town.

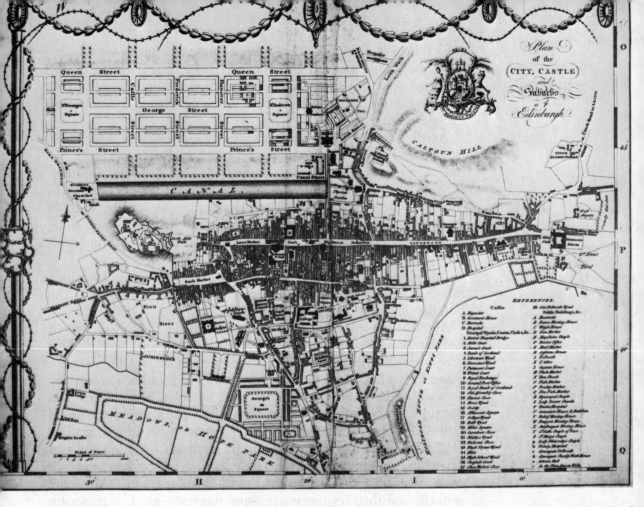

The houses were different, too. By this time, architects had rediscovered the building ideas of the Greeks and Romans and tried to copy them. One of these architects, Robert Adam, had travelled from Scotland to visit Roman remains in Italy. Adam designed Charlotte Square which is still one of the most beautiful squares in the world.

These houses were much larger than the tenements of the Old Town. The rooms were beautifully designed with large windows which gave majestic views out over the Forth to the hills of the north. Yet at first people were not keen to move: they had become attached to the Old Town—despite its smells! They did not want to leave the cosiness of the closes, the convenience of the shops and the company of their neighbours.

Soon, however, the better-off families were moving in large numbers to fill the grander houses of the New Town. This movement of richer families to newer, finer, houses was also happening in other towns in Scotland. In Aberdeen, Perth, Montrose, Dumfries, Ayr, Elgin, Dundee—as well as Glasgow—new houses were being built for the wealthy on the outskirts of the town. In these pleasant

110

Charlotte Square,
Edinburgh

suburbs the well-to-do enjoyed a life of considerable ease and
luxury.

But what was life like for those who could not afford to move?
They still had to suffer all the discomforts of the tenement closes.
As more people flocked to the towns looking for work, the overcrowding became worse. In some places whole families had to
share a single room with no proper heating or sanitation. These
people were desperately poor and could scarcely feed themselves,
far less buy furniture or pay for repairs.

Soon what had once been respectable tenement homes became
dreadful slums. Here is a description of one such slum in Glasgow
in 1839: 'In the lower lodging houses, ten, twelve and sometimes
twenty persons of both sexes, and all ages, sleep on the floor, in
different degrees of nakedness. These places are generally as regards
dirt, damp and decay such as no person in common humanity would
stable his horse in.' Conditions were made even worse in the 1840s
by the arrival of thousands of Irish folk driven from their homes by
a terrible famine.

You must remember that there was no Local Authority Housing
Department or Social Work Department to help these unfortunate
people. In the largest towns there were 'workhouses' for folk who
were poor and unemployed and there were 'hospitals' for the old
people and for orphans. In Glasgow in 1830, about five thousand
poor folk, or 'paupers' as they were called, received help. But in
most towns and all the country parishes, people had to pay a 'poor
rate' or 'poor tax'. Unemployed and old folk were given money
and continued to stay in their own homes. In addition, towns and
parishes gave licences to some poor men and women to beg. The

111

'gaberlunzie man' with his blue gown and big licence-badge was quite a common sight.

Other common sights were the funerals of slum dwellers. Thousands died because their living conditions were so bad. It was estimated that half the children born in Glasgow died from illness before they reached ten years of age.

Yet at first little or nothing was done to make the towns healthier. Epidemics of killing diseases such as *cholera* and *typhus* came year after year. From February to November 1832 cholera raged in Glasgow: 6208 people caught the disease and of these 3005 died. After an awful epidemic in 1848, however, Parliament and the Town Councils of the big towns began to do something about it. The first Public Health Act was passed and the big cities were compelled to arrange proper sanitation and safe water supplies. They began to appoint doctors as Medical Officers of Health to look after such important matters. After about 1860 some Town Councils turned their attention to housing and began to clear away some of the worst slums.

The problems of poverty remained, however. The little help received from the parish was not enough. Thousands of working families had to struggle to survive. Many more years were to pass before any real effort was made to tackle the misery and squalor of their lives.

THINGS TO DO

1 Explain in your own words why Glasgow grew so rapidly in size after 1707.

2 Why did better-off families move away from the older parts of our towns and cities?

3 On page 110 you read about the new style of architecture used to build Edinburgh's New Town. This was called 'Classical' because it copied the style of the Greeks and Romans or 'Georgian' because it was most popular during the reigns of George III (1760–1820) and George IV (1820–1830). If you live in or near one of the towns mentioned on page 110 find out if there are any Georgian buildings still standing. If so, you should try to make a visit and find out what you can about it. In Edinburgh much of the New Town has been preserved. The National Trust for Scotland has restored the house at 7 Charlotte Square as a Georgian House which is open to visitors.

4 On pages 111–12 you read about the health problems facing working families. If you live near a graveyard dating from the early nineteenth century, a visit will show you just how bad things were. You would see gravestones like this showing the tragic deaths of young children. The stones should give you other information too, such as the jobs done by people in those days and the Christian names that were popular then.

5 In 1766 Edinburgh Town Council organised a competition for a plan for the New Town. The prize was to be a gold medal and the Freedom of the City. Design a poster for this competition.

6 We know much more about events in Scotland from 1707 onwards because we have so much more evidence to study. Interesting sources are the accounts left by visitors to Scotland of what they saw and did. Many of these can be borrowed from your local library and are well worth looking up to see what your town or district was like then. Among the visitors to Scotland at the start of the nineteenth century was the famous poet William Wordsworth and his sister Dorothy. She kept a diary of their travels. Imagine that you are Dorothy Wordsworth. Write her diary entries for the visits to Glasgow and Edinburgh.

7 In 1833 a famous Edinburgh writer, Robert Chambers, described what happened when the better-off families moved to the New Town. Read the passage carefully then answer the questions below.

> The fine gentlemen who daily exhibit their foreign dresses and manners on Princes Street [in the New Town] have no idea of a race of people who roost in the tall houses of the Lawnmarket and the West Bow [in the Old Town], and retain about them many of the primitive modes of life and habits of thought that flourished among their grandfathers.
>
> Edinburgh is in fact two towns in more ways than one. It contains an upper and under town—the one a sort of thoroughfare for the children of business and fashion, the other a den of retreat for the poor, the diseased and the ignorant.

(a) Why do you think 'the fine gentlemen' had no idea about life in the Old Town?

(b) You have read already about one of 'the primitive modes of life' of the Old Town. What was it?

(c) What evidence is there in the passage to confirm that it was the richer people who had moved to the New Town?

(d) What were the differences between the houses of the New Town and the Old Town?

(e) What do you think the differences between the lives of 'the fine gentlemen' of the New Town and the 'people who roost' in the Old Town would be?

(f) Do you think Chambers approved the fact that Edinburgh was now 'two towns'?

15 The struggle between Britain and France

You will remember that in the fourteenth and fifteenth centuries there were long wars between England and France. These wars are called the Hundred Years' War, and in them England was fighting to conquer France.

In the eighteenth century there was a second and greater Hundred Years' War between France and Britain, fought for a greater prize. This time they fought for control of the trade, the empty lands and the sea-roads of the world. Of course the fighting was not continuous, and there were long periods of peace, but we can say that for rather more than a hundred years the two countries were in opposite camps.

At first sight all the advantages seem to lie with France. In 1700 there were three or four times as many Frenchmen as there were Englishmen. Even when Scotland united with England, Britain did not have nearly as many men as France. Then the French army was much larger and better organised than the British. The French navy was almost as large as Britain's, but Britain had one great advantage: she had no frontiers to guard. France had to keep up a vast army to guard her frontiers against Britain's allies. Britain could do with a small army and keep herself strong at sea, using her fleet to seize colonies and carry troops to fight in India and America.

Just look at this list of the wars in which England, then Britain, fought against France in the second Hundred Years' War:

War of the League of Augsburg	1689 to 1697
War of the Spanish Succession	1702 to 1713
War of the Austrian Succession	1740 to 1748
Seven Years' War	1756 to 1763
War of American Independence	1775 to 1783
Revolutionary and Napoleonic Wars	1793 to 1815

During most of these wars British troops took no great part in the land-fighting in Europe. In the war of the Spanish Succession, however, under the Duke of Marlborough, the British Army won many victories. Later, as we shall see in Chapter 17, in the Napoleonic Wars, it drove the French out of Spain and, helped by the Prussians,

Marlborough

finally defeated them at the Battle of Waterloo. Usually, however, we relied upon our allies to do the land-fighting in Europe while we fought at sea and in the colonies.

In these wars Britain gained lands overseas, especially in the Seven Years' War. In fact, for Britain, this war lasted for almost nine years and gave us control of North America and India.

We last looked at these colonies in Chapter 6. By the middle of the eighteenth century, thousands of colonists had made their homes in the New World.

As you can imagine, life for the first colonists was hard—especially in the north where there were no slaves to do the heavy work. The pioneer farmer usually had to clear the forest before he could make his fields: cutting down trees, digging up stumps and burning the wood. From some of the logs he had to build his wooden house and barns. Much of the furniture had to be hand-made. For his wife the days were equally hard. She had bread to make, meat to salt for the long winter, wool to spin and skins to cure for clothing as well as all the other work which housewives have everywhere.

Life was made harder by the Indians. The settlers traded with them, exchanging rum, axes, knives and cloth for valuable furs, but they knew all the time that they might hear the whooping war-cries of an Indian raid, or see their thatched houses set alight by Indian fire-arrows. In 1675 the Wampanoag Indians led an attack in which more than a thousand colonists were killed. The

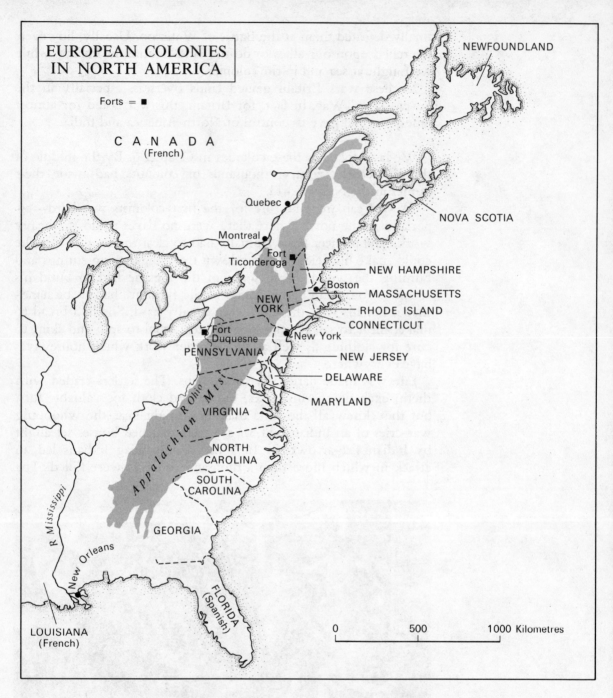

EUROPEAN COLONIES IN NORTH AMERICA

Forts = ■

NEWFOUNDLAND

CANADA
(French)

Quebec

NOVA SCOTIA

Montreal

Fort
Ticonderoga

NEW HAMPSHIRE

Boston

MASSACHUSETTS

NEW
YORK

RHODE ISLAND

CONNECTICUT

Fort
Duquesne

New York

PENNSYLVANIA

NEW JERSEY

DELAWARE

R Ohio

MARYLAND

VIRGINIA

Appalachian Mts

NORTH
CAROLINA

SOUTH
CAROLINA

R Mississippi

GEORGIA

New Orleans

FLORIDA
(Spanish)

LOUISIANA
(French)

0   500   1000 Kilometres

settlers lived with their guns beside them and became skilled backwoodsmen and marksmen, especially the Irish-Scots who settled in Pennsylvania.

Gradually the colonies prospered. From their farms and forests, rich cargoes of sugar, cotton, tobacco and timber were shipped to Britain. As you know, these products played an important part in our Industrial Revolution. In return, the colonies bought the

116

cotton, woollen and iron goods made in Britain's factories and foundries. So you can see why colonies were so important to Britain.

But it was not only British colonists who moved into North America. The valley of the St Lawrence river was settled by French people, whose descendants still live there. Today in Canada one person in every four speaks French. Until 1666 these French colonists suffered from the attacks of the Iroquois, the best led and fiercest of the Indian nations. In that year the Iroquois were defeated and the way was open to the west. French fur-traders and missionaries pushed further and further into Canada, up the St Lawrence and through the lakes in canoes and open boats. Others from the south settled along the Mississippi, creating the new state of Louisiana. This was a real danger to the British colonists, for if the French in Canada and the French in Louisiana joined up they would stop the British colonies from spreading westwards.

There was competition in India, too. Both the French and the British had built trading posts. At the start of the eighteenth century India was ruled by an emperor, known as the Mogul. The country was very wealthy. Living among a population of many millions, the European traders had to be careful not to offend the Indians. Here you can see one European being received at the court of a rich Indian prince.

India was very different from the North American colonies. The European settlers in India were few in number. They came to trade, not to hunt or farm. The land had been farmed for hundreds of years by the Indians living in countless villages. The Indians had a rich culture and Europeans were astonished at the beauty of the many temples and palaces filled with fine works of art. Perhaps the best known temple is the Taj Mahal.

From 1707 onwards, however, the Mogul Empire began to break up. The various princes of India fought among themselves for power. Each prince hoped that with the help of European weapons and soldiers he would be able to defeat his rivals. On the other hand, the French and British trading companies hoped that with the help of Indian princes they would be able to increase their wealth and power.

At first things favoured the French. The French governor of Pondicherry, Dupleix, was a brave man who was determined that south India should be French. In the War of the Austrian Succession the French captured Madras but were forced to hand it back when war ended. Even after the peace treaty, however, fighting continued between the princes and both French and British troops took part. This gave a chance for Robert Clive to prove his skill as a soldier and to win control of India from the French.

117

In his first campaigns Clive showed his genius with a very small force—six officers, two hundred British and three hundred Indian soldiers. He captured the great town of Arcot and held it against ten thousand enemy troops for fifty-three days in spite of fierce attacks on the gates by armour-plated elephants. As a result of his victory a prince who was a friend of Britain was made ruler of the south-east of India, the Carnatic.

Further north, at Calcutta, Clive had to act to save the British trading-post there. In 1756 the ruler of Bengal, Suraj-ud-daula, had imprisoned sixty-nine of the British in a small, over-crowded cell; and during the night all except twenty-six died. This was the 'Black Hole of Calcutta'. To avenge this, Clive was sent north with an army of about three thousand men, of whom some nine hundred were British. He recaptured Calcutta and fought Suraj-ud-daula's forces at Plassey in 1757. It was an outstanding victory over very great odds, for Suraj-ud-daula had nearly fifty thousand men. After the battle Clive appointed as ruler of Bengal a prince who was friendly to Britain.

One more step was needed to weaken French power, for in the Deccan, the great plateau of south India, the French were still strong. From Bengal a small force was sent to capture Masulipatam and its French garrison. Once it was in British hands the ruler of the Deccan hurried to become an ally of Britain. By 1763 French power in India was broken, and the British merchants had the trade

East India Company troops at Bombay

between India and Europe in their own hands. We should remember the words 'British merchants'. For it was the great East India Company, 'John Company'—not the British government—that ruled India. Gradually the Company came more and more under the control of the British government, but its rule did not finally end until 1858.

118

Meanwhile, what was happening in North America?

There, the war began in 1754 when the French tried to join their colonies in Canada and in the Ohio Valley. This would have put a stop to any expansion to the lands of the West. The French challenge had to be met.

When the French built a fort, Fort Duquesne (where Pittsburgh now stands) some soldiers under a young colonel called George Washington were sent from Virginia to drive them out. Washington and his men were taken prisoner. This was serious, and in 1755 the British government sent a regular soldier, General Braddock, with regular troops to drive out the French. The redcoated soldiers, with fifes shrilling and drums beating at the head of the column, made their way slowly westwards towards Fort Duquesne. But all the way they were shadowed by silent redmen who knew how to remain unseen in the woods. Just before Braddock reached Fort Duquesne the Indians and their French masters struck. Two-thirds of the British force were killed or wounded, including General Braddock. Fair-haired scalps hung in the wigwams afterwards.

The next two years were difficult years in North America. Until William Pitt became Prime Minister in 1757 things went badly for Britain. They might have been worse but for Sir William Johnson, the king's agent for Indian affairs, who had a wonderful gift for dealing with Indians and managed to keep both the Mohawks and the Iroquois friendly.

Pitt's leadership changed everything. We should remember that it was Pitt who encouraged Highlanders to join the British army. In North America these Highland soldiers distinguished themselves first at the attack on a French fort, Ticonderoga, and then at Quebec. The year 1759 was the wonderful year when victory followed victory in Europe, at sea, in India and in North America.

William Pitt

Let us take a closer look at the capture of Quebec, the key to Canada. The man given the job of capturing the town was General James Wolfe. Many people were surprised at Pitt's choice of leader, for Wolfe was only thirty-two years old. He had almost ruined his career after the Battle of Culloden when he refused to kill wounded Highlanders. Pitt knew, however, that Wolfe was an officer of great skill and courage.

In 1759, the expedition left on its journey to Quebec. The town stood high above the St Lawrence River, guarded by a hundred guns and a large garrison. The French defenders were led by the clever General Montcalm. It was not going to be easy.

First, the attackers had to make their way up the treacherous St Lawrence River. Here Wolfe was helped by the skilful navigation of young James Cook, later to be famous as an explorer. Wolfe tried several times to capture Quebec but each time his

attacks were beaten off. In June and July the French tried twice to destroy the British fleet with fire ships. The Indian allies of the French frightened Wolfe's men by their sudden raids. Their victims were scalped and their prisoners cruelly tortured to death.

By the end of the summer, Wolfe was in despair. The onset of winter could force him to withdraw. There was one last chance. Spies reported that there was a narrow path up the steep cliffs behind the French lines. Wolfe decided to launch a final attack here.

What kind of men did Wolfe lead into action? Most of them were from poor families, glad of a meal and the pay of 2½p a day in return for three years' service. Some had been tricked into joining up by recruiting sergeants; others were criminals on the run from the law. Their scarlet coats earned them the nickname 'lobsters'. They also wore a waistcoat, scarlet breeches, white gaiters and buckled shoes. In their haversacks, the soldiers carried spare clothes and six days' supply of bread. Each man was armed with the famous 'Brown Bess' musket, accurate up to about sixty paces, a sword and a bayonet. On their heads they wore tall, peaked caps or black three-cornered hats—depending on which regiment they belonged to.

In those days each regiment had a different number. The first regiment was the Royal Scots, who still carry the title of 'The First of Foot'. Among Wolfe's soldiers was the 78th Regiment, a High-land regiment made up mostly of Frasers, including men who had fought against Wolfe at Culloden.

Discipline had to be very harsh to prevent men running away under fire. Offenders were whipped with the 'cat o'nine tails' and the minimum punishment was twenty five lashes. The maximum was three thousand! Few survived this.

Wolfe was a firm but fair commander. His men respected him and were in good heart as they prepared to attack. One of his men composed a tune in honour of him:

Come each death-dealing dog who dares venture his neck,
Come follow the hero who goes to Quebec,
And ye that love fighting shall soon have enough;
Wolfe commands us my boys; we shall give them hot stuff.

At one o'clock in the morning of September 13th thirty boats slipped from the British fleet under cover of darkness. Wolfe and 1700 men headed upstream for the path. When they were challenged by French sentries, Captain Fraser of the 78th replied in French that they were friends carrying supplies for the garrison. They were allowed to pass.

The British and their Indian allies landed beneath the steep cliffs. They climbed silently up to the Plains of Abraham. The French

120

sentries were killed and the signal given for the rest of the troops to land. By dawn 4500 men were drawn up ready for battle.

Montcalm was taken by surprise. He ordered an immediate attack. At a distance of forty paces the redcoats opened fire. The French fell in hundreds, the survivors turned and fled. Wolfe had been wounded twice; now, in the moment of victory, he was shot in the chest. He was told that the French were beaten. 'Now, God be praised' he said, 'I will die in peace.'

Montcalm was also mortally wounded. Next day he, too, died. On September 18th, Quebec surrendered. Wolfe had won a famous victory but at the cost of his life.

After Quebec had fallen the way up the St Lawrence was open. Other British forces had taken Fort Duquesne and were advancing towards the Great Lakes. When peace came France was glad to surrender all her lands in North America. In this one war Britain gained Canada and all the rest of North America as far west as the Mississippi, for we had also taken Florida from Spain, the ally of France.

As you can imagine, there were tremendous celebrations in Britain. This is how one man at the time described the feeling: 'Our bells are worn threadbare with ringing for victories. One can never afford to miss a single copy of a newspaper for fear of missing a British victory somewhere.'

In the rejoicing, few people could have thought that twelve years later the redcoats would again be fighting in North America. Even fewer people would have imagined that they would not be fighting the French, but the British colonists—their own kith and kin.

THINGS TO DO

1 Explain in your own words why colonies were so important to Britain.

2 What were the differences between the British settlements in India and North America?

3 From what you have learnt about the life of the redcoat in this chapter, draw a recruiting poster for the British Army.

4 Here is part of a British soldier's account of the fighting round Quebec. He was a Grenadier like the one shown here. Read the passage carefully and answer the questions below. Then use the information here and in the chapter to help you write a letter home describing the campaign to capture Quebec.

> As soon as we landed, we fix'd our Bayonets and beat our Grenadier's March, and so advanced on. During all this time their Cannon play'd very briskly on us; but their Small Arms, in their Trenches, lay cool 'till they were sure of their Mark; then they poured their Small-Shot like showers of Hail, which caus'd our brave Grenadiers to fall very fast.

(a) What was a 'Bayonet'?

(b) What evidence is there in the passage to show that the men went into battle to music?

(c) What instruments do you think would be played?

(d) What do you think is meant by 'their Small Arms'?

(e) What evidence is there in the passage to show that the French soldiers held their fire?

(f) Why do you think they would do this?

(g) What evidence is there in the passage to show that British casualties were heavy?

(h) This passage describes one of the earlier unsuccessful attempts made by Wolfe to capture Quebec. How did the British manage to overcome the strong French defences?

16 The USA is born

The Seven Years' War left Britain as the strongest power in North America. She owned a great belt of land stretching the whole way down the eastern coast, from Hudson's Bay to Florida. It seemed that all was well, but in fact the driving out of the French had weakened Britain.

Up till now the colonists had realised that they needed British soldiers and British ships to protect them from the French. When the French were driven out, British forces no longer seemed necessary. The British government in London decided, however, to keep an army of 6000 soldiers in North America. This, of course, cost a good deal of money and the government felt that it was only fair that the colonists should pay part of this cost. The colonists did not agree. They resented very much having to pay a share of the cost of defence, especially when they were not represented in Parliament. We shall see that, twenty years after the victory over France, Britain lost the original thirteen colonies in North America.

The trouble began almost at once. An Indian chief, Pontiac, raised a rebellion against the white settlers—the greatest Indian rising there ever was. His men killed many settlers around the Great Lakes and burned many of the log forts and stockades before they were finally defeated. One reason for the rising had been that the Indians feared that they would lose their lands to the white settlers. Look again at the map on page 116.

To prevent further trouble the British government ordered settlers not to cross the Appalachian Mountains until treaties were made with the Indians. To the men in the colonies this seemed to be nonsense. For them the land to the west was the Land of Promise: rich, fertile land from which the French had been driven. It seemed to them that the British government was deliberately favouring the Indians. So they ignored the Proclamation Line, as the boundary was called, moved west down the great Ohio River, and defied the government in London and the British soldiers in the forts beyond the mountains.

To raise the money needed to pay for the soldiers in North America the London government tried to increase the amount of money which they received from the colonists. There were two

George III

main ways of doing this: by customs, the taxes paid on goods coming into a country; and by excise, the taxes paid on goods made or sold inside the country. The customs officers were never popular. Even during the war with France, when they tried to stop American merchants trading with the enemy, they were hated, for the colonists loathed the laws which hindered their trade.

In 1764 Parliament at Westminster put heavy customs duties on such foreign goods as silk, sugar and wine. This Act, the Sugar Act, was very unpopular. In the following year the Stamp Act was passed, and this was still more unpopular. It laid down that all legal documents, newspapers, advertisements, playing cards, and so on, had to be stamped before they were sold. This excise duty affected a great many people and there was such an outcry that the Act was repealed in 1766. But the damage was done. The colonists saw that the British Parliament meant to tax them, although the colonies were not represented in Parliament.

Quite clearly, Britain had misjudged the mood of the colonists. These people were not prepared to be pushed around by a government, five thousand kilometres away. To them, King George III and his ministers were interfering in their country. After all, they had done all the hard work necessary to make the colonies prosper. They had cleared the forests, raised the crops, built the villages and towns, fought the Indians. Now it seemed that Britain wanted to get the benefits from all their efforts. Some of the leading colonists began to meet secretly. Representatives from the different colonies discussed what actions should be taken. The tension mounted.

Trouble broke out in 1770 in Boston when a crowd of rowdies surrounded a patrol of British troops, throwing stones and jeering at the soldiers. The troops opened fire and killed five of the mob. The colonists called this 'The Boston Massacre'.

A few years later Boston was the centre of more trouble. Until 1773 it had been difficult to sell tea from British India in the colonies because tea smuggled from Holland was cheaper. The Tea Act of 1773 reduced the price of British tea so much that it sold cheaper than Dutch tea. But there was still a tax on the British tea, and many people in the colonies thought that the price had been reduced simply to make them pay the tax. A band of colonists disguised as Red Indians boarded a tea-ship in Boston harbour and threw the tea overboard. All up and down the coast others followed their example. It was open rebellion, and the 'Boston Tea Party' is usually thought of as the beginning of the break-away from Britain.

The war began with a little skirmish. In April 1775 the British governor of Boston, General Gage, sent a force of troops to seize a gunpowder magazine at Concord. During the night Paul Revere and William Dawes, two men of Boston, rode out to warn the 'minutemen', colonists who said they were ready to march at a minute's notice to resist the British. So when the British forces arrived at a little village called Lexington fifty 'minutemen' tried to stop them. Shots were fired and the British decided to return the twenty kilometres to Boston. More 'minutemen' arrived and hounded the retreating redcoats. By the end of the day, 273 British and 95 colonists had been killed. This little battle began a war which lasted for eight years and ended with the defeat of the British and the setting up of the United States.

At first, most people thought that the 'rebels', as the British now called them, could be beaten easily. After all, Britain had a large army of trained soldiers and the strongest navy in the world. These men had only recently defeated the might of France. Yet they were to be humbled by the Americans. Why was this?

We have seen already that the British government had made mistakes. Now, they underestimated the American soldiers. The Earl of Sandwich, First Lord of the Admiralty, thought that the Americans were 'raw, undisciplined, cowardly men. The very sound of a cannon would carry them off [make them run away]'. He was quite wrong. The Americans were used to fighting. They had plenty of experience against the Indians and the French. Many of them were skilled marksmen, able to make good use of the forests in carrying out surprise attacks. The British in their red coats made easy targets. Remember, too, that the Americans felt that they were fighting for their freedom.

In 1776 the leaders of the colonists met and signed a statement of their beliefs that 'all men are born free and equal' and declared that the colonies were independent of Britain. This document is called the Declaration of Independence, and you will find part of it on page 129. The Americans still keep the day on which it was signed, July 4th, as 'Independence Day'.

In the actual fighting both sides did badly at first. The well-drilled redcoats (and the German regiments which King George III hired to help them) won some victories but their casualties were heavy. They were rather at a loss to know how to deal with the Americans who refused to fight pitched battles; who fired from behind trees and who were difficult to catch.

The Americans for their part were often short of weapons, of powder, of shoes, even of food. An attempt to invade Canada was defeated with heavy losses. They had one great advantage: in George Washington they had a great leader, a man who was absolutely unshakeable. This was the same George Washington who as a young man had been captured by the French when fighting for Britain. Later he became the first *President* of the United States, but his greatest work was done during the war when he kept together his poorly-equipped soldiers and led them to victory.

Washington

Signature of the
Declaration of
Independence

Britain had no Wolfe to command its armies; our generals were
poor choices and no match for Washington.

At first neither side could claim any definite victory, but in
October 1777 the colonists had their first success. At Saratoga
General Burgoyne and his army of 4500 men had to surrender.

The victory was a very important one. Up till now other European
countries had been watching the war, expecting the British to win.
Now they realised that the Americans had a chance. France, Spain
and Holland came into the war against Britain and we had to fight
on sea as well as on land, in Europe as well as in America. For
example, the Spanish besieged Gibraltar, French troops landed in
America, and a great sea battle—the Battle of the Saints—was
fought between the British and French fleets in the West Indies.
The Americans, too, were creating a navy. Paul Jones, the son of a
Scots gardener from Kirkcudbright, was one of its founders and
was one of the first to fly the 'Stars and Stripes' in a ship of war. In
his ship the 'Bonhomme Richard', he raided the British coast and
even defeated a Royal Navy frigate, the 'Serapis'. At one time he
sailed up the Forth and threatened Edinburgh but he was driven off
by a storm.

By 1782 Britain was ready to think of peace. On October 17th
1781, the army of Lord Cornwallis had been forced to surrender

at Yorktown. Like General Burgoyne, Cornwallis found himself surrounded by enemies and cut off from help. It had been hard enough for the British to supply their armies at the start of the war. The 5000 km journey could take as long as ten weeks. Now, the Royal Navy was no longer in control of the seas. At Yorktown, French ships prevented British reinforcements reaching Cornwallis. With the help of his French allies, Washington pressed home his attack. Cornwallis had no choice but to surrender his army. As the redcoats marched out to hand over their weapons, the British bands played a favourite tune 'The World Turned Upside Down'.

And so it had. The war was becoming very expensive for Britain and unpopular too. King George III reluctantly accepted that 'the raw, undisciplined, cowardly men' had beaten Britain. In 1783 the Peace of Versailles ended the war and left the colonists free of British rule, free to form their own country—the United States of America.

Of course not everyone in the colonies had rebelled against Britain. Many had remained loyal, including such people as Flora MacDonald and most of the Highlanders who had gone to settle in the Carolinas. After the war was over many of these loyalists left the United States to settle in Canada, in Ontario and New Brunswick. During the war the people of Canada had remained

127

loyal to Britain, for the French Catholics thought that life would be better for them under British rule than under the rule of the Puritans of New England. The arrival of the new settlers in Ontario and New Brunswick meant that Canada now had a large number of British settlers. So one result of the British defeat in America was that Canada began to grow into an English-speaking colony.

When the people of the United States began to think how they should govern themselves, they gave up the idea of having a new king to replace George III. Instead they set up a *republic* and elected George Washington as President. In place of Parliament they set up Congress. This, like Parliament, has two Houses. One is called the House of Representatives and corresponds to our House of Commons; the other is called the Senate, in which there are two representatives from every State, large and small. Congress, like Parliament, makes laws for the whole country. In addition, each State has the right to make laws which apply to its own members only.

This young country grew very quickly. Settlers pushed westwards into the new lands till they reached the Pacific Ocean. When the War of Independence started there were fewer than two million people in the colonies. Today the population of the United States is over 215 million and the United States is one of the two greatest Powers in the world.

THINGS TO DO

1 Explain in your own words why you think the colonists chose to fight Britain.

2 William Eden was a British *diplomat* sent to negotiate a peace with the Americans. This is part of what he wrote about the loss of the American colonies:

> It is impossible to see what I can see of this magnificent country and not go nearly mad at the long train of misconducts and mistakes by which we have lost it.

What mistakes do you think Britain made during these years?

3 Why do you think the colonists were able to beat Britain?

4 On page 124 you read about the Boston Massacre. Use this information and this picture (opposite) to help you to write a newspaper article for a British paper, choosing a suitable headline. Now try to write an article about the same incident for an American paper. Do you think this picture was drawn for a British or an American paper?

128

5 Why did it take so long for news to reach Britain?

6 Read carefully this part of the American Declaration of Independence. Try to understand what it means. Do you agree with what it is saying? Organise a class debate to discuss this.

> We hold these truths to be self-evident, that all men are created equal, that they are endowed by their Creator with certain unalienable rights, that among these are life, liberty and the pursuit of happiness. . . . Whenever any form of government becomes destructive of these ends, it is the right of the people to alter or to abolish it, and to institute a new government . . . as shall seem most likely to effect their safety and happiness.

17 The French Revolution

The peasants' burden:
a contemporary cartoon

A thrill of excitement ran through Europe in 1789.

The French parliament, the States-General, which had not met for more than one hundred and fifty years, was called together. To us there is nothing very thrilling in the idea of the meeting of a parliament, but in 1789 almost every country in Europe, except Britain, was ruled by a king without any parliament. No one could be sure where this change in France would lead to. The king, Louis XVI, was not particularly eager to call it, but his hand was forced. France was almost bankrupt; taxes were appallingly heavy; many of the people were desperately poor. In fact, the cost of helping the American colonists in their struggle had finally ruined France. To find the extra money he needed, Louis XVI had no choice but to turn to the States-General. But (like the Parliament of Charles I that we read about in Chapter 4) the States-General was in no mood to help the king. Several of its members had fought in America and they brought back to France the ideas of the Americans—where the people governed the country, not a king. So when the States-General met, it took charge and began to put right many of the things which were wrong in France. The power of the nobles was taken away, taxes were spread more evenly, laws were reformed, and so on.

In all this there was nothing to worry about. The trouble came from the people, the labouring people both in Paris and in the country, who thought that the States-General was not going fast enough. In Paris, on July 14th, a mob seized the royal fortress-prison, the Bastille, killed the guards and captured arms. July 14th, 'Bastille Day', is still kept as a national holiday in France. (Incidentally inside that huge fortress, the mob found only seven prisoners to set free.)

The capture of this royal stronghold was the signal for revolt. In the country many of the *peasants* attacked the nobles' castles, burned them and took the land. Some of these nobles fled to foreign countries and took with them stories of what was happening in France. Everyone realised that this was revolution, especially when crowds of hungry people from Paris marched to the royal palace at Versailles and forced the king and his family to return to Paris.

Storming of the Bastille

At first the States-General had hoped to give France a government rather like that of Great Britain, where the king ruled with the help and advice of parliament, but obviously that would succeed only if the king agreed. In 1792 Louis and his family tried to flee from France. He was arrested and tried. The sentence was death both for himself and for the queen, the hated Marie Antoinette: death by the guillotine, a machine for cutting off heads cleanly.

On the morning of January 21st 1793, Louis said a tearful farewell to his family before being driven through packed streets to the Place de la Revolution where he was to be executed. He took off his coat and mounted the scaffold. He tried to talk to the crowd but a roll of drums drowned his last words.

Here is part of a report printed in the 'Edinburgh Evening Courant' describing his last moments: 'The head of Louis was then struck off: and being exhibited a thousand cries were heard of "Vive La Nation, Vive La Republique Française!" Some volunteers dipt their pikes; others their handkerchiefs in the blood of the tyrant.'

People in Britain were horrified by his death. 'We can but conclusively consider that Louis the sixteenth has died a Martyr.

131

AND BE HIS BLOOD UPON THE HEADS OF THE MURDERERS.'

Louis did not die alone, for a very large number of nobles were also tried and executed. The heavy carts carried them from prison to the public squares in Paris and other towns where the tall guillotines were set up and the crowds gloated over the deaths of the aristocrats. It was the Reign of Terror. According to Robespierre, one of the leaders of the Revolution, 'Revolutionary government owes every protection to good citizens: to the enemies of the people it owes only death.' But many of these first leaders, including Robespierre, were sent to the guillotine during the Reign of Terror.

But we must not think of the French Revolution simply as a time when nobles were killed. Many great reforms were made which have lasted till today. The watchwords were *Liberty, Equality and Fraternity*, and these ideas are the basis of what we mean by democracy today. All the laws which prevented men from being free and equal were repealed. Schools were built to give all French children, not just the rich, the chance to learn. Even the systems of measurement were changed and the metric system which we now use was brought in.

Outside France men watched carefully what was happening. To some it was the greatest event they had ever known. They saw that the changes in France might be an example to their own countries. This was very worrying to the rulers. In Britain, for example, few people had any say in the running of the country. As we shall see in Chapter 19, MPs were chosen by a tiny handful of property-owners. Many people thought this was wrong, particularly when the government did nothing to help them. We

132

have seen already the misery caused by the Industrial Revolution. The mood of the people was becoming bitter. The government for its part was worried in case a revolution started in Britain. Even before 1789, there had been signs of trouble. Here is a report of an incident in Glasgow:

> In 1787, the cotton manufacturers [the employers] proposed to reduce the price of weaving on which a number of the workers stopt work, and after parading the streets on 3rd September burned and destroyed a number of webs [weaving machines] in the Drygate and Calton. Provost Riddell called out the military, under the command of Colonel Kellet, when the *Riot Act* was read; the mob refused to disperse, three men were killed and several wounded.

Thomas Muir

When news of the French Revolution reached Britain, the government was determined to keep control. In many towns there were demonstrations by people wanting to be allowed to vote. They were known as Radicals. Amongst their leaders was Thomas Muir of Huntershill near Glasgow. He and others were arrested and put on trial in 1793. This trial was most unfair. The judge, Lord Braxfield, hated the Radicals and he made his feelings very plain to the jury. As he said to one of them: 'Come awa' Maister Horner, come awa' and help us to hang ane o' they damned scoundrels.'

One of the leaders was indeed hanged, his only crime being to demand the right to vote. Muir was sentenced to fourteen years transportation to the recently-discovered colony of Botany Bay in Australia. In 1796 he escaped on board an American ship sent to rescue him and, after many adventures, he reached France where he died in 1799. Today, a monument stands to this 'Friend of the People' on the Calton Hill in Edinburgh.

The execution of Louis led to war in Europe. This long war, which lasted from 1793 to 1815, began when the French revolutionaries declared war on Austria, hoping to spread the ideas of the revolution all over Europe. The French army seemed to be in bad shape, but although many of the officer-nobles had left, the newly-appointed officers and the soldiers had something that made up for their lack of skill. They believed passionately in France and in the revolution. The stirring words and music of the 'Marseillaise', which was written at this time, gives us some idea of the spirit of France. In a short campaign the Austrians and Prussians were driven from France. Belgium was conquered, then Holland. A British army which landed in Holland under the Duke of York was defeated and forced to retreat. Everywhere France was victorious at first. Soon she was to be served by the greatest soldier of his age.

Napoleon Bonaparte, a Corsican, had been an artillery officer of the royal army in France. When the revolution came he stayed on and made a name for himself by helping to drive a British force out of Toulon. His great chance came when he was given command of the army of Italy. In 1796 he began to conquer Italy, which was then a collection of small independent states. By 1797 the campaign was over: Italy was conquered and large parts of it made into republics like France. Austria and Prussia had made peace and Britain alone remained at war with France.

The next year Napoleon tried to knock Britain out of the war by an attack, through Egypt, on our trade in the Indian Ocean. He succeeded in landing a great army in Egypt and defeating the Egyptians, but a British fleet under Horatio Nelson caught his ships in Aboukir Bay at the mouth of the Nile, destroyed them and so cut off the French army. In France men did not understand how serious this naval defeat was, for they thought of Napoleon simply as a great hero who had conquered Egypt. When he came back to France he was welcomed everywhere and made head of the government, with the title of First Consul. By 1802 both France and Britain realised that neither had much hope of victory: it was a war of elephant against whale. The Peace of Amiens ended this first stage of the war.

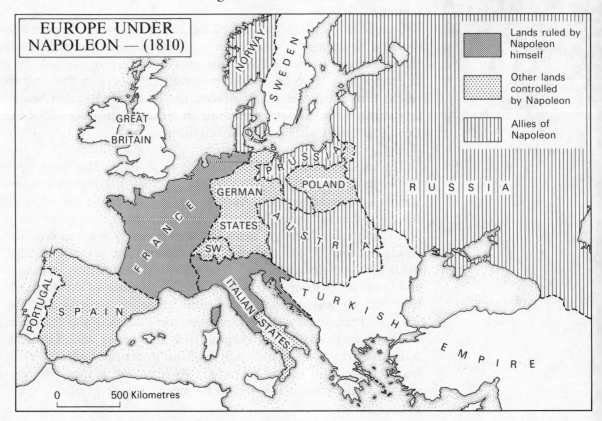

EUROPE UNDER NAPOLEON — (1810)

Lands ruled by Napoleon himself

Other lands controlled by Napoleon

Allies of Napoleon

0   500 Kilometres

134

After a short-lived peace, war broke out again in 1803. France and Spain fought on one side; Britain, Russia, Austria (and later Prussia) on the other. Napoleon's first plan was to invade Britain, by carrying a large army over the English Channel in rafts and flat-bottomed landing-craft. A great army was assembled on the French coast and prepared for the invasion. In Britain great preparations were made to meet the invasion: men were enlisted in the Fencibles and Militia—the 'Home Guard' of the time; bonfires were built on high ground to be lit if the enemy landed; above all, the Navy was ordered to seek out and destroy the French fleet. The Navy succeeded in its task. On October 21st 1805, Lord Nelson shattered the combined French and Spanish fleets at Trafalgar, to give Britain the mastery of the seas for the next hundred years. Like Wolfe at Quebec, however, Nelson died at the moment of victory.

Even before Trafalgar, Napoleon had been forced to withdraw his troops from the Channel and hurry eastwards, for Russia and Austria had *mobilised* against him. In this campaign Europe was shown how great a soldier Napoleon was. At Austerlitz in 1805 the Austrian army was defeated; at Jena in 1806 the Prussian army was defeated; and finally after a long march across Poland, Napoleon forced the Russians to make peace at Tilsit. All Europe was subdued, except for Britain. Against Britain Napoleon tried a new weapon—blockade. The countries of Europe were forbidden to trade with Britain. The weapon was two-edged: it caused unemployment in Britain, but it stirred up much ill-feeling against Napoleon in Europe, where men needed British goods.

Indeed, it led to a renewal of the land-fighting. The Portuguese refused to stop trading with Britain and, when French troops invaded Portugal, Britain was able to send troops to fight the French there and in Spain. This war, which we call the Peninsular War, did not end till the British, commanded by the Duke of Wellington, had driven the French from Spain and had occupied the south of France.

In the east, too, Napoleon's blockade caused trouble. The Tsar of Russia disliked it very much, for it prevented British manufactured goods from reaching Russia. Finally he decided to pay no attention to Napoleon's wishes. Once more Napoleon led a great army eastwards, this time to disaster. In June 1812 he crossed the Russian frontier at the head of his army of about 500 000 men. Slowly the French made their way across the great Russian plain, defeating the Russians at Borodino. Moscow was captured in September but Russia was not defeated. The city of Moscow was set on fire. In October the order to retreat was given. As Napoleon's forces marched back into Europe, they were attacked repeatedly by Russian cavalry. Winter came on early, and the bitter cold of Russia killed thousands of men. Only about 40 000 men of that great army came back.

That was the beginning of Napoleon's downfall. In 1813 the Austrians, Russians and Prussians combined to beat him at Leipzig in the 'Battle of the Nations'. France was invaded, and in the end Napoleon gave up the throne of France and went into exile on Elba. Europe seemed to be at peace again.

In 1815 another storm burst upon Europe: Napoleon came back from Elba. His soldiers came flocking back to join him and serve under the red, white and blue flag. At Waterloo in Belgium the last battle of the war was fought. All day long the red-coated British troops under the Duke of Wellington held the fierce French attacks. As evening came on, the Prussians under Blücher came to help, and the French were finally defeated. The casualties for both sides

136

were very heavy. The British lost 15 000 men, the Prussians 7000 and the French 25 000. As he looked over the battlefield now covered with bodies, Wellington said to one of his officers 'I have never fought such a battle, and I trust I shall never fight such another.' Napoleon was sent to St Helena (where he died in 1821) and Paris was occupied by the allies.

But Napoleon's work did not all end in 1815. The great work he did to reform French law survived and France today lives under the Napoleonic law code. In addition, the glory of Napoleon's conquests lived on in Frenchmen's memories. Years after his death, his body was brought back to Paris to be re-buried in the magnificent tomb where it now lies.

In the long wars Scotsmen of all ranks had played a great part, none greater than that of Sir John Moore. He fought bravely in the Peninsular War but, sadly, was killed at the battle of Corunna. At sea, the Scots commander, Admiral Duncan, won a great victory over the Dutch fleet in 1797 at Camperdown. Ordinary men, too, played their part in the army and navy of King George III. This was the time when many famous Highland regiments were added to the British army—the 79th, Cameron Highlanders, the 92nd, Gordon Highlanders, the 91st and 93rd, Argyll and Sutherland Highlanders, as well as others now disbanded.

At home the war had meant prosperity for many. Farming was very profitable because food was scarce. The iron workers (and therefore the coal miners) had plenty of work to supply the weapons needed for Britain and her allies. Carron in particular was very busy making the famous guns, the carronades, which were much used at this time. Sail-makers, too, were busy. On the other hand, Napoleon's blockade kept our goods out of many European countries and there was, as a result, a good deal of unemployment as the war went on. We should remember as well that food was dear. Many went hungry both in the Highlands, where sheep-farming was spreading, and in the manufacturing towns of the Lowlands.

We began by saying that the rulers of Europe were shocked in 1789. They suffered many more shocks before 1815, and when Napoleon was defeated they resolved never again to allow France to become a danger to Europe. For a long time the Great Powers tried to put down any attempts to give ordinary people any say in the running of any country. No one paid any attention to the wishes of the people, unfortunately. The rulers thought that the danger from France had ended when Napoleon was defeated: they did not understand that the ideas of the French Revolution—Liberty, Equality and Fraternity—were more dangerous to them than even the French armies.

THINGS TO DO

1 Explain in your own words why there was a revolution in France in 1789.

2 What was the Reign of Terror? Why do you think it was introduced?

3 Why did the French Revolution frighten the government in Britain? What happened to the Radicals who supported the French Revolution?

4 What part did the Royal Navy play in the war against France? Why do you think control of the seas was so important to Britain?

5 'At home the war had meant prosperity for many.' (See above.) Explain in your own words what you understand by this.

6 On page 131 you read an account of the execution of Louis XVI. Imagine that you are one of the thousands who have come to Paris to see the event. Write a letter home telling what you witnessed. You can write either as a supporter of the Revolution or as a supporter of Louis.

7 As you read on page 137, Napoleon died in exile on St Helena in 1821. Write a short obituary for the 'Edinburgh Evening Courant'.

8 On Saturday June 24th 1815 'The Edinburgh Evening Courant' carried this exciting news:

> An express from London has this moment reached the Post Office with the glorious intelligence of the total overthrow of the French army commanded by Bonaparte, on the 18th of June in the neighbourhood of Charleroi. The following is the substance of the report:
>
> Major Percy, son to Lord Beverley, has within this hour and a half, arrived with the account of the greatest victory ever known obtained by the Duke of Wellington at Charleroi.
>
> The French attacked his Grace's position on Sunday 18th at daylight, and continued to attack, and to be repulsed the whole day; about seven in the evening the Duke began generally to charge and drove them straight before him, and obtained the greatest victory ever heard of.
>
> The result is three eagles and 150 pieces of cannon taken by the British, that is, Lord Wellington's army. General Blücher in his pursuit, took 60 pieces more. A day so contested and so ended has been obtained by immense loss. I can give no names, not having seen the returns. Lord Wellington is safe.

(*a*) 'The total overthrow of the French army in the neighbourhood of Charleroi.' What name do we give to this battle?

(*b*) How did the news of the battle reach Edinburgh?

(*c*) Who was Bonaparte?

(*d*) Who was the Duke of Wellington?

(*e*) From what you have learnt about the battle, is this report accurate?

(*f*) What do you think an 'eagle' was? (If you look carefully at the picture on page 137, you should get the answer.)

(*g*) Who was General Blücher?

(*h*) What evidence is there in the report to show that casualties have been heavy?

(*i*) What were the casualties for the battle?

(*j*) As you can see it took nearly a week for the news of this important battle to reach Britain. We are so used to our 'instant news' that it is hard for us to appreciate the suspense as people waited to hear what had happened. Remember, the war had been going on for nearly twenty years. Imagine that you have just heard the news of the battle. Write a short paragraph to describe your feelings.

WELLINGTON BOOT
Head of the Army

18 Britain in 1815

The coming of peace after the long, hard, years of war was greeted with great celebrations. Everywhere people rang church bells, lit bonfires, marched in parades and decorated the streets of their towns and villages. A grateful nation honoured the hero of the hour, the victor of Waterloo. In London a new bridge was named after the battle—and so was a village in Perthshire! In Edinburgh a magnificent statue of 'The Iron Duke' was erected. Is there a street or building near you named after Wellington or Waterloo?

The government, of course, was very popular. It had brought peace and victory—and victory had not always seemed certain. Indeed, at one time Napoleon had prepared an invasion of Britain and only the 'wooden walls' of the Royal Navy had held him back.

The Prime Minister was Lord Liverpool, who had taken over when the previous leader, Spencer Perceval, was *assassinated* in the House of Commons. Lord Liverpool led a Tory government, opposed in Parliament by the Whigs. We read in Chapter 5 how these names, Tory and Whig, began. Now, more than a century later, what did they stand for?

First, the Tories believed firmly that a country should be ruled by a monarch—by a king or a queen. After all, they had spent several years fighting the French republicans who had executed their king and queen. The Tories were determined that sort of thing must never happen in Britain: the government of the country should stay as it was. So, even after the defeat of Napoleon, any suggestions that more people should have the vote, or that working people should be allowed to have trade unions, were frowned upon. Such Radical ideas, according to the Tories, were dangerous and could lead to revolution and bloodshed.

The Whigs also supported the monarchy. At first, some of their leaders had welcomed the French Revolution—but the Reign of Terror and the years of war had made them change their minds. The Whigs still wanted to see some changes, however. Men such as the Scottish lawyer Henry Brougham believed that Parliament should be *reformed*. They wanted to give the right to vote to middle-class people—to men like factory-owners and merchants—but

not to all men and women. For the Whigs, too, were still frightened that this might lead to revolution in Britain.

Although everywhere there were cheers for victory, there was also widespread discontent in 1815. Let us look at some of the problems.

Unfortunately for the supporters of the monarchy, poor King George III was a very sick man. He had been on the throne since 1760 but, from 1811 until his death in 1820, he was quite unable to reign. The Prince of Wales, took over as Regent—but he was very unpopular. He was fat, lazy and spent a lot of his time enjoying himself—as this cartoon shows. When many poor folk were starving for bread, people were annoyed at the amount of money he spent on clothes, gambling and his pleasure-seeking friends. His palace at Brighton cost more than £150 000 to build: a fortune in those days.

So here was one problem for the government: the monarchy, the Royal Family, was not popular. Indeed, things did not improve for several years. The Prince Regent became King George IV in 1820. When he died in 1830 he was succeeded by his brother William IV, 'Sailor Billy', who reigned until 1837. Then the throne passed to his niece Victoria, who was only eighteen years old. As we shall see, during her long reign the people's support for the monarchy was restored.

But in 1815 other, even more serious, problems faced the government. As we have already seen, the Agricultural and Industrial Revolutions caused much distress and misery.

In the countryside, the 'Improvements' had led to many families losing their jobs. The new enclosed farms did not need so many workers to run them—and the farm workers who were left were very poor. Before, as tenant farmers, they had all shared part of the land to farm for themselves. Now, most of them were landless labourers working for a farmer. Their wages were very low: no more than 30p to 40p a week. With the prices of things such as bread, soap and candles increasing, many of them found it hard to make ends meet.

In the mines and factories (as we have read in Chapter 12) conditions were often dreadful. Long hours, very unpleasant working conditions, harsh discipline and low pay made life miserable for many workers and their families. Remember, too, that at this time there were no Factory Inspectors to see what conditions were like. As we shall see later, some workers had made attempts to form trade unions to try to improve conditions. But in 1799, when the war with France was at its height, the government made trade unions illegal. Can you think why?

The end of the war actually made matters worse. About 200 000

soldiers and sailors were *demobilised*. With France defeated, they were no longer needed in the armed forces. They came flocking home, happy the war was over and looking for work. But many were disappointed, for them there were no jobs to be found. The small *pensions* they were given were not enough to feed their families. What were they to do?

The end of the war brought hardship to others, too. Can you think why hundreds more people lost their jobs? Why was there less work in the iron industry, in textiles and in shipbuilding?

Even for those fortunate enough to be in work, times were hard. As you can imagine, the war had cost the country a lot of money. Britain's National Debt (that is, the money owed by the government) had risen from £247 million in 1792 to £902 million in 1816—and this had to be paid from taxes. During the war, the government had introduced an *Income Tax* to help to pay the bills. Obviously most of this tax was paid by wealthy folk. Now, in 1816, the government ended this tax. In its place, they put taxes on everyday things such as sugar, tea, soap and tobacco—which were bought by poorer people too. There was even a tax on windows— which made householders brick up the ones they could do without!

As we have already seen, the cost of food went up during the war years. Bread was, of course, an important part of the diet of working people. The government introduced a law which stopped cheaper grain from abroad from coming into Britain. This helped the farmers but it meant dearer bread in the shops.

142

To make matters worse, the wages of some workers were actually reduced. The hardest-hit of all were the handloom weavers. In 1802 their wages had been 70p a week; by 1812 they had fallen to 32p and by 1817 they were only 22p.

How did such people manage? The whole family had to work or beg in the streets. Some were driven to stealing—but they took terrible risks. At that time a person could be hanged for over a hundred different offences, including theft. Even stealing a small article such as a pocket handkerchief could mean transportation for many years.

Remember, too, that there was no government help: no unemployment pay or social security. The little money given by the parishes to paupers was just not enough to make ends meet. The New Statistical Account tells us that some of the weaver families in Glasgow were so poor that they could not afford fires to heat the little food they had.

In 1817 Henry Brougham described, in a speech in the House of Commons, how bad things were: 'Everyone is aware that there exists in the country a great and universal distress. We have known former times of great national suffering but no man can find an example of anything like the present.'

Some Town Councils did try to do something to help, however. Here is how Lord Cockburn, a famous lawyer, described the situation in Edinburgh: 'The year 1816 closed bitterly for the poor. There probably never were so many people destitute at one time in Edinburgh. Work was given and some permanent good was obtained from the labour of the relieved [those people who were given help]. Bruntsfield Links were cleared of whins, and of old quarries; walks were made for the first time on the Calton Hill; and a path was cleared along the base of the cliff of Salisbury Crags.' Paid work such as this was also provided in Glasgow and other towns. It was still not enough, however, and desperation drove many people to protest publicly.

Lord Cockburn
(a photograph taken
in the 1840s)

Even before the war ended, some workers broke into factories and smashed the hated machines which were putting them out of work. In the countryside, farmhouses were set on fire. The government reacted sternly. The machine-breakers, called Luddites (we think from the name of one of their leaders, Ned Ludd) were executed if they were caught. As there were no proper police forces, regiments of soldiers were sent to troublesome parts of the country—and this, in fact, made matters worse.

The worst incident in Scotland took place on August 29th 1797 at Tranent in East Lothian. There a demonstration got out of hand. The Riot Act was read and troops were called in. The demonstrators threw stones at the troops; the angry soldiers opened fire. Ignoring

143

the orders of their officers, they pursued the fleeing people. This is how an eyewitness described what happened: 'The cavalry rode through the corn fields and gave no quarter [killed on sight]; the soldiers dispersed in small parties, firing at those they came up with in the fields; a young boy was killed, begging hard for his life.' By the time the killing stopped, twelve villagers had been killed and many more wounded. No one was ever punished for this: in fact, the government hoped it could be an example for others.

The troubles continued after the war. In 1816 a large demonstration in London was broken up by troops. The next year the same thing happened in Derbyshire and the leaders were arrested: four were hanged and fourteen transported. Riots and demonstrations continued in Scotland too: at Bonnymuir near Falkirk, for example, a group of weavers and colliers clashed with soldiers. Later, three of their leaders were also hanged.

Perhaps the best-known demonstration of all, however, took place at Manchester in 1819. There a large crowd of working men and their families gathered at St Peter's fields to listen to Henry Hunt, a well-known Radical. The atmosphere was rather like a good-humoured football crowd. Men carried banners demanding the vote and cheap bread. But troops were on hand to control the crowd—and the *magistrates* decided to arrest Hunt. The crowd panicked. So did the soldiers and, as at Tranent, they lost their heads. They charged at the seething crowd, hacking at the unarmed people with their swords. Eleven people were killed and several hundred wounded. Among the dead was a young man who had fought for his country at Waterloo—and this incident became known as the Peterloo Massacre.

Here is a contemporary cartoon of Peterloo. Do you think it was drawn by a supporter of the government or a supporter of the demonstration?

Again, no one was punished for these deaths. Instead, the government congratulated the magistrates for their actions. Strict orders were given to stop any further meetings like Peterloo: now anyone could be arrested without trial and sent to prison.

One group plotted to murder the Cabinet, the leading members of the government. But they were arrested and executed.

By 1820, however, things were calmer. There had not been a revolution in Britain. Many people thought that the government had exaggerated the danger. So the threat of revolution passed and the government at last began to think about reforms.

Capture of the
Cato Street Conspirators

145

THINGS TO DO

1 The farm workers, the factory workers, the demobbed soldiers and sailors: take each of these groups and write a short paragraph saying in your own words what problems faced them in 1815.

2 What problems faced the government of Lord Liverpool after the war? How did they try to deal with them? Do you think they did the right things to solve these problems?

3 The Peterloo Massacre was well reported in the newspapers of the time. Imagine that you are a newspaper reporter for 'The Scotsman'. Write a report of the incident as though you were present at St Peter's fields, Manchester. You can write your report as either a supporter of the government or of the Radicals.

4 Here is part of a report which describes conditions in Glasgow after the war. Read it carefully then answer the questions below:

> In 1819 the working classes were again thrown into great distress from want of employment. The seeds of discontent which had been widely sown took deep root in this part of the country and ended in what has been called Radicalism. At this alarming crisis, when thousands of workers paraded the streets, demanding employment or bread, upwards of 600 persons were employed at spade work or breaking stones for the roads. The magistrates of Glasgow employed 340 weavers at spade-work in the Green [Glasgow Green—a park in the city] for upwards of four months, and it is only justice to those individuals [the weavers] to say that none of them left their work to attend political meetings in the Green, although thousands marched past them with their radical ensigns [flags] accompanied by well-dressed females carrying caps of liberty.

A French Revolution poster

(a) 'What of employment'. Why were so many unemployed at this time?

(b) 'Seeds of discontent'. What had the workers to complain about?

(c) What evidence is there in the passage to show that there were Radical demonstrations in Glasgow at this time?

(d) What help was given to some of the unemployed?

(e) Why do you think none of them left their work to attend political meetings'?

(f) What sort of messages would you have expected to see on the 'Radical ensigns'? (The picture of Peterloo on page 145 should give you some ideas.)

(g) What were 'caps of liberty'?

(h) Is there any evidence in the passage to show that there was violence at these demonstrations?

19 Votes for the people!

As you read in Chapter 3, our Members of Parliament (MPs) have to be elected at least once every five years. Notice that we say 'our' MPs, because these men and women are our representatives at Westminster. This idea of electing representatives is called democracy. The word 'democracy' comes from two Greek words: 'demos' meaning 'people' and 'kratos' meaning 'strength'. So it means 'power to the people'.

The first democracies probably began in Greece about 3000 years ago. Then the people lived in small *city-states*. All the citizens could meet together to discuss how to run the city and to choose the leaders. Now, of course, it is impossible for the 55 million people living in Britain to do that. So, to do the job for us, we choose our MPs. At present there are 635 of them, representing people from Shetland to Land's End.

Today men and women vote—and vote freely for the *candidate* of their choice. You will think that this is only fair—and may be surprised to learn that it was a long, long, struggle before it became possible.

In 1820 there were actually more MPs in Parliament—658—but they were chosen by very few people. In Scotland, out of a population of about two million, only 3000 were allowed to vote!

And you would think that each MP would, as far as possible, represent approximately the same number of people? You will be surprised. In 1820 the growing towns of Glasgow, Rutherglen, Renfrew and Dumbarton—with a total population of about 158 000—had to share one MP. Edinburgh and Leith, with a population of about 138 000 also shared one MP. But the small county of Cornwall, with only 295 000 people, had forty-two MPs! Why was this?

The answer is that the rules for the election of MPs had been made about two hundred years before. And, as you know, there had been great changes during that time. The Agricultural and Industrial Revolutions had altered the face of the countryside. Large factory towns had grown up; fewer people were needed on the land.

But Parliament had not moved with the times. Towns such as Birmingham, Leeds and Manchester had no MPs to represent

them. Yet this mound that you see in the photograph had two MPs of its own! This is Old Sarum in Wiltshire: once a bustling village, but by this time the people had gone. Such a place, where the MP really had nobody to represent, was called a 'rotten borough'.

In other places, too, MPs were not chosen by votes but by people already in power. In country areas about 160 landowners were able to choose about 300 MPs. So nearly half the membership of the House of Commons was decided by 160 people! Obviously an MP chosen like this would do his best to please the landowner who had sent him to Parliament. It was said that the MP was 'in his pocket' and such places were called 'pocket boroughs'. Again, in other places things were not much better. About fifty-six towns had fewer than forty voters each. In Edinburgh the Town Council (which was not elected—the Council itself chose any new members!) chose the MP and ordinary folk had no say in this at all.

Even where there were elections, things were not much better. Elections took place in public: not, as today, in private. A wooden platform known as the hustings was set up. There the candidates made their speeches and then the voters had to say openly who they were voting for. And there was plenty of time for money to be spent on bribes or threats to 'persuade' people, for an election could last for two weeks! (Nowadays, as you know, one day is set aside.)

Obviously Parliament needed to be reformed: that is, changed for the better. But, as we have seen already, both the Tories and the Whigs were suspicious of any reforms. They still feared revolution.

After 1820, however, the chances of reform had improved. Despite Peterloo and the Cato Street Conspiracy there had been no revolution. Some new younger men had entered Parliament and joined the government. Among them was Robert Peel. As *Home Secretary* he helped to improve conditions in overcrowded prisons and in 1829 he formed the first modern police force: the Metropolitan Police Force of London. Soon these 'peelers' or 'bobbies' (nicknamed after Robert Peel) were familiar figures, patrolling the streets in their frock coats and top hats.

Encouraged by these changes, people pressed for the right to vote. Huge demonstrations and rallies were held; speeches were made demanding the reform of Parliament. This is how Lord Cockburn described one parade in Glasgow in 1831:

> The whole people in that place [Glasgow] and in the adjoining towns walked in procession into the Green [Glasgow Green], divided into their crafts, societies, villages and parishes, with colours and emblems. It is stated that, including spectators, there were perhaps 80 000 or 100 000 persons at least assembled, with about 500 flags and 200 bands of music.

In 1830 a new Whig government came into power. The Prime Minister, Lord Grey, introduced a Reform Bill which was passed in Parliament in 1832. The 'rotten boroughs' lost their MPs and these *seats* were given to the new industrial towns. Glasgow was given two seats, as was Edinburgh; Greenock and Paisley each received one.

This contemporary cartoon shows the reformers chopping down the 'rotten tree' with its nests of 'rotten boroughs'. Notice, however, that some people are trying to hold the tree up. So, although there were great celebrations up and down the country at this break-through, there was also bitter disappointment. There was still no secret *ballot*. There was no attempt to stop bribery and *corruption*. The 1832 Reform Bill gave the vote to only a few thousand extra people—mostly landowners, factory owners and businessmen—all of whom had to own property before even they could vote.

No wonder ordinary working folk felt cheated. Up and down the country, groups of them met to discuss what to do. From such meetings came a powerful organisation known as the Chartists. Who were they and what did they want? You have probably heard about petitions. Perhaps you have been asked to sign a petition at school about wearing uniforms or having a disco. A petition is a request, backed up by lots of signatures, asking for something to be done. In the 1830s one of the ways of trying to get Parliament to take action was to present a petition to the MPs. This had been done for hundreds of years and, in fact, can still be done today.

The Chartists decided to present a petition, known as the People's Charter, to Parliament. They asked for six things:

1 UNIVERSAL MANHOOD SUFFRAGE
   ('The vote for every man over 21')
2 SECRET BALLOT
   ('Voting in secret, not on the open hustings')
3 EQUAL ELECTORAL CONSTITUENCIES
   ('Each MP to represent the same number of electors')
4 NO PROPERTY QUALIFICATIONS FOR MPs
   ('Any man to be allowed to stand for election')
5 PAYMENT OF MPs
   ('MPs to be paid a salary so that working men could afford to give up their jobs and stand for Parliament')
6 ANNUAL PARLIAMENTS
   ('A General Election each year, so that Parliament keeps in touch with the people')

Three times the Chartists presented their petition. In 1839 they collected 1 280 000 signatures; in 1842 three million and in 1848 two million. Obviously they attracted huge support. Each time a large procession was organised to carry the petition to Parliament: in 1842 the procession stretched for nearly 10 km! Each time, however, the government refused to accept the petition.

Despite their massive support, then, the Chartists failed. Why was this?

First, the Chartist leaders were divided regarding the methods they should use. One group believed in using violence; another group believed in peaceful means such as petitions and persuasion. But, whatever the methods they used, the government acted firmly. Several leaders were arrested and imprisoned; troops and the new 'bobbies' were used to control their meetings. In 1848 the old Duke of Wellington was brought out of retirement to organise the defence of London. Thousands of troops and police were posted in the city in case there was trouble when the petition was presented to Parliament. But nothing happened: the huge crowds melted away and returned peacefully to their homes.

Secondly, the Chartists failed because people saw that some reforms were already being made.

In 1807 the first step had been taken to end the dreadful slave trade—when British ships were forbidden to carry slaves. We read in Chapter 6 how the first African slaves had been taken from their homes to work in the colonies of the New World, where they were sold. The man who did more than anyone else to stamp out this cruelty was William Wilberforce. In 1833 his efforts were rewarded when Parliament freed all the slaves in the British colonies.

Wilberforce

150

A slave auction

In that same year a Factory Act was passed by Parliament. Now children under nine were not allowed to work in mills and factories; children between nine and thirteen could work only 48 hours a week; young people of thirteen to eighteen could work only 69 hours a week. To us these hours seem far too long, of course, but at that time it was an improvement—and Factory Inspectors were appointed to see that the law was kept. Then, in 1842, a Mines Act stopped women and children working underground.

Perhaps the most important reform of these years, however, was the repeal of the Corn Law in 1846. We read in the last chapter how this law made bread very dear in the shops: now a massive campaign was organised to end this. In 1839 the Anti-Corn Law League was formed and, unlike the Chartists, the League was supported by many MPs. The government at first refused to give way but then a disaster in Ireland forced them to change their minds. By 1840 the population of Ireland had grown to more than eight million. Most of them were desperately poor and their only food was potatoes. In 1846 the potato crop failed and the people were starving. Many came to settle in Glasgow and Liverpool; many more made the long journey to the USA, nursing a deep hatred of Britain. The government was forced to act. Cheap food had to be allowed into Ireland. In June 1846 Sir Robert Peel, now Prime Minister, persuaded Parliament to end the Corn Law.

151

"THE RIGHTS of WOMEN" or the EFFEC

These reforms, then, helped working people. But what about the reform of Parliament? Although the Chartists had failed, changes did come. In 1867 the vote was given to working men in the towns and cities. In 1872 voting was made secret and in 1884 the vote was given to working men in the countryside. Now most men over twenty-one had the vote.

But still there were no votes for women.

Indeed, women were very badly treated by the law in those days. Before 1872 married women had to give all their possessions to their husbands. So if a married women had her purse stolen, the police would note that the purse belonged to the husband! Few women were allowed to go to university. Better-off girls were taught to 'make their homes attractive', as one of them said, not to pass exams. Most of the better jobs were closed to women. Those who did work were paid much less than men, even if they were doing similar jobs. We call this sort of unfair treatment *discrimination*.

Some women were determined to do something about it. In 1903 the Women's Social and Political Union (WSPU) was formed to compaign for the right to vote. They soon became known as Suffragettes (from the Latin word for 'vote') and their leader was Mrs Emmeline Pankhurst. Like the Chartists, they held meetings and sent petitions to Parliament. And, again like the Chartists, their requests were turned down by the government.

152

LADIES CANDIDATE — THE GENTLEMENS CANDIDATE

VOTE for SCREW DRIVER The great Political Economist

DO Not vote for Ignorent Puppies

The friends
Sir Charles
Darling
are requested to
meet this five
in the Assembly
Rooms — The Hon.
Mrs Manley in
the Chair
Tea & Coffee at
— 7 oClock

Designed & etched by George Cruikshank

Pub.d by D Bogue 86 Fleet Street London

EMALE ENFRANCHISEMENT

Arrest of
Mrs Pankhurst

Why was this? Some argued that women were not strong enough to vote; others that women were not clever enough to understand politics. This cartoon shows another argument put forward by opponents. Can you see what it is? Do you think it is fair? One politician said that if women were given the vote Britain would become the laughing stock of the world.

When it was obvious that the government was not going to listen to peaceful persuasion, the WSPU turned to other means. Here is part of a report from a London newspaper of March 2nd 1912: 'The West End of London last night was the scene of an unexampled outrage on the part of the militant suffragettes. The women "furthered their cause" by doing thousands of pounds' worth of damage to the windows of West London shopkeepers. Bands of women paraded Regent Street, Piccadilly, the Strand, Oxford Street and Bond Street, smashing windows with hammers.' (Do you think the newspaper supported the Suffragettes or not?)

The papers were soon full of other stories. Women set fire to the contents of pillar boxes, attacked the homes of politicians, chained themselves to railings and interrupted public meetings. Their constant cry was 'Votes for Women!'

Many women were arrested and put in prison. There, some went on hunger strike and refused to eat. The government could not let them starve to death so they were force-fed. This is how one Suffragette described this terrifying experience: 'Two of the

153

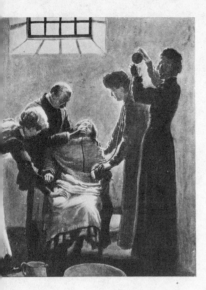

wardresses took hold of my arms, one held my head and one my feet. One wardress helped to pour the food [about a pint of milk and egg]. The doctor got the gag between my teeth until my jaws were fastened wide apart, far more than they would go naturally. Then he put down my throat a tube which seemed to be much too wide and something like four feet in length. I choked the moment it touched my throat until it got down. Then the food was poured in quickly: it made me sick a few seconds after it was down. The horror of it was more than I can describe.'

Many voices were raised in protest against this cruelty. Among them was a Scottish MP, Keir Hardie, whom we will be reading about later: 'Women, worn and weak by hunger, are seized upon, held down by brute force, gagged, a tube inserted down the throat, and food poured or pumped into the stomach. Let British men think over the spectacle.' Later, the government introduced a law which allowed women who weakened themselves through hunger striking to go free until they got their strength back. Then they were re-arrested to complete their sentence. The Suffragettes called this 'The Cat and Mouse Act'!

The WSPU campaign continued. There were more outrages and arrests. In June 1913 Emily Davidson threw herself in front of

the king's horse running in the Derby and was killed. Still the government refused to give women the vote.

But, suddenly, everything was changed. In 1914 war broke out between Britain and Germany. Men were needed to fight. Led by Mrs Pankhurst, women played their part in the war effort. Suffragettes, such as Dr Elsie Inglis from Edinburgh, went to the battlefields to tend the wounded. Others worked on the land, in offices, drove buses, delivered coal and—perhaps most dangerous of all—made shells in munitions factories.

154

Their efforts helped to win the war. When peace came in 1918, the vote was at last given to the women of Britain. But even then there was still discrimination. Women had to be thirty before they could vote! Not until 1928 were men and women over twenty-one voting as equals. Women became Members of Parliament and Ministers but fifty years passed before Britain had its first woman Prime Minister, Margaret Thatcher.

So you can see what a long, hard, struggle it was to win the vote for the people. You should remember this when you in turn can vote. You should remember, too, that you have the right to be elected as a representative. Some of you reading this book will, in time, be elected as Councillors for your District or Region; some of you will be elected as MPs. Now there is something to think about!

THINGS TO DO

1 Say in your own words what was wrong with Parliament before 1832.

2 Why were working people disappointed with the 1832 Reform Bill?

3 Who were the Chartists and why did they not succeed?

155

4 Look again at the six points of the Peoples' Charter on page 150. The only point not now a law in this country is 'Annual Parliaments'. Why do you think this has never been accepted?

5 On pages 152–5 you read about the discrimination against women. What other forms of discrimination have you heard of? Perhaps you could organise a class debate to discuss one of them.

6 Try to organise a Suffragette rally in class. One group should take the part of the Suffragettes preparing posters and a speech on why there should be votes for women. The rest of the class should prepare the part of the passers-by with questions and comments. Perhaps the actual rally should be held in the playground!

7 It is 1918 and the government has just announced that women over thirty can now vote. Write a newspaper article for your paper telling the story of the fight by women to win the vote.

8 Here is a report from the 'Scotsman' newspaper written in 1914. Read it carefully then answer the questions below in sentences.

THE SUFFRAGETTES
RELEASE OF MRS PANKHURST
AFTER FOUR DAYS' IMPRISONMENT

After being in Holloway Prison since Wednesday last when she was arrested outside the offices of the Women's Social and Political Union, Mrs Pankhurst was on Saturday released on licence granted under the 'Cat and Mouse' Act. While in prison she had been on both hunger and thirst strike, and her early release was due to the fact when she was arrested she was not in the best of health.

This is the eighth or ninth time the militant leader has been arrested under the sentence of three years penal servitude [hard labour in prison] passed upon her.

She was taken in an ambulance to an address in the West End [of London].

(*a*) Who was Mrs Pankhurst?

(*b*) What was the Women's Social and Political Union?

(*c*) Why do you think it had been started?

(*d*) What was the 'Cat and Mouse Act'?

(*e*) What had happened before to women who went on hunger-strike?

(*f*) Why do you think Mrs Pankhurst was described as 'the militant leader'?

(*g*) What evidence is there in the passage to show that this sort of thing had happened before?

(*h*) What evidence is there in the passage to show that Mrs Pankhurst was unwell as a result of going on hunger-strike?

THE CAT AND MOUSE ACT
PASSED BY THE LIBERAL GOVERNMENT

THE LIBERAL CAT
ELECTORS VOTE AGAINST HIM!
KEEP THE LIBERAL OUT!

BUY AND READ 'THE SUFFRAGETTE'

156

20 'Unity is strength'

Have you already guessed? This shows a meeting of the Trades Union Congress (TUC). Each year the leaders of Britain's most important trade unions come together to discuss their work. These men and women represent more than eleven million people. The largest union, The Transport and General Workers' Union (TGWU), has over two million members. Other unions are much smaller but you can see that the TUC is a very powerful organisa-

157

tion. The government usually consults the TUC before deciding policies and union leaders are often seen on TV discussing Britain's affairs.

So trade unions and their leaders play an important part in the life of the nation. Unfortunately you usually hear about their work only when their members are on strike or in dispute. The sight of a march of strikers or of a clash between strikers and the police provides a lively news story for TV, radio or newspapers. An argument on TV between a trade union leader and a representative of employers is usually interesting to watch—although it does not often help matters.

So what does a trade union try to do for its members all the time?

1 It tries to make sure that its members receive a fair wage for the work they do.

2 It tries to make sure that hours of work and holidays are fair.

3 It tries to improve the working conditions of its members—with particular attention to matters of health and safety.

4 It tries to protect the jobs of its members.

When new machinery is introduced into a factory, the union will try to make sure that jobs are not lost. If a factory is to be closed, the union will try to stop this to save its members from unemployment.

5 It collects subscriptions from its members.

Part of this money is used to look after its members when they are sick or unemployed and pensions are given to the families of members who die before they retire from work.

6 A trade union helps its members to improve their education by organising courses and lectures.

Some members who do well on these courses may be offered full-time jobs working for their union. They may travel round a district visiting work places to talk to their members. Others may become shop stewards. In each place of work the day-to-day business of the union is carried out by shop stewards (in some large factories there may be more than a hundred) elected by the members of the union.

Now, as more than half the people working in Britain today are members of trade unions, most of you will join one when you begin work. But less than two hundred years ago you might have been arrested and transported for doing just this! Let us see how trade unions have grown from small groups of workers hounded by the law to the position they hold today.

The first trade unions were started in the eighteenth century. Groups of workers such as carpenters, *wrights*, weavers and printers

Early trade union card

A cartoon poking
fun at early
trade unionists

began to meet together—often in inns, where they could talk about their work over a drink. They made sure that their wages were fair and that their hours of work were not over-long. Each week, the members put aside a few pence into a fund. This money would be used to pay members and their families in times of sickness or hardship. With no Welfare State as we know it today, these payments must have been a great help.

These early unions were not popular with employers. They resented any attempts to increase wages or shorten hours of work. As they saw it, this would mean less profit for themselves. So the employers opposed these 'combinations' of workers. Those who joined a combination, or a union, were liable to be sacked. As there was no unemployment pay in those days, people did not want to lose their jobs so members often met in secret.

At the end of the eighteenth century the French Revolution and the war with France brought more problems for the infant trade unions. The government was afraid that workers meeting together could be plotting revolution. So the Combination Acts of 1799 and 1800 made it illegal for workers to 'combine', to meet together as a union. The meetings continued in secret, however—but at great risk.

During the war years there were some strikes but the leaders were quickly arrested and some transported. Those workers who refused to go back to work were replaced by others desperate for a job—in spite of the terrible conditions of work. Some workers turned to violence in protest: you have already read about the Luddites who smashed machines, set fire to factories—and risked death if they were caught.

The end of the war in 1815 brought even greater unemployment and poverty, as you know, but after 1820 things did begin to improve. The revolution had not come and other people saw that these workers' unions were not like the revolutionary groups in France. As you read in the last chapter, the government made some reforms: among these, in 1824, the Combination Acts were repealed.

Many unions were now formed. The result was a wave of strikes by workers anxious to improve their conditions. In some cases, however, a union was formed to try to stop matters getting worse. This is what the Glasgow cotton-spinners did. 'The cause of the cotton-spinners forming themselves into an association [a union] was·to resist, as far as their moral power and united efforts would allow them, a gradual reduction in wages made upon them by the masters [the employers].'

This union, like so many others at this time, was broken by the employers. The wages of these Glasgow cotton-spinners were actually reduced by about 20 per cent. Can you imagine that happening today? How were the employers able to do it? In the words of one cotton-spinner, 'At the period of our strike in 1824 I happened to be secretary of our association [union] and for that I was kept three years out of employment. A number of our late committee are still kept out of employment; some of them had to leave the country and go to Belgium to get work; they have been informed by their employers that dismissed them that they could not be employed again.' As you can see, workers were not only sacked for belonging to a union but were also 'blacklisted' by employers. This meant that no one would employ them. With so many people out of work, it was easy for employers to recruit new workers to replace those they had sacked.

Often workers were made to sign a promise that they would not join a union. All this created bad feelings among the workers themselves. The union members sometimes attacked these 'scabs' or 'blacklegs' as they were called. Lord Cockburn described a series of outrages in Scotland at this time: non-union men had acid thrown at them; their houses were burned and, in some cases, they were murdered. Although these were the actions of a few men, union members as a whole were regarded as trouble-makers.

Many working people hoped that things would be improved

peacefully when they got the vote. But, as we have seen, they were disappointed by the Reform Act of 1832. What was to be done?

One man who had an answer was Robert Owen, the owner of the New Lanark mills (page 93). In 1833 he tried to organise all the workers of Britain into one huge union. This Grand National Consolidated Trade Union (GNCTU) would force the government and employers to improve conditions by calling on all workers to 'down tools' and stop work. In other words, there would be what we call a *general strike*. But the GNCTU failed miserably. Although nearly a million people joined, they were poorly organised and divided among themselves. The government and the employers were united against it. What finally ended Owen's plans was an incident in the English county of Dorset.

Robert Owen

In March 1834 six farm labourers from the village of Tolpuddle met to join the GNCTU and took an oath to support the union. They were arrested and charged with conspiracy: that is, plotting against the government in secret. They were found guilty and sentenced to transportation for seven years—a savage sentence which caused an uproar. What had the men done wrong? As George Loveless, one of these 'Tolpuddle martyrs', said at the time, 'If we have violated [broken] any law it was not done intentionally. We have injured no man's reputation, character, person or property; we were uniting together to preserve ourselves, our wives and our children from utter degradation [misery] and starvation.' Even people who were opposed to the unions saw that this punishment was harsh and after two years the men were pardoned. But the GNCTU was finished.

In 1851, however, a new union was formed and this time it did succeed. This was the Amalgamated Society of Engineers (ASE). Its members were skilled workers: they could not be replaced easily so employers did not sack them for joining a union. They were well organised and well led. Engineers were also better paid than other workers so they could afford to pay a higher subscription. Each week the 11 000 members gave a total of £500 to their union. This money was used to look after members in times of hardship. Above all, the ASE avoided strikes and so it was more acceptable to both the employers and the government.

Soon other groups of skilled workers followed the example of the ASE. In 1868 representatives from these 'model' unions, as they were called, met in Manchester and formed the Trades Union Congress. In 1875 an Act allowed trade union members to 'picket' peacefully. This meant that workers on strike were allowed to wait outside a place of work to try to persuade others to join their strike.

All this, however, helped only the skilled workers. The unskilled

161

Match girls on strike

workers had no unions of their own: they were too poorly paid to afford large subscriptions and, being unskilled, they could easily be replaced. But two famous strikes helped to change this.

In 1888 the match girls at Bryant and May's London factory went on strike. A well-known Londoner, Miss Annie Besant, sympathised with them and started a publicity campaign to win support. The public were horrified to hear how bad their conditions were. The phosphorous in the matches caused the jawbones and gums of some of the girls to rot away. The Company gave way and met the demands of the strikers.

The next year there was a huge docks strike, again in London. The unskilled dockers were paid threepence halfpenny (1½p) an hour for hard, back-breaking, work. They went on strike for sixpence, 'a tanner' ($2\frac{1}{2}$p) an hour. They won tremendous support for their cause. Huge processions were held to attract the attention of other people. The leaders of the strike, John Burns (later to become on MP) and Ben Tillet were able men and excellent organisers. Money poured in to the strike headquarters to help to support the men. After several weeks the employers gave way and agreed to pay 'the dockers' tanner' as it was called.

Other unskilled workers now formed their own unions. In 1888 there were 750 000 trade unionists; by 1914 this had grown to four million.

Most of the men members of these trade unions now had the vote and they wanted to use it to persuade Parliament to improve the lives of working people. The question was: which political party should they support? Both the Tories (now named Conservatives) and the Whigs (now called Liberals) tried to win the new voters over. Many people, however, felt that a new party was needed—a party committed to helping the workers. One man did more than any other to bring this about. His name was Keir Hardie.

Keir Hardie was born in 1856 at Laighbrannoch, a village near Holytown in Lanarkshire. His family were desperately poor and could not afford to send young Keir to school. At the age of eight he was working for a few pence a week as a message boy. Then he had a job in the Govan shipyards and at ten was working as a trapper in a coal-mine. Helped by his mother, he learned to read and write. Later he hewed coal during the day and studied at night. When he tried to organise a strike for higher wages, he lost his job and his home—a cottage belonging to the mine. And, when he tried to get work at another mine, he found that he had been blacklisted. No pit-owner in Lanarkshire would employ him.

He moved to Cumnock in Ayrshire and, as a journalist, became interested in politics. By this time two working men were Members of Parliament but they had stood for election as Liberals. Hardie believed in a party for the workers themselves and he became a *Socialist*. Socialists wanted to see industries and farms owned by the people as a whole, not by private owners: they should be *nationalised* and belong to the whole nation. Socialists wanted to see more working people becoming MPs. Only then, they thought, would the problems of long hours and low pay be solved and socialism brought about.

In 1892 Keir Hardie was elected MP for West Ham in London. Over the page you see his election poster. Do you understand his plans? He shocked MPs by turning up at Parliament in a cloth cap and a red tie and accompanied by a brass band! He had arrived— and he wanted people to know it.

VOTE FOR

Home Rule.

Democratic Government.

Justice to Labour

No Monopoly.

No Landlordism

Temperance Reform.

Healthy Homes.

Fair Rents.

Eight-Hour Day.

Work for the Unemployed.

KEIR HARDIE.

Already, in 1888, Hardie helped to set up the Scottish Labour Party—the first Labour Party in Britain. In 1893 the Scottish Labour Party joined other societies to form the Independent Labour Party (ILP) and Keir Hardie became its first Chairman. In 1899 he helped to form the Labour Representation Committee with members of the TUC. A year later this became the Labour Party: Keir Hardie was chosen as its first leader and the secretary was another Scot, Ramsay MacDonald from Lossiemouth.

The Labour Party grew in strength. In 1906 fifty-three MPs who supported its ideas were elected. These MPs were able to persuade the Liberal government of the day to help working people. Unemployment pay was introduced; so were old age pensions.

Outside Parliament the trade unions were much more powerful than before. In 1914 the miners, railwaymen and transport workers were together planning a great strike. Then, in August, the war with Germany broke out. Thoughts of the strike were laid aside as thousands of workers came forward to fight for their country. Only a few voices spoke out against the war—among them Keir Hardie's. He was saddened that working men were marching off to fight working men from Germany. He spoke out bravely against this, trying to convince people that the war was wrong. He wore himself out in this work and died in September 1915.

As we shall see, only eight years later his old colleague Ramsay Macdonald became Prime Minister of the first Labour government.

164

THINGS TO DO

1 Say in your own words what problems faced the early trade unions.

2 What was the GNCTU and why did it fail?

3 'Glasgow Cotton-Spinners' Strike Broken', 'Tolpuddle Labourers Found Guilty' Write a newspaper story for each of these headlines. (The information on pages 160 and 161 will help you.)

4 Why did the Amalgamated Society of Engineers succeed as a union?

5 Show how the strikes of the match girls and the dockers helped the unskilled workers.

6 Organise a class discussion on the work of our trade unions today.

Hardie speaking against the war, 1915

21 The health of the people

Imagine that you are a young worker about 150 years ago in one of the factories that have sprung up in Scotland.

One day in 1840 your hand has been caught in a machine and terribly injured. You are taken away to a hospital, a rather dirty, dull and smelly place. You are met, perhaps, by a 'nurse'—an unkempt old woman—and taken to a doctor who looks more like a workman in his grubby and stained old coat. He looks at your hand, shakes his head sadly and says that as far as he can see there is nothing he can do to save it. You are taken to a smaller separate room, perhaps given a drink of spirits, and made to lie on a table. There and then, with nothing to deaden the pain, the surgeon amputates. Then your arm is bandaged and you are carried off to bed.

That is not the end of your troubles, for in a day or two it is clear that your arm is poisoned. The doctors do what they can, but a bad poisoning, called gangrene, has set in. However, let us look on the bright side and say that after long weeks of suffering you are able to go home. You are maimed and unable to do heavy work again, but you think yourself lucky. You might have died from the shock of the operation, or from the poisoning that followed it. Many people did.

But you have not been home many days before an epidemic of that fearful disease called cholera sweeps through the town. It caused many deaths in your street three years ago—so you sit at home, wondering if your family will be lucky this time.

We last looked at life in the growing towns and cities in Chapter 14. There we saw how the overcrowding and the poverty produced terrible living conditions. In Edinburgh and elsewhere, the better-off families escaped to the pleasant suburbs, leaving the old tenements to the poorer folk. Remember, there was no District Council to provide decent homes for the incomers. They had to find shelter for themselves as best they could. Whole families often lived in a single room. The results were dreadful. Here is part of a contemporary description of a close in Edinburgh's Old Town.

In the Middle Meal Market Stairs are 59 rooms, almost all separate dwelling-houses, entered by a steep, dark, stone stair common to the whole. In these dwell 248 individuals (adults, 197, children under five,

51) divided into 56 families. And in this huge congeries [collection] of dens, there is no water, no water-closet, no sink. The women, living in the fifth, or highest floor, have to carry all their water up the close, and up these stairs. It is not difficult to imagine the state of wet and filth in which they must continually be.

In these conditions, it is not surprising that the killer diseases of cholera and, later, typhus claimed so many lives. In the great cholera epidemic of 1832, there were 1886 cases in Edinburgh. Of these 1065 died.

People were terrified by the arrival of the disease and tried to find out what caused it. Their medical knowledge was scanty. Some blamed a lack of education; others, a lack of religion. In 1840, when another cholera attack threatened, Edinburgh's Board of Health published this information sheet for its citizens. It you look closely at the second paragraph you can see that some of the advice was indeed useful. But what, according to the Board of Health, seemed to cause the disease?

Edinburgh Board of Health.

As the EPIDEMIC CHOLERA has now unfortunately appeared in several Towns in the North of England, the BOARD of HEALTH in Edinburgh think it their duty again earnestly to impress upon their Fellow-Citizens, of all ranks, the danger to which they will expose themselves, in the event of the Disease reaching this City, by indulging to any excess in the use of Strong Liquors, and especially of *Ardent Spirits*.

The BOARD can confidently assure their Fellow-Citizens of the good effects which have been found to result from Cleanliness in Person and Habitation, Warm Clothing, and Regular Habits, in checking the progress, and diminishing the fatality, of this Pestilential Disease; but they feel themselves especially called upon, by the experience of every great Town in which CHOLERA has prevailed, to state, that nothing disposes the Human Body to be attacked by it so much as *Intoxication*; and that *Habitual Drunkards*, particularly those living in the lowest, the dirtiest, and the worst-aired parts of Towns, have been, in all Countries, its most constant Victims.

The following are the expressions used on this subject, by some of those who have witnessed the ravages of the Disease in India, in Russia, in Poland, in Germany, and in England :—

INDIA.

" Persons of sober, regular habits, enjoyed greater immunity than the *drunken and dissipated*, who kept irregular hours, and were frequently exposed to the vapours and cold of the night, after a debauch."—*Jamieson's Report on the Cholera in Bengal*.

" In India, it has been almost invariably found, that regular habits, nourishing diet, and cleanliness, gave those exposed to the Disease the best chance of escape; while exposure to fatigue or to cold, particularly during sleep, poor diet, and above all, *intoxication and dissipated habits*, have been found powerfully to predispose to Cholera."—*Hamilton Bell's Letter to Sir Henry Halford*.

" All who have seen the Disease are aware how frequently an attack of it has succeeded *intoxication*."—*Hamilton Bell, on Cholera*.

" *Intemperance in Drink* has been already strongly adverted to, but the fact of its great influence in producing the Disease cannot be too much insisted on."—*Orton, on Cholera*.

RUSSIA.

" The effects of previous *intemperance* upon the system seemed to predispose it more than any other cause to the Disease."—*Lefevre, on the Cholera at St Petersburg*.

" It had been observed at Moscow and Riga, that any great Festivals, where the Lower Orders were assembled, and where *Intoxication* was a common consequence, were always followed by a marked increase in the ensuing Day's List of Invalids."—*Same Work*.

POLAND.

" Three Warsaw Butchers went to a Tavern, abandoned themselves to every sort of excess, and drank till they were so intoxicated, that they were carried home senseless. A few hours had scarcely elapsed, when the miserable Men were seized with all the symptoms of Cholera, which advanced with such rapidity, *as to prove fatal to the whole Three within Four Hours*."—*Brierre de Boismont, on the Cholera in Poland*.

GERMANY.

" The great majority of Persons attacked with Cholera in Berlin, consists of those who are exposed to the usual causes of Disease,—namely, cold, fatigue, *and particularly intemperance in food and drink*."—*Dr Becker's Report on the Cholera in Berlin*.

SUNDERLAND.

" Its victims have been the infirm, the aged, and the *intemperate*."—*Letter from Dr Gibson*.

By Authority of the BOARD,

Printed by Neill & Co.   JOHN LEARMONTH, *Lord Provost*.

Remember that at that time even doctors had very little idea as to how infections spread. Gradually, however, it was seen that there was a link between disease and dirt—particularly dirty drinking water. Here is part of another description of an Edinburgh close, written in 1850:

This is truly a horrible place. It is a cellar several feet below the level of the close, and entered by steps descending to it. Before the entrance there is a large pool of filth of the worst aspect and odour collected, and it is over this pool that all who enter must either wade or spring to get to the upper step in order to get down to the cellar. In this place they can sometimes of a night enjoy themselves with a fiddle and a dance. This is surely the horrible dance of death with the cholera standing at the door.

Children suffered terribly in these conditions. One third of all children born died before they reached the age of five. It was quite common for families to have eight or nine children; sadly, it was all too common for five or six of these youngsters to die in childhood. Those who survived often had to beg for food or

scavenge in the piles of rubbish fouling the streets and closes. Many children had to steal to stay alive.

Gradually, voices were raised in protest. Demands were made that something must be done to help the poor in the slums.

At first it was left to individual men and women to do something to help. In Edinburgh Dr Thomas Guthrie opened up 'Ragged Schools' for the children of the streets. This table, prepared by Dr Guthrie in 1852, shows the background of the children admitted to his schools:

Found homeless, and provided with lodgings	72
Children with both parents	32
With the father dead	140
Mother dead	89
Deserted by parents	43
With one or both parents transported	9
Fatherless, with drunken mothers	77
Motherless, with drunken fathers	66
With both parents worthless	84
Who have been beggars	271
Who have been in the Police Office	75
Who have been in Prison	20
Known as children of thieves	76
Believed to be so, including the preceding	148

Dr Thomas Guthrie

Work like this was carried on in other towns and cities of Britain. It became clear, however, that this *charitable* action was not enough. Much more had to be done to tackle the problems of ill-health and poverty.

In 1842 a government committee led by Edwin Chadwick prepared a report on the health of the people. The report proved once and for all that dirty living conditions encouraged disease. In 1848 Parliament passed a Public Health Act which encouraged towns to appoint Medical Officers of Health and to make sure that supplies of clean drinking water were brought to people's homes. At first, however, little was done. Then in 1861 Prince Albert, the husband of Queen Victoria, died after drinking infected water at Windsor. After that a law was passed which said that clean water had to be provided. Attempts were also made to clear away some of the worst of the slum housing. But progress was slow.

While this was going on some exciting new discoveries were being made by doctors: discoveries which helped to save lives.

First of all men had to find out more about the body and how it works. This study is called 'anatomy'. A great deal of work was carried on at Edinburgh University. There are gruesome stories of 'body snatchers' who stole corpses from graveyards in the night. You may have heard of the terrible Burke and Hare who, before they were caught, made quite a business of killing people to supply to the unsuspecting doctors. In such ways more was learned about the working of the human body.

Next, it was necessary to find some way of reducing the pain

169

and shock of an operation. If a way could be found to make the patient unconscious, surgeons would not have to hurry and would be able to do more delicate operations. Before 1800 Humphry Davy had discovered that if he breathed nitrous oxide, 'laughing gas', he became unconscious; and about 1840 an American dentist showed that ether had the same effect. A German doctor discovered chloroform and James Simpson, a native of Bathgate, began to use it for his operations in the hospital at Edinburgh. Old-fashioned doctors tried to stop Simpson's new methods, but slowly his ideas were followed. They became much more popular when it was announced that Queen Victoria had been given chloroform when she was in hospital. One great danger of operations was ended.

But the second danger remained: infection and gangrene. A German, Robert Koch, and a Frenchman, Louis Pasteur, found that the trouble is caused by living things in the air so tiny that they cannot be seen by the naked eye. These we call 'microbes', and they are the cause of many diseases.

A Glasgow surgeon, Joseph Lister, realised that wounds were infected by microbes in the air and on the hands and instruments of the surgeon. So Lister tried to kill them by using carbolic acid, which is still used as a disinfectant. His method was to have a spray

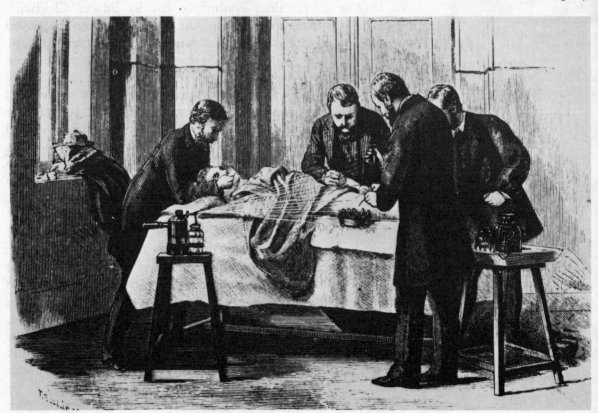

in the operating-room which sprayed the area of the operation. The surgeon, patient and attendants were soaked and other doctors thought it a huge joke. But they were more serious when they saw that Lister's patients healed quickly and cleanly. The old, dirty, slipshod methods were at an end.

Koch and Pasteur went on to find out more about microbes. Koch, for example, found the microbe that causes the illness known as tuberculosis. Pasteur made the discovery that when a disease microbe attacks a person, the body begins to build a defence against it. This is why you usually catch diseases like mumps and measles only once.

After this discovery Pasteur went on to make more experiments. He began to breed specially weak disease microbes and never let them grow strong and dangerous. Then he gave injections which contained these weak microbes. As he expected, the microbes were too weak to do any real harm, but the body built up a defence just as if it was in danger—and the protection stayed on. So began the idea of inoculation. You may have heard how, years before, Edward Jenner had begun something similar: vaccination against smallpox.

About the middle of the nineteenth century doctors began to use their three most important 'tools'. First came the stethoscope, then the clinical thermometer, and then the hypodermic syringe which was invented by Alexander Wood, an Edinburgh doctor.

All these changes meant that trained and skilled nurses were needed to replace the slovenly old women who had worked in hospitals before. Florence Nightingale, 'The Lady with the Lamp' to soldiers in the Crimean War, began a school for nurses in London and did more than anyone else to improve the training of nurses.

Florence Nightingale

These were of course important changes but they did little at first to help ordinary people. With no National Health Service as we know it, few working people could afford to pay for medical treatment. Indeed, it was found that many families scarcely had enough money to buy food let alone medicine.

In London, Charles Booth studied the lives of the poorest people and found that 30 per cent of London's population were trying to live on less than £1 per week. In York, in 1899, Seebohm Rowntree (whose family owned the famous chocolate firm) did another study. His results were the same. Thousands of people were living in dreadful poverty.

The contemporary photograph over the page of a Glasgow close shows the sort of housing many had to put up with. Notice the state of repair of the buildings, the single water-tap to serve all the families of the close and the open ditch in the middle. At the end of the court would be an outside toilet: again, to be shared. What evidence is

171

there to tell us that the families had no gardens of their own?

Poor housing, low wages, unemployment and ill-health made life miserable for many. Yet they were poor through no fault of their own. Rowntree worked out that at least £1.08 was needed to keep a family with three children out of poverty. But 30 per cent of families earned less than this. Even to live on £1.08 meant having no luxuries at all. No pocket-money for the children; no tobacco for father, no new clothes for mother. The family lived in constant fear of illness or unemployment as this would mean no money coming into the home. Sometimes mother and children had to go without food at mealtimes so that the father could eat to keep up his strength for working.

The children often suffered terribly. Here is part of a description written in 1909:

Nearly the whole of the children of a slum quarter may go on year after year suffering from adenoids, inflamed glands, enlarged tonsils, defects of eyesight and chronic ear discharges which will eventually prevent many of them from earning their livelihood.

172

In 1899 Britain was at war with the Boers—the Dutch settlers in South Africa. An appeal went out for recruits to join the British Army. Half of the men who volunteered had to be turned down because they were unfit. Clearly something had to be done.

In 1906 a new Liberal government was elected. It had the support of the Labour MPs we read about in the last chapter. Liberals like the young Lloyd George and Winston Churchill were determined to act. From 1906 to 1914, several important reforms were made. Let us look briefly at what was done for the children, the unemployed, the sick and the old folk.

The children	Free medical inspections and free school meals for those most in need.
The unemployed	Labour Exchanges were set up to help those looking for work to find jobs. Unemployment pay was started for some jobs, such as building, where men were often out of work because of bad weather.
The sick	A National Insurance Act was passed to give money to workers when they were off sick. The worker, his employer and the government put money aside each week. All these savings went to the worker when he was ill. This poster was issued by the government to explain what the Insurance Act meant.

THE RIGHT TICKET FOR YOU!
YOU ARE TRAVELLING ON A SAFE LINE

GOVERNMENT LINE
1913
MALE WORKER PAYS 4ᴰ
EMPLOYER PAYS 3ᴰ
STATE PAYS 2ᴰ

YOUR RETURN
DURING ILLNESS
10/- Per Week FOR 26 WEEKS
5/- AFTERWARDS (TILL 70) WHILE INCAPABLE OF WORK
FREE DOCTOR & MEDICINE
30/- Maternity Grant
SANATORIUM BENEFIT

AND ARE ASSURED
A SAFE RETURN

The old folk

An old-age pension was introduced: men and women over seventy got 25p a week from the government. Now, working people at least had something to keep them going when they retired. (Many, however, still had to end their days in workhouses such as this.)

All this of course cost a lot of money. In 1909 the *Chancellor of the Exchequer*, Lloyd George, needed to raise an extra £15 million to pay for these benefits. He decided to get the money by taxing the rich. The House of Lords objected to this and refused to agree to his *Budget* with its new taxes. Two General Elections were fought in 1910 before the Lords gave in. The Budget was passed and the new taxes became law. A start had been made to improving the welfare of the people.

Much of course still remained to be done to combat the dreadful poverty. But at least it was a beginning. Unfortunately any plans for further reforms were shattered in August 1914 with the outbreak of the First World War.

Lloyd George

THINGS TO DO

1 Why were Victorian towns and cities so unhealthy?

2 What advances were made in medical care during these years? Why did the improvements not benefit everybody?

3 Imagine that you are a newspaper reporter sent to interview Dr Guthrie about his work for the children of Edinburgh's slums.

174

Use the information on pages 166–9 to help you write a report of your interview.

4 Lloyd George described his 1909 Budget as 'a war budget against poverty'. What do you think he meant by this? What measure did the Liberals take to combat poverty between 1906 and 1914?

5 Here is part of Rowntree's report on the living conditions of working people in York. He is describing how a family of two adults and three children could manage to live on £1.08 per week. Imagine that you are a Liberal candidate standing for the 1906 General Election. Use this information, together with what you have learnt from the chapter, to make a speech saying what you think should be done by the government to help.

> They [the family] must never spend a penny on a railway fare or omnibus. They must never purchase a half-penny newspaper, or spend a penny to buy a ticket for a popular concert. They cannot save nor join sick clubs [clubs that paid you money when you were off work ill] or a Trade Union, because they cannot pay the necessary subscriptions. The children must have no pocket money for dolls, marbles or sweets. The father must smoke no tobacco and must drink no beer. The mother must never buy any pretty clothes for herself or for her children. Finally the wage earner must never be absent from his work for a single day.

Here is Rowntree's diet for children of 8–16 years. It was the most nourishing diet that could be devised for a cost of 2s 7d [13p] a week.

	BREAKFAST	DINNER	SUPPER
Sunday	Bread 6 oz	Boiled bacon 3 oz	Bread 6 oz
	Margarine $\frac{1}{2}$ oz	Bread 3 oz	Margarine $\frac{1}{2}$ oz
	Tea $\frac{3}{4}$ pt	Potatoes 8 oz	Cocoa $\frac{3}{4}$ pt
Monday	Bread 3 oz	Potatoes 16 oz	Bread 6 oz
	Milk $\frac{1}{2}$ pt	Bread 2 oz	Veg. Broth $\frac{3}{4}$ pt
	Porridge $\frac{3}{4}$ pt	Cheese $1\frac{1}{2}$ oz	Cheese $1\frac{1}{2}$ oz
	Sugar $\frac{1}{2}$ oz		
Tuesday	"	Veg. broth $\frac{1}{2}$ pt	Plain cake 6 oz
		Bread 3 oz	Milk $\frac{3}{4}$ pt
		Cheese $1\frac{1}{2}$ oz	
		Dumpling 6 oz	
Wednesday	"	Boiled bacon 3 oz	"
		Bread 3 oz	
		Potatoes 3 oz	
Thursday	"	Cocoa $\frac{3}{4}$ pt	Bread 6 oz
		Bread 6 oz	Broth $\frac{3}{4}$ pt
		Cheese 2 oz	Cheese $1\frac{1}{2}$ oz

175

Friday	”	Boiled bacon 3 oz	Plain cake 6 oz
		Bread 3 oz	Cocoa $\frac{3}{4}$ pt
		Potatoes 8 oz	
Saturday	”	Suet Pudding 12 oz	Bread 6 oz
			Milk $\frac{3}{4}$ pt

In addition, lunch of bread 2 oz, cake 2 oz or biscuits 2 oz on weekdays only.

(a) How would you describe the food contained in this diet?

(b) Do you think this was a good diet for children?

(c) Why do you think the family only had bread, cheese and cocoa for Thursday dinner compared with the bacon, bread and potatoes for Friday dinner?

(d) Are there any luxuries in this diet?

(e) Why was such a diet necessary?

(f) Compare this diet with your own. What are the main differences?

(g) Give as many reasons as you can why your diet is different.

Slum children window-shopping in 1910

176

PART THREE

War and Peace

View of the Earth
from Apollo 17

22 The gathering storm

In January 1901 Queen Victoria died. She had reigned since 1837 and had lived through some remarkable times. During the years she had been on the throne, Britain had become the most powerful country in the world. How had this happened?

The answer is that Britain had been the first country to have an Industrial Revolution. All over the world the products of our factories and mines were sold; money from our banks was invested; British skill and know-how were at work. Everywhere, it seemed, people were buying British goods and turning to British engineers and craftsmen to build roads, railways and bridges. What was more, most of the world's trade was carried to the four corners of the globe on British ships.

In 1851 Prince Albert, the husband of Queen Victoria, had organised an exhibition to show to the rest of the world what Britain could do. This Great Exhibition, as it was called, was housed in the specially-built Crystal Palace in London's Hyde Park. Thousands came to marvel at the examples of British expertise. Truly, as it was said, Britain was now 'the workshop of the world'.

In 1887 Queen Victoria celebrated her Golden Jubilee. In London the decorated streets were packed to see the huge parade in honour

Crystal Palace

of her fifty years on the throne. The cheering crowds were treated to the sight of troop after troop of soldiers representing the many countries of Britain's huge Empire. Indians, Africans, Australians, Canadians, New Zealanders, all marched past in their colourful uniforms.

What pride there was in that Empire! In all, it covered some 31 000 000 square kilometres. Four hundred million people were subjects of Queen Victoria. The Union Jack fluttered bravely over an Empire on which, it was said, 'the sun never set'. It was no wonder they sang songs such as 'Land of Hope and Glory' and 'Rule Britannia' with such enthusiasm.

We have seen already how this Empire started in the sixteenth century and how it grew. Much had been gained from the wars with France; much more was added by the brave explorers who risked their lives travelling into the unknown: men such as Captain James Cook who had been present at Quebec in 1759. His voyages of discovery gained Australia, New Zealand and several Pacific Islands for Britain.

Scotsmen played their part, too. Mungo Park, from Foulshiels near Selkirk, explored the river Niger in West Africa. The most famous, however, was David Livingstone of Blantyre, born in 1813. His parents were poor and when he was ten he went to work in a cotton mill. He worked from six in the morning until eight at night, but still he managed to teach himself Latin and Greek, and to read many books on travel and science. When he was twenty-three he went to Glasgow University, working in the mill during his holidays to pay his fees. By the time he was twenty-eight he had qualified as a doctor and went out to Africa as a missionary.

From Cape Town he travelled north to join the mission of a fellow-Scot, Dr Robert Moffat, whose daughter he later married. He made his way north into swampy country where he discovered Lake Ngami. Further on he reached a great river, the Zambesi. His aim now was to pioneer new routes to the east and the west which would be easier for missionaries and traders than the route he had followed. His journeys took him through dense jungle and treacherous swampland. He travelled down the mighty Zambesi river. On the way to the coast he came to a huge water-fall, where the river, over 750 metres wide, suddenly drops more than 130 metres. This he named the 'Victoria Falls'. When Livingstone reached the mouth of the Zambesi, he had crossed the continent of Africa from coast to coast.

By this time Livingstone was famous. The outside world had heard no news of him for four years however, and a New York newspaper sent out a search party under the command of Henry

M. Stanley. You have probably heard the story of his meeting with Livingstone. Livingstone refused to return home with Stanley, saying that he had too much work to do in Africa. One morning in 1873 his native porters opened the door of his tent. They found him kneeling by the side of his bed, his head resting on his arms. The travels of David Livingstone from Blantyre were over.

Explorers and missionaries like Livingstone were followed by traders and settlers. By the end of the nineteenth century, hundreds of thousands of people of British descent were living and working in lands very far away from home. They took with them their British way of life including, of course, their sports—especially cricket. In the cool of an evening, sitting outside their homes, they would talk of family and friends back in 'the old country'.

Britons in India—a picture taken in the 1890s

While Britain was winning this Empire, other countries had not been standing still. They, too, saw cottage industries being replaced by factories; saw big increases in their populations and a rapid growth of their cities. They, too, wanted a share of the wealth to be made from trading. By 1901, when King Edward VII succeeded his mother, Britain's lead was being challenged.

Where did this challenge come from? Let us look briefly at the growth of three of these countries.

180

France

You might have expected that France would be Britain's main rival. After all, in the eighteenth century, the two countries had fought a second Hundred Years' War. France was still rich and powerful but during the nineteenth century did not modernise as much as others. Why was this?

You remember how, in 1815, French troops had been beaten at Waterloo. Napoleon *abdicated* and was imprisoned on the island of St Helena. The Allies who had beaten Napoleon decided to restore the family of the executed Louis XVI. This meant a return to some of the old ways. The ideas of Liberty, Equality and Fraternity were pushed aside—but not forgotten. In 1830 there was another revolution but this time without the bloodshed of 1789. Louis Philippe was then chosen as king but he in turn was overthrown in 1848 by a third revolution. A new republic was declared: at its head Louis Napoleon, nephew of the famous emperor. Four years later, this Napoleon made himself emperor, too. It seems strange that the French should have wanted another emperor. After all, the last one had been defeated heavily at Waterloo. But the magic of the name Napoleon was enough to sweep him to power.

At first things went well. There were no wars of conquest against other countries. Instead, roads and railways were built; industries developed and trade was encouraged. The crowded streets of Paris were transformed into the beautiful avenues that we can visit today. Napoleon even organised a Great Exhibition of his own to show off French products.

Unfortunately for France, however, this Napoleon tried to imitate his uncle. He wanted to increase the strength of France by fighting victorious wars. In 1870, France went to war against the German state of Prussia. Prussia was helped by other German states, and together they totally defeated France. Napoleon was captured and the country invaded; Paris was surrounded and ordered to surrender. For four months, the city held out against the German attacks; the only contact with the outside world was by balloon. The people were starving: even the animals in the famous Paris zoo were killed and sold for food. The city was forced to give in.

The victorious Germans imposed a terrible peace treaty. France had to pay £200 million to the Germans and hand over the French border counties of Alsace and Lorraine. Napoleon was allowed to come and live in Britain. (Later, his only son was killed fighting for the British army in Africa.) Meanwhile, another republic was set up to replace the rule of the emperor. France never forgot or forgave the defeat by Germany. Sooner or later the French would seek revenge.

The United States of America

Carnegie

Across the Atlantic, the USA had made incredible progress. In 1790, the population had been about four millions. By 1913 this had grown to ninety-seven millions! We have seen already how hundreds of thousands of British folk emigrated to America. During the nineteenth century these were joined by people from every country in Europe. In all some thirty-three millions had emigrated to the USA by 1914. They all came seeking a new life in the young republic. Many found fame and fortune. Amongst them was Andrew Carnegie, a penniless young lad from Dunfermline who became a multi-millionaire as the owner of the giant United States Steel Corporation.

Many of these settlers moved out from the boundaries of the original thirteen states and headed westwards across the great plains of America. They faced dangers and hardships: attacks from hostile Indians, disease, the burning heat of the desert or the freezing cold of the high passes through the snow-capped Rocky Mountains. Wars were fought against the Indians, the Spanish and the Mexicans as the Americans pushed further west. Vast areas of land were bought from the French, the Spanish, the Indians and the Russians, who sold Alaska to the Americans. From these lands, new states were created and added to the Union. But one terrible problem remained.

We have read in Chapter 6 how slaves were first brought to America. Although Britain had ended slavery, it was still allowed in the USA. By 1861, about five million slaves were working for their masters, most of them on the cotton plantations in the south of the country. Many Americans thought that slavery was very wrong, but the southern states were prepared to defend what they saw as an important part of their way of life.

In 1861, these eleven southern states broke away from the Union and set up their own government known as the Confederacy. A civil war broke out between the Confederacy and the twenty-three states of the north who supported the Union. The war went on for four years. There were some bloody battles, thousands of soldiers on both sides were killed. Large areas of the land and many towns were destroyed as the armies fought backwards and forwards for the decisive victory. In the end, it was the states of the north that won. They had more men to call on and most of the important factories were in the north. The Confederacy was slowly ground into defeat and forced to surrender.

Lincoln (centre)

During the war, President Lincoln, the leader of the Union, had freed the slaves. After so many years of slavery there were tremendous problems of prejudice to resolve. Sadly, Lincoln did not get the chance to repair the damage caused by the war. Five days

182

after the surrender of the South he was shot dead by an assassin. The newly-freed blacks faced a desperate struggle to win acceptance as equal citizens of the reunited USA.

Despite this continuing problem, America went from strength to strength. The wealth produced by its farms, factories and mines was enormous. In 1901, Carnegie's US Steel Corporation produced more steel than the whole of Britain. There was competition for Britain in other areas too, but most of what America produced was sold in America itself to the rapidly-growing population. The USA was too busy with its own affairs to bother overmuch with what was happening in Europe. So the threat to Britain did not come from America, it came from Germany.

Germany

In 1815 Germany was not a united country: about two hundred states—some as small as our Border towns—made up what was called Germany. The strongest state was Prussia, and under Prussia's leadership these states came to be united. One man more than any other achieved this. His name was Otto von Bismarck, Chancellor first of Prussia, then of Germany.

For many years Prussia had been well-known for the strength of its armies. You may remember how Prussian soldiers had helped to win the battle of Waterloo. Between 1860 and 1871 these armies won startling victories over the Danes, the Austrians and, as we have seen, the French. In 1871, a new German Reich or Empire was set up with William I, King of Prussia, as ruler. He was known as the Kaiser. (Can you guess where this word 'Kaiser' came from?)

Guided by Bismarck, Germany made alliances with Austria and Italy. Bismarck did not want to risk any more wars. It was hoped that an alliance could be made also with Britain. After all, Frederick, the heir to the German throne, was married to Vicky, the eldest daughter of Queen Victoria. But when old Kaiser William I died in 1888, Frederick had cancer and clearly did not have long to live. He reigned for only ninety-nine days before he, too, died.

The new Kaiser was his son, William II. He was a proud, arrogant, young man who liked nothing better than wearing military uniform and inspecting his soldiers on parade. William dismissed Bismarck and set about building up Germany even if this meant annoying other countries. German industries grew at a tremendous pace. By 1914 the Germans were producing more iron than Britain and almost as much coal. The Germans led the world in the new chemical and electrical industries. The German motor car industry was far ahead of Britain's. Clearly Britain was no longer 'the workshop of

Bismarck

183

the world'. British industries had fallen behind, for they had not kept pace with new developments.

Next, the Kaiser demanded that Germany should have colonies like Britain and France. Germany deserved 'a place in the sun'; countries like Britain must accept the strength of the new Reich. Most lands, however, had already been shared out by the other European countries and Germany could win only about 2 500 000 square kilometres—mostly in Africa—with about 12 million people. How did this compare with Britain's Empire? Do you think the Kaiser would be satisfied with this?

To defend his new Empire, the Kaiser ordered a navy to be built. This was too much for Britain. As an island, Britain felt she needed to have control of the seas and so the Royal Navy was kept larger than the fleet of any other country. The battleships being built by the Germans were seen as a threat and as a challenge—and King Edward VII detested his rude nephew. Something had to be done. In 1906 a new type of battleship was launched by Britain. HMS 'Dreadnought' was bigger, faster and had larger guns than any other ship afloat. Work was started on other ships.

What would the Germans do? They started to build their own 'Dreadnoughts'. The race was on. Between 1908 and 1914 both

HMS *Dreadnought*

countries spent millions of pounds building these huge battleships. By 1914 Britain had twenty-nine; Germany had seventeen. The tension between the two countries rose.

Britain in the meantime was so worried about what it saw as 'the German threat' that other measures were taken. The British army was modernised and a special Expeditionary Force of 100 000

184

men prepared for foreign service in the event of war. Britain also made treaties with France and Russia in case of trouble from Germany.

And yet in the summer of 1914, British people had something else to worry about. They believed that a civil war was about to break out in Ireland.

Since 1800 Ireland had been ruled from Westminster. This suited the Protestants of the six counties of Ulster in the north but not the Catholics of the south who made up the majority of Ireland's population. They resented this control and were angry after years of unfair treatment which had stopped them owning land or holding important jobs. These wrongs were put right but this was not enough. Some of these Irishmen stood as Irish *Nationalist* MPs and went to London determined to persuade Parliament to give Ireland its independence. Others turned to violence and formed the 'Sein Fein' ('Ourselves Alone'). A series of murders and bombings shocked the people of Britain.

Attempts were made in Parliament to give independence to Ireland but they all failed. In 1912, there were fifty-three Irish Nationalist MPs. They persuaded the Liberal government to try again and an Act of Parliament was passed which promised Ireland its independence in 1914.

This was unacceptable to the Ulster Protestants. Led by Edward Carson and encouraged by some Conservatives, they openly prepared to fight. The Nationalists also recruited men and got ready for war.

But then events in Europe overtook what was happening in Ireland. In the summer of 1914 the gathering storm-clouds of war with Germany brought a halt to the threat of civil war. For the moment at least, Ulstermen and Nationalists gave up their differences to fight the common foe.

THINGS TO DO

1 Try to explain in your own words what you understand by the term 'workshop of the world'. Was this an accurate description of Britain in 1851? In 1914?

2 You read on page 179 how it was said that 'the sun never set' on the British Empire. What do you understand by this?

3 'Land of Hope and Glory' and 'Rule Britannia' were two popular songs of those times. There were many others. Popular writers such as Rudyard Kipling and Robert Louis Stevenson set many of their stories and poems 'on the frontier' of the Empire. You should try to borrow some of these from the library to appreciate the pride that there was then in the Empire.

4 Class work. Try to make a collection of postage stamps from the lands of the Empire before 1914. Mount each country's stamps on a sheet of white paper and make a class display.

5 'Britain needed to have control of the seas' (page 184) Why do you think control of the seas was so important to Britain? What steps did Britain take after 1906 to retain control of the seas? Do you think control of the seas is still as important for Britain?

6 It is 1911: thirty years since the German Reich was created. Imagine that you are a German newspaper reporter. You have been asked to write an article describing the progress of Germany over the thirty years. What would you write?

Now try to write about the same events but this time as a British newspaper reporter.

Children waving Union Jacks

23 The First World War

Kaiser William II

In 1914 an American visitor said that Europe was like a huge gunpowder barrel, just waiting for a spark to blow it up. What did he mean?

We have read already about the tension between Britain and Germany. The naval race to build Dreadnoughts, the competition for colonies and the challenge of German industries worried and angered the British. They saw the Kaiser as a dangerous, warlike, man: King Edward VII had died in 1910 and King George V had an intense dislike for his arrogant German cousin. Yet the 'spark' that led to war did not come from a clash between Britain and Germany.

There was no love lost between France and Germany either. The French could never forget the defeats of 1870. They improved their army and built heavy defences all along the border with Germany. From these forts the French soldiers glowered at the Germans and waited for the order to attack. Only then could the shame of 1870 be forgotten.

The Germans also made their own preparations for war. An army of nearly two million men was kept ready to strike. Millions of other Germans were given military training and were ready to leave their peacetime jobs to join their regiments. The German generals prepared a plan for war. The German armies would take a 'short cut' round the French forts and attack France through Belgium. They would be able to move quickly over the flat countryside and conquer the French before their allies, the Russians, had time to attack.

So France and Germany were also squaring up for a fight. But still the 'spark' did not come from a clash between them.

The 'spark' came from another quarrel: between Austria (an ally of Germany) and Russia (an ally of France).

There had been bad feeling between Austria and Russia for many years. If you look at the map on page 194 you will see that in 1914 the Austrian Empire stretched across much of central and southern Europe. This Empire contained people of many different nationalities, all wanting their freedom from Austrian rule.

Archduke Ferdinand and his wife just before they were shot

German machine gun team

Sir Douglas Haig

In the area known as the Balkans, the Slav peoples looked to small, independent, Serbia to help them to create a country of their own.

On June 28th 1914, the Austrian Archduke Franz Ferdinand and his wife were shot dead in the Balkan town of Sarajevo. Their assassin was Gavrilo Princip, a young student who seemed to have been helped by Serbia. The Serbs were prepared to apologise, but the Austrians declared war. Russia began to mobilise her armies to help Serbia; France came to the help of Russia; Germany came to the help of Austria.

The 'powder barrel' had exploded.

As planned, the German armies marched through little Belgium—in spite of the brave resistance led by King Albert. Britain and other countries had promised to help Belgium if she were attacked, and so this brought Britain into the war on August 4th 1914.

On August 6th the British Expeditionary Force (the 'BEF') crossed the Channel and landed in France. They were soon in action: at Mons in Belgium they fought bravely against the German invaders but were forced to retreat. The German armies swept on towards Paris and were only stopped at the great battle of the Marne. They were pushed back just beyond the River Aisne and there they dug trenches from which they could fight. The French and British armies did the same, and for four long years the two sides faced each other across an empty 'No Man's Land'.

You have probably heard of the horrors of this trench warfare and of the terrible battles which killed hundreds of thousands of men and turned 'No Man's Land' into a nightmare land of barbed wire, shell-holes, shattered trees and broken buildings. These battles were not like the battles of the past, over in a few hours or a day or two: they dragged on for months and months.

The battle of the Somme was fought for five months in 1916, from early July to late November. The British forces, commanded by Sir Douglas Haig, were determined to push the German army back.

For five days and nights the British guns hammered at the German lines. It was the heaviest bombardment ever known and the noise of the firing could be heard in London! The generals believed that no-one would be left alive in the German trenches.

At 7 a.m. on the first of July the firing stopped. The officers in the British front line had their orders: they checked their watches, blew their whistles and led their men 'over the top'. The British 'tommies' struggled through the barbed wire and the shell holes towards what was left of the German trenches.

Many Germans had been killed by the shelling; many others had been driven mad by the constant noise. But others were alive, deep underground in their concrete dugouts. Now they scrambled

'Over the top'
(filmed during the Battle
of the Somme, 1916)

Gas casualties

to the surface, dragging their machine guns with them. Quickly they set up their weapons and watched as line after line of British soldiers advanced towards them. Then came the order. Firing five hundred rounds a minute, the guns cut down the khaki figures like scythes cutting corn. On that first day of the battle sixty thousand British soldiers were killed, wounded or captured. It was the worst disaster ever suffered by the British army. Yet the generals continued the attack for another five months! During that time more than half a million Britons and Frenchmen, and more than half a million Germans, were killed, wounded or captured—all in this one drawn-out battle. And what was gained? The answer is nothing. At the end of it all, both sides dug deeper into the winter mud. Now exhausted, they gathered their strength for another attack.

In the trenches living conditions for the men—British, French and German alike—were dreadful. Mud, rats and lice were constant companions. So, too, was the smell of rotting bodies lying in 'No Man's Land'. Long periods of silence would be shattered by the crash of an exploding shell or the crack of a *sniper's* rifle; then screams of pain and shouts of 'Stretcher bearers!' Nor was there any peace at night. The ghastly landscape would be lit up by the glow of star shells or the flash of gunfire. Shadowy figures would creep out on patrol or to try to reach wounded comrades out there in 'No Man's Land'.

How could it end? Both sides tried new weapons. In 1915 the Germans began to use gas which could blind a man or destroy his lungs: at first there was no protection but soon gas masks were issued. In 1916 the British used tanks for the first time, but they

189

moved slowly and broke down easily. It seemed there was no way of breaking the deadlock.

All this had a terrible effect on the soldiers. Many of those who survived wrote down their experiences in stories and poems. A.A. Milne, the author of 'Christopher Robin' served in the trenches and this is what he thought of it:

> Same old trenches, same old view,
> Same old rats, as blooming tame,
> Same old dug-outs, nothing new,
> Same old smell, the very same,
> Same old bodies out in front,
> Same old strafe from 2 till 4,   [enemy bombardment]
> Same old scratching, same old hunt,
> Same old bloody war.

The Home Front

How did the war affect those back home in Britain?

At first a great wave of loyalty swept through the country. Suffragettes, trades unionists, feuding Irishmen, all rallied to support their country in its hour of need. Everybody was anxious to play his or her part. Thousands of young men answered the call of the recruiting posters. In the first five weeks of the war a quarter of a million men had 'joined up'.

Soon, however, many more were needed to replace the slaughter of the battlefields. In 1916 Britain had to introduce conscription. This meant that all fit men had to join the armed forces unless they were doing essential war work such as coal-mining or making weapons.

Women, too, played their part. With the menfolk away at the front, women had to take on their jobs. Women worked on the land, drove buses and trams, replaced coalmen, carpenters, plumbers and engineers. Thousands of women risked their lives making shells; thousands more brought comfort to the wounded as doctors and nurses. By 1918 more than forty thousand women were serving in uniform as soldiers, sailors or airwomen. Although they did not actually fight, they released men from work such as driving and signals.

There were other changes, too. The government introduced *censorship* of newspapers and encouraged propaganda stories against the Germans, describing acts of cruelty. There were many such stories but they have never been proved.

The anti-German feeling gathered pace. Shops with German names were attacked and people with German-sounding names were regarded as traitors. The First Sea Lord, Prince Louis von Battenberg, was forced to resign—although his loyalty was never

A famous recruiting poster showing Lord Kitchener

A Scottish ambulance driver, Mairi Chisholm, at the Front

190

in doubt. (He changed his family name to Mountbatten.) On the day his resignation was announced, the newspapers reported the death of his nephew killed in action. Even the Royal Family felt it necessary to change their name from Saxe-Coburg to Windsor.

War in the air

The anti-German feeling grew when the Germans used airships called Zeppelins to bomb cities such as London and Edinburgh. This new form of attack was very frightening although the raids were tiny compared with those of the Second World War.

Aeroplanes played an increasingly important part in the war.

At first the machines had just been used for spotting enemy movement. Soon, however, there were squadrons of fighter planes piloted by 'aces' who battled it out with the enemy in 'dogfights' high above the trenches. By 1918, British bombers could fly as far as Germany itself to repay the damage caused by the Zeppelins.

War at sea

There was little fighting between the battleships of Britain and Germany. Even in the battle of Jutland in 1916, Admiral Jellicoe and the German Admiral Scheer were careful not to risk their fleets too much. For by this time the Germans had decided to try to end the war quickly on the sea since they could not end it quickly on land. They built submarines, known as U-boats, hoping to starve Britain into surrender by sinking merchant ships bringing food and supplies. They nearly succeeded: in the month of April 1917 over four hundred ships were sunk. Britain was forced to introduce *food rationing*.

But in the long run the U-boat campaign was unwise, for it was this that made America decide to enter the war on the side of the Allies in 1917. The U-boats were defeated by the help of the American navy; by grouping the ships in convoys protected by warships; and by new weapons such as the depth charge.

Remember we know this as the First World War. There had been much fighting elsewhere, though on a smaller scale. In 1915, after the Turks sided with Germany, the Allies tried to capture Constantinople so that ships could move between Russia and western Europe. Thousands of troops, many of them from Australia and New Zealand, were landed at Gallipoli. They fought most gallantly, but the attack was a failure. In 1917, however, the Turkish possessions in Mesopotamia and Palestine were conquered and General Allenby entered Jerusalem. Allenby's forces had been helped by T. E. Lawrence, 'Lawrence of Arabia', who led tribesmen against their Turkish rulers.

Meanwhile, fighting flared up again on the Western Front. At Passchendaele, in 1917, the mistakes of the Somme were repeated. For fourteen days, the British guns bombarded the German positions. Over four million shells turned 'No Man's Land' into a shattered sea of mud. After one hundred days of fighting, the British had lost 300 000 men. It was one of the most awful battles of the war—yet, again, scarcely any ground was won.

The year 1917 was important for another reason. Russian armies fought the German troops on the Eastern Front most bravely although they were badly armed, sometimes possessing only one rifle between three soldiers. The Emperor of Russia's government

Stretcher bearers in the mud of Passchendaele

Tank going into action at Courcelette

had never been well organised: now it was overthrown by a revolution and the new government made peace with Germany. (You will read more about this in the next chapter.) Now Germany could concentrate all her forces on the Western Front.

On March 21st 1918 came the greatest German attack of all the war. The whole of the British Fifth Army was pushed out of the way. In the space of sixteen days, the Allies lost 230000 men. But the German troops never crossed the River Marne and now the Allies counter-attacked. It was the turning-point of the war.

The Allied forces on the Western Front were put under the command of one man—the French Marshal Foch. He could call on over a quarter of a million American soldiers who had arrived in France, fresh and eager to fight. By this time, too, the British had several hundred tanks ready for battle. These were bigger and faster than the earlier ones. They struck terror into the hearts of the Germans. The German army went into retreat. Thousands surrendered as the Allies swept forward.

The armies of Germany were not finally defeated, but things looked hopeless for her. Her ports were blocked and her allies beaten. The German people lost hope. They rebelled against the government that had led them to disaster, and the Kaiser fled to Holland. At 11 a.m. on November 11th 1918, the guns stopped firing and men laid down their arms.

Everyone was glad the killing was over, and everyone agreed that it must never happen again. The leaders of the Allies met at Versailles. Of these leaders the most important were the 'Big Four': Lloyd George from Britain, Clemenceau from France, Orlando from Italy, and President Wilson of the United States.

193

GREAT BRITAIN

HOLLAND

RUSSIAN EMPIRE

GERMAN EMPIRE

BELGIUM

FRANCE

AUSTRIA HUNGARY

SWITZERLAND

RUMANIA

PORTUGAL

SPAIN

ITALY

SERBIA

BULGARIA

GREECE

TURKISH EMPIRE

ALBANIA

MONTENEGRO

EGYPT

EUROPE AND MIDDLE EAST, 1914

At Versailles the victorious Allies blamed Germany for starting the war. Her colonies were taken away from her; she was ordered to pay large sums of money to the Allies; her army and navy were made very small; and she lost valuable lands to other countries. Some of these lands Germany had taken years before (such as Alsace-Lorraine and part of Poland) but she also lost for a time the rich coalfields of the Saar valley. In years to come ordinary Germans felt that they had been unfairly treated, and asked why they should go on paying for the unwise acts of the ex-Kaiser and his generals.

Outside Germany, too, tremendous changes were made. The old Austrian Empire came to an end, and from its vast territories were carved out a tiny Austrian republic and the new states of Czechoslovakia and Hungary. Yugoslavia and Poland, new states created by the peacemakers, also had large pieces of former Austrian territory, as did Rumania. The little Baltic countries of Estonia, Latvia, and Lithuania, which had been yielded by Russia to Germany in 1918, were allowed to remain in existence as independent states. Finland also became a separate state.

These changes, and also some that took place in the countries of the Middle East, can be seen on the map on page 195.

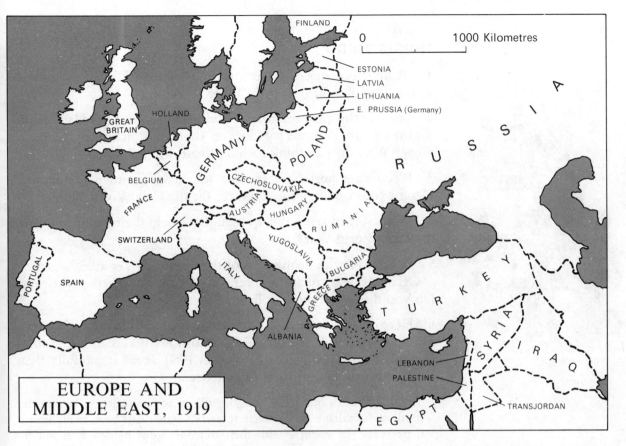

EUROPE AND MIDDLE EAST, 1919

Map labels: FINLAND, 0 1000 Kilometres, ESTONIA, LATVIA, LITHUANIA, E. PRUSSIA (Germany), GREAT BRITAIN, HOLLAND, GERMANY, POLAND, RUSSIA, BELGIUM, CZECHOSLOVAKIA, FRANCE, AUSTRIA, HUNGARY, RUMANIA, SWITZERLAND, YUGOSLAVIA, BULGARIA, PORTUGAL, SPAIN, ITALY, GREECE, TURKEY, ALBANIA, SYRIA, IRAQ, LEBANON, PALESTINE, TRANSJORDAN, EGYPT

Who caused all this re-drawing of frontiers and setting up of new nations?

It was the work, above all, of the American President, Woodrow Wilson. He was determined that if possible none of the peoples of Europe should have to live under 'foreign' rule. So Czechoslovakia was made for the Czechs and Slovenes to live in, Hungary for the Hungarians, and so on.

Wilson had one other great idea, and he insisted that it should be made part of the peace treaty. This idea was that the nations of the world should band together in a league and promise to settle any disputes peacefully instead of by war. So the League of Nations was born and big headquarters were built at Geneva. Everybody hoped that this was the beginning of a great period of peace for the world.

While the peacemakers were at work, the nations sadly counted the cost and honoured their dead. In all, over ten million people had been killed. Of these some 750 000 were British (equal to nearly the entire population of Glasgow). In every church and village, memorials were put up in honour of those who had given their lives for their country. Surely, people thought, such a terrible thing could never happen again?

195

THINGS TO DO

1 'A huge powder barrel just waiting for a spark.' Why was there so much tension in Europe in 1914?

2 Look at this cartoon. It appeared in 'Punch'—a popular British magazine—in 1914. What do you think the picture is trying to show? Why do you think such a picture was published?

3 Recruiting posters were used to encourage men to join up. Design your own recruiting poster for the First World War.

4 What sort of work did women do to help their country during the First World War?

5 What were the main terms of the Treaty of Versailles?
  Germany was made to accept the blame for starting the war. Do you think that this was fair?

6 Here is part of an eye-witness account of a battle on the Western Front. It was told by an old Scottish soldier, Lance-Corporal Magnus Hood, just before he died in 1980. Read it carefully then answer the questions below in sentences.

THE TRIUMPH OF "CULTURE."

> The objective of our attack was the village of Courcelette. Barring the road to the village was a sugar refinery, which had been made into a fortress by the enemy, with their machine guns hidden well underground until the attack started. The attack had been held up at this point, and a party of us had to rush up with more ammunition, bullets and grenades, to the 21st Battalion, lying in shell holes in front of the refinery. As we reached them we saw a landship, named the LS Creme de Menthe, pass ahead, and go right up to the walls of the refinery, its guns blazing. It seemed to lean against one of the walls which collapsed, and the monster roared into the fort, while we could see the Germans streaming out behind it, offering an excellent target to the riflemen in the shellholes.

(*a*) What was the objective of the attack?

(*b*) Why was the attack held up?

(*c*) What cover was there for the attacking troops?

(*d*) Why do you think such attacks cost so many casualties?

(*e*) What do you think the 'landship' was?

(*f*) What part did it play in the attack?

(*g*) This was the first time Corporal Hood had ever seen a 'landship' in action. Do you think he was impressed?

7 Imagine that you are a soldier serving in the trenches of the Western Front. Write a letter home to your family describing your experiences. (Such letters were censored by the soldiers' officers before they were sent home. Can you think why?)

196

24 Russia —the road to revolution

May Day parade
in Moscow

Today, the country we know as Russia is one of the world's strongest *super-powers*.

Indeed, in terms of size, Russia is the largest country in the world. One-sixth of the Earth's surface is Russian. From the Baltic Sea in the West to the Pacific Ocean in the East, Russia stretches a vast 9000 kilometres. Today about 254 million people live in Russia. With its rich reserves of coal, iron and oil, Russian industry is very powerful.

In 1957 Russian scientists succeeded in putting the first *satellite* into space. This was followed in 1961 when the Russian Yuri Gargarin became the first man in space. Since then Russia and America have spent many millions of pounds in a 'space race' with each country trying to get ahead of the other in the exploration of space. This competition between the two super-powers has its darker side. Today Russia and America threaten each other and

197

the world with their rockets. These missiles with their *nuclear warheads* are capable of destroying mankind completely.

Yet, at the start of this century, Russia was one of the most backward countries of Europe. The population of some 160 million was thinly scattered across the broad land. Some were clustered in towns with white-walled houses grouped round the churches with their onion-shaped domes. Most, however, lived in straggling villages of unpainted log huts. Geese and pigs wandered freely through the muddy streets. Men, women and children worked all summer planting and harvesting the crops before the coming of the first September frost. Then, for six long months of winter, the open country became a wasteland of freezing whiteness. Inside their huts, the people sat round their stoves hoping that their supplies of food would last.

Russian peasants
pulling a barge

Most of these people were simple peasants who worked the land in much the same way as in Scotland before the Agricultural Revolution. It was only in 1861 that they were freed, on the orders of the government, from a kind of slavery known as serfdom. They still remained desperately poor with famine an ever-present threat. It was little wonder that many of them cast longing looks at the huge estates of the wealthy land-owners.

It was only at the end of the nineteenth century that Russia had its Industrial Revolution. Factories were built in the largest towns—St Petersburg and Moscow. As had happened in Britain, people flocked from the land looking for work. Again, as in Britain, conditions were often dreadful: long hours in unpleasant working conditions for very little pay, then home to a cramped slum put up by the factory owner. Trade unions were forbidden; workers who complained could be fined, beaten or sacked. Strikes were often put down by force. In 1912 at Lena in Siberia, two hundred striking miners were shot dead by troops sent by the government.

What was this government that could free serfs and shoot down strikers? The government of Russia was in the hands of one man— the Tsar. (Notice again the word Tsar: does it remind you of any other titles used by rulers?) The Tsar of Russia was what we call an autocrat—that is, he had complete power. His orders were carried out across his huge empire by an army of ministers, governors, civil servants, tax collectors and police. Some 20 000 agents of the Okhrana, the Tsar's secret police, kept a watch on any opponents. There was no parliament: the Tsar chose his own advisers and decided his own policies.

In 1914 the Tsar was Nicholas II. He was a polite, handsome, devoted family man, but quite unfitted to rule Russia. For one thing, he had not been trained for the job. His father Alexander

Nicholas, Alexandra
and Alexis

III had died suddenly in 1894, when Nicholas was twenty-six. In his own words he said, 'What am I going to do? I am not prepared to be a Tsar, I know nothing of the business of ruling. I have no idea of even how to talk to ministers.' Poor Nicholas was not very clever and found it hard to concentrate on the tremendous problems facing him. One Russian claimed that the new Tsar was unfit to run a village post office—let alone a country the size of Russia.

Nicholas had married a German princess, Alexandra—a grand-daughter of Queen Victoria. Being German, she was not popular with the Russians. To make matters worse, she tried to make Nicholas act like a strong ruler. 'Never forget you [Nicholas] are and must remain autocratic Emperor. How they [the Russians] all need to feel an iron will and hand—you are the Lord and Master in Russia and God Almighty placed you there and they shall bow down before your wisdom and firmness.' But it was not to be. Wisdom and firmness were qualities that Nicholas just did not have.

The royal couple were very happy together. Alexandra gave birth to four daughters. Then in 1904 came the birth of the longed-for son and heir. The joy of the parents quickly turned to grief and despair when it was discovered that the baby Alexis suffered from haemophilia. This meant that if he was cut or bumped his blood could not clot. The slightest knock could see him bleeding to death. Poor Alexis had several such accidents. On each occasion he suffered terrible pain from internal bleeding as the bruising spread through his joints. Several times he nearly died.

Then it seemed that the prayers of his worried parents were answered. A rough peasant from Siberia, Gregory Rasputin, turned up in St Petersburg claiming to be a man of God. He was introduced to the royal family. He visited the sick boy and somehow managed to help him. How Rasputin did this we are still not sure. He may have used hypnotism to calm Alexis down and stop his bleeding. Nicholas and Alexandra became devoted to the man they called 'Our Friend'. He became their trusted adviser. Alexandra in particular was very much under his spell. 'Now hearken [listen] unto Our Friend,' wrote Alexandra to her husband. 'He has your interest at heart—it is not for nothing God sent him to us. Only we must pay attention to what he says.'

Rasputin and admirers

As the years went past this is just what happened. The Tsar decided policies and appointed Ministers under the guidance of Rasputin. The trouble was that the rest of Russia did not see a devout holy man. They saw a dreadful rogue who seldom washed, drank too much and enjoyed the company of women. How do you think this would affect the people's respect for the Tsar?

For many years there had been opposition to the autocracy. As there was no parliament in Russia some of these opponents

Lenin in 1892

Marx

turned to violence. Nicholas's grandfather, Alexander II, had been killed by a terrorist bomb. There had been attempts on his father's life, too. Several terrorists were arrested and hanged in 1887. Among them was a young student Alexander Ulyanov. His younger brother Vladimir swore revenge.

Vladimir Ilich Ulyanov was born in 1870, the son of a school inspector. He was very clever at school and seemed to have a bright future ahead of him. The death of his brother changed that. From then on he worked for the overthrow of the autocracy that he hated. He became a *revolutionary*, a follower of Karl Marx, and changed his name to Lenin.

He believed in the ideas of Karl Marx, who had died in 1883. Marx was a German scholar who read and wrote about many things—including history, politics and economics. He argued that the world was divided between the 'haves' and the 'have-nots'. The 'haves' (whom Marx called 'capitalists') had the money, or capital, to own the land and the factories. This gave the capitalists great power to control the 'have-nots' (whom Marx called the 'proletariat'). The 'have-nots' owned nothing. They were forced to work for the capitalists in order to live. They had to put up with low wages and bad conditions. Marx thought that things would get worse and worse for these workers and their families. Naturally they would resent this. Tension would build up until the proletariat reached breaking point. There would be a revolution and the capitalists would be overthrown.

Some capitalists, however, might escape and try to regain control. So for some time the proletariat would need to keep a tight hold on the government. There would need to be a secret police force and strict censorship. Enemies of the revolution would have to be searched out and destroyed. We call this sort of government a *dictatorship*. Once the enemies had been eliminated, Marx said, the dictatorship would no longer be needed. There would be no more landlords or factory bosses. Everybody would have a share in the wealth of the country. They would hold things in common.

Here, of course, is the origin of the word 'communist': a communist is someone who believes in the sort of revolution described by Marx. Lenin read about Marx's ideas and became a communist. While other opponents of the Tsar believed in working for a parliament similar to that of Britain, Lenin believed in a revolution that would destroy the autocracy.

The Okhrana were everywhere, however, and in 1895 Lenin was arrested. After a year in prison he was exiled to Siberia, then in 1900 he was allowed to leave Russia. For the next seventeen years Lenin lived abroad. He talked and wrote about the revolution he hoped to see in Russia. His ideas attracted followers: some joined him abroad, others worked in Russia itself. Most of these followers were

Stalin—photograph from the records of the Okhrana

educated people like Lenin himself; others came from peasant families. Among them was a young man known as Stalin—'the man of steel'. He led some daring bank robberies to get money for the revolutionaries. When he was caught, he too was sent to Siberia. Lenin set high standards for his followers, who came to be known as *Bolsheviks*. He wanted people who were prepared to give everything for the revolution. 'We must train people who shall devote to the revolution not only their spare evenings, but the whole of their lives.' So Lenin watched and waited.

Meanwhile what was happening in Russia?

Opposition to the Tsar continued to grow. Indeed, in 1905 there had been an attempted revolution. At that time Russia was at war with Japan. The Tsar had expected easy victories; instead the Japanese triumphed on land and sea. In January 1905 a huge peaceful demonstration of workers and their families in St Petersburg was fired on by troops. Some five hundred were killed and many more wounded. This was the signal for a series of strikes and riots. In St Petersburg a workers' council known as a 'soviet' was set up. Here representatives from the different factories met to discuss what to do. One of the leaders of this soviet was a young man called Leon Trotsky. Soon other soviets were set up.

The situation was serious for Nicholas. In October 1905 he agreed to hold elections for a parliament, or Duma as it was called. This was enough for most people. They wanted to see Russia governed like Britain with a monarch agreeing to accept the decisions of the people's representatives in parliament. They did not want a bloody revolution. The soviets, however, wanted more. But now they had few supporters. In the end they were put down by force and the leaders arrested. Once again the Tsar was in power. He quickly showed that the Duma was not going to be like the British parliament. When it disagreed with Nicholas, he dismissed it. The autocracy seemed as strong as ever.

We have seen already how important the year 1914 was for Europe. The nations plunged into a terrible conflict. Russia went to the aid of Serbia and found herself at war with Austria, Germany and later Turkey.

Great things were expected from the Russians. Their huge army of some 3.5 million men was expected to flatten all opposition. But the Russian army was only strong on paper. The soldiers were mostly uneducated peasants, poorly trained and poorly equipped. Sometimes there were not enough rifles to go round and a man had to wait until a comrade with a rifle was killed or wounded before he could fight back. The officers came from noble families and had little time for their men. The Russian commanders relied on mass

Tsar Nicholas
at the Front

frontal attacks to beat the enemy, but these tactics were useless against the rapid fire of the machine-guns. After two years of war, the Russians had lost nearly two million men. Not surprisingly, the Russians began to grumble.

In 1916 Nicholas himself took charge at the front—but he had no military training at all! To make matters worse, he was continually told what to do by Alexandra whom he had left in charge at St Petersburg (now renamed Petrograd). 'Now, before I forget, I must give you a message from Our Friend, prompted by what he saw in the night. He begs you to order that one [Nicholas and the Russian army] should advance nearer Riga.'

Who, people asked, is really running Russia? Seeing the danger, some members of the royal family decided to get rid of Rasputin. In December 1916 he was brutally murdered. But the damage had already been done.

The winter of 1916–1917 was bad even by Russian standards. With so many men away at the war the harvest had been a poor one, and now there was widespread hunger and discontent. In March 1917, people took to the streets demanding bread. At first neither Nicholas nor Alexandra realised how serious the situation was. The Tsar remained at the front and sent orders for the troops in Petrograd to put down the riots. Instead, the troops joined the demonstrators in the streets. The Tsar's government was helpless. When Nicholas tried to return to the city his train was stopped by railway workers. He could go no further. Now the Tsar of Russia, too, was powerless. In a panic he decided to give up the throne and abdicate. In the space of a few days, the autocracy that had lasted for hundreds of years had collapsed. The Tsar and his family were now prisoners.

Who then was to govern Russia?

202

The leaders of the Duma hastily formed themselves into a temporary, or Provisional, government. They would run the country until elections could be held. They faced tremendous problems, however. With the Tsar gone, people imagined that things would improve overnight: that in some way the bad working conditions, the shortages of food and the demands of the peasants for land could all be put right. Of course they could not. To make matters worse, the Provisional government decided to continue the war against Germany and her allies. Instead of the Tsar being blamed for the defeats and the losses, the people's anger now turned against the Provisional government. Then, in Petrograd, a new soviet was set up. Representatives of all the workers met with soldiers. It soon became clear that in the city the soviet had more power than the Provisional government. As in 1905, more soviets sprang up elsewhere in Russia.

Where was Lenin in all this? When the March revolution broke out he was still in exile in Switzerland. In a fever of excitement he tried to return to Russia and received help from an unusual ally. The Germans provided him with a train and money to get back. (Why do you think the Germans did this?)

On his return to Petrograd Lenin was given a hero's welcome. He at once set about attacking the work of the Provisional government. Lenin worked tirelessly, making speeches and encouraging his supporters. It was not just in the city that the Bolsheviks were at work. Some of them went to the front to persuade the soldiers to stop fighting. Many soldiers joined the Bolsheviks; others deserted their regiments and headed for home. Lenin's simple message of 'Peace, Bread and Land' appealed to the millions of Russians fed up with the shortages and the war.

Lenin speaking in Petrograd. Trotsky is standing on the right

In July his first attempt to seize power failed. Lenin had to escape to neighbouring Finland until things quietened down. In the autumn he returned in disguise. This time things were much better planned. Early on the morning of November 7th 1917 the Bolsheviks went into action in Petrograd. The most important places in the city were seized. By nightfall only the Winter Palace, headquarters of the Provisional government, was left. Then that, too, was taken by force and Petrograd was in the hands of the Bolsheviks.

The news was sent all over Russia. 'To the Citizens of Russia. The Provisional government has been overthrown. State power has passed into the hands of the Petrograd Soviet of Workers' and Soldiers' Deputies. Long live the Revolution of workers, soldiers and peasants!' Remember, however, that the Bolsheviks held only Petrograd. Lenin had seized power—but could he hold it?

THINGS TO DO

1   Explain in your own words what 'autocracy' means. How does this form of government differ from ours?

2   What problems faced Tsar Nicholas II? Why do you think he found it difficult to cope with them?

3   'We must train people who shall devote to the revolution not only their spare evenings but the whole of their lives' (page 201). Write a short paragraph to show whether you think Lenin lived up to what he expected from his followers.

4   What part did the First World War play in the Tsar's downfall?

5   On page 203 you read of the work of the Bolshevik agitators at the front. Prepare a speech that you would make to the troops to persuade them to stop fighting the Germans and support Lenin.

Street fighting in
Petrograd, July 1917

25 The Roaring Twenties

Berlin street scene,
July 1919

In Britain and the lands of her Allies, the news of the cease-fire was greeted with great rejoicing. People sang and danced in the streets. At last, it was all over!

It was very different in Germany, however. The news of the surrender came as a great shock. The censorship of German newspapers had hidden the truth from the German people. Now, having been promised victory for so many years, it was hard to believe that the German army had been defeated. The brave soldiers must have been 'stabbed in the back' by the politicians who made the peace. This of course was far from the truth. Faced by the superior numbers of the Allies, the German soldiers were in full retreat when the surrender was agreed. Even so, many Germans refused to believe that this had happened.

205

Among them was a young Austrian corporal serving in the German army. He had fought in the trenches and had been wounded at the battle of the Somme. In November 1918, he was in hospital recovering from having been gassed. When he heard the news of the surrender he collapsed on his bed in tears. Later he wrote 'So it had all been in vain. In vain all the sacrifices and hardship. In vain the hours in which with mortal fear clutching at our hearts we nevertheless did our duty; in vain the death of two millions. Had they died for this? So that a gang of wretched criminals could lay hands on the Fatherland?' The soldier's name was Adolf Hitler.

The coming of peace brought problems for the victors and the defeated alike. For one thing, there was the terrible cost of the war itself. Over 10 million had been killed: six deaths for every minute of the war. The cost of fighting for those four years was over £75 000 million: £3500 for every minute of the war. Now all countries had to try to rebuild their shattered strength. For the millions of 'demobbed' servicemen who now returned to civilian life there was the problem of finding a job. In fact, for many of them, there was no job to be found. The hardships of life in the trenches were exchanged for the hardships of life 'on the dole'.

I KNOW 3 TRADES
I SPEAK 3 LANGUAGES
FOUGHT FOR 3 YEARS
HAVE 3 CHILDREN
AND NO WORK FOR
3 MONTHS
BUT I ONLY WANT
ONE JOB

The Peace Treaty itself caused difficulties. No-one was happy with it. Britain and France felt that Germany had been let off too lightly. 'Hang the Kaiser!' was one demand. 'Make Germany pay!' was another. The Americans felt that Britain and France had been too hard on Germany. The Italians (who had joined the Allies in 1915) were disappointed with the small amount of land they gained from Austria and they felt that they deserved more.

You can probably guess how the Germans felt about the Peace Treaty. Here is part of a German newspaper article for June 28th 1919. 'Today in the Hall of Mirrors [at the palace of Versailles], the disgraceful Treaty is being signed. Do not forget it. The German people will with increasing labour press forward to reconquer the place among nations to which it is entitled. Then will come vengeance for the shame of 1919.'

So people in each country had something to grumble about. The task for most ordinary folk, however, was to try to forget about the war and 'get back to normal'.

Russia after the war

Meanwhile what was happening in Russia? In the last chapter we saw how the Bolsheviks managed to seize power in Petrograd. Soon they captured Moscow as well, but this did not mean they controlled the whole country. You must remember that the Bolsheviks—or Communists as they called themselves after March 1918—were a very small group. Out of a population of about 160 million, fewer than 250 000 were followers of Lenin.

Lenin's opponents, known as the Whites, took up arms against the new Soviet government. This called for drastic action by Lenin. To him, the revolution was in danger from the Whites—a mixture of supporters of the Tsar, the Provisional government and other revolutionary groups. So all political opposition was declared illegal: the press was censored and a new, terrible, secret police—the Cheka, later known as the KGB—was set up to destroy the enemies of the Communists. It has been estimated that as many as fifty thousand people were executed by the end of 1918 in this so-called Red Terror.

Trotsky and Red Army soldiers

Amongst the victims were the former Tsar Nicholas and his family. Since the revolution, the royal family had been held prisoners by the Communists. Now at Ekaterinburg in the Urals, the decision was taken to execute them. The whole family was shot and bayoneted to death in a cellar. Over three hundred years of Romanov rule had been brutally ended.

One of the first acts of the Soviet government had been to make peace with the Germans. In March 1918, the Germans presented their peace terms to the Russians, who had a terrible price to pay. By the treaty of Brest-Litovsk Russia lost about a quarter of her population, a third of her railway system, a third of her best farming land and three-quarters of her heavy industry.

The Allies were shocked at what the Russians had done. So Allied troops—British, American, French and Japanese—were sent to Russia. They were supposed to help the Whites but they had little to do and most of their time was spent guarding their bases. In the end they withdrew in June 1919 once the Versailles Treaty had been signed. Although the soldiers had done no real fighting, the Soviet government never forgave the Allies for siding with their enemies, the Whites.

With the withdrawal of the Allies, the Communists could turn all their attention to winning the civil war. Trotsky was given the job of beating the White armies. Almost out of nothing he created the famous Red Army. Each unit of this army had a Cheka group attached to it. Anybody not pulling his weight was shot. By 1921, the civil war had been won by the Red Army. The Whites were disorganised and poorly led. Above all they lacked the ruthless will of the Communists to win.

Starving Russians

These were terrible years for the Russian people. It has been estimated that between 1914 and 1921 over 14 million Russians died as the result of fighting. Remember, that is nearly three times the present population of Scotland. Now hunger and disease swept the ruined land and by 1922 another 5 million had died. Moreover, Lenin had exhausted himself in the struggle. In January 1924, he died aged fifty-three.

207

The nation was stunned. Who could succeed the great man? Trotsky was the most able of the Communists but he was not trusted. Some people thought that he had ambitions to become another Napoleon. So it was Stalin who took over the leadership. He was a dangerous, violent man but determined to build up Russia's strength. He introduced a Five-Year Plan for Russia's factories and farms. Targets of production were set. If these were reached, the workers were rewarded. If they were not, then the workers were punished. Any opponents were swept aside.

The results were staggering. By 1930, Russia was hot on the heels of other industrial countries, but a heavy price was paid. Hundreds of thousands of Russians had been executed or sent to work in terrible labour camps. Many people in Britain and elsewhere who had welcomed the Russian Revolution were shocked and worried about what was being done. Other events, however, were to cause even greater worries. Let us look at what was happening elsewhere.

Britain after 1918

unemployed

As you have read, the end of the war was greeted in Britain with joy—but the rejoicing did not last for long. By 1919, four million men and women had been demobbed. With the coming of peace Britain's wartime industries, such as munitions, no longer needed so many workers. So hundreds of thousands became unemployed. Britain had run up huge debts during the war: for example, we owed £842 million to the United States. Much of what Britain owned overseas had to be sold to help pay for the war. During the 1920s, British industry had to struggle to compete with our foreign competitors. All this meant long unemployment queues and low wages for those lucky enough to have a job.

There was another problem for the British government in Ireland. You read in Chapter 22 how a civil war had nearly broken out there. The outbreak of war in 1914 had stopped it for the moment at least. Then, in 1916, some of those who wanted an Ireland free of British control had staged an armed uprising in Dublin. This had been put down by force by the British army and fifteen of the Irish leaders were executed by Britain.

At the end of the First World War it was clear that any attempt to force the six counties of Ulster into a united Ireland would fail. There was an outbreak of violence with murders and bombings. In 1921 Lloyd George, who was still Prime Minister, suggested that Ulster should remain part of Great Britain but that the rest of Ireland, to be known as Eire, should have its independence. This was agreed but many Irishmen were not satisfied. There was a bitter civil war in Eire and it was some years before law and order were restored. Even so there were still Irishmen who were determined to make

Ulster part of Eire even if it meant using force. The problem for Britain was still there.

In 1924 a General Election was held in Britain. Although the Conservatives had the most MPs (258) they did not have a majority as Labour (191) and the Liberals (159) could outvote them. So King George V asked Ramsay Macdonald, the Scottish leader of the Labour Party, to form a government. He became the first Labour Prime Minister and on January 22nd 1924, King George V wrote this in his diary: 'Today 23 years ago dear Grandmama [Queen Victoria] died. I wonder what she would have thought of a Labour Government!'

The Labour government lasted for only nine months before it was defeated but it had shown itself able to run the country. The Labour party now replaced the Liberals as the main opponents of the Conservatives.

The new Conservative government was led by Stanley Baldwin, an easy-going millionaire. The country faced severe economic problems. In 1926 rising unemployment and a reduction in wages produced Britain's first *General Strike*. It was led by the miners who were being asked by their employers to accept a cut in pay and a longer working week. The miners' slogan was 'Not a penny off the pay, not a minute on the day!' The TUC supported them and asked other workers to come out on strike, too. For nine days, Britain was brought almost to a standstill. There was a rush of volunteers to do jobs such as driving buses. The army was used to escort food convoys from the docks. For most of the time the

atmosphere was good-humoured and there were football matches between strikers and policemen! But there were clashes and injuries, too, and strikers were arrested. In the end the TUC called off the strike, leaving the miners on their own. After another three months on strike they were forced to accept the cuts in their wages.

Later, things did improve slightly. British industry and trade picked up. There was more money to spend and more to spend it on after the wartime shortages. The theatres, cinemas, dance halls and the new night clubs did a roaring trade. Indeed, people talked of the 'Roaring Twenties'. Cheaper motor cars made it easier for people to travel to places of entertainment. There was more entertainment in the home, too. In 1922 the British Broadcasting Corporation (the BBC) made its first wireless broadcasts. Cheaper gramophones meant that folk could buy records of all the popular tunes. In 1926, John Logie Baird from Helensburgh produced the first TV pictures though BBC programmes did not come until 1936.

Women, especially, could enjoy themselves much more. It was no longer considered 'shocking' for girls to be seen unescorted in public—or, indeed, to be seen smoking and drinking. Women's fashions changed, too, with short skirts being all the rage. In 1928 these 'flappers', as they were called, were able to vote for the first time on equal terms with men.

Times certainly had changed!

But other changes were to plunge the world into a terrible economic *depression* and to lead to a Second World War. We must first look at events in Italy.

'Flappers'

Mussolini

Mussolini and Hitler

Many Italians after the war were poor, hungry and restless, and many men were ready to listen to an ex-soldier named Benito Mussolini. He told them that Italy could find greatness again only if the whole nation gathered round a leader who had full power. As a badge for his party he chose the 'fasces' of ancient Rome. This was a bundle of tightly bound rods with an axe: the sign of the ruler's powers in ancient Rome. Mussolini's followers were known as Fascists, or 'Blackshirts' from the uniform they wore.

In 1922 Mussolini was strong enough to lead a march on Rome at the head of thirty thousand followers. He demanded control of the government and King Victor Emmanuel agreed. So Mussolini, now known as 'Il Duce' or The Leader, made himself a dictator and punished or imprisoned anyone who opposed him. He kept the Italian Parliament in being, but all members had to be Fascists so it was completely under his control.

By this time there was a similar movement in Germany. As you

Hitler and General Ludendorff. Both were on trial in 1923 for trying to seize power

German shopkeeper, 1922

already know, the Germans hated the Treaty of Versailles, which they considered had punished them harshly. Events in Russia made many of them afraid of Communism. Many Germans, too, disliked the Jews who, they said, had too much wealth and power in Germany. They were ready to listen to the ideas of the ex-army corporal Adolf Hitler, who became the leader of the small National-Socialist or Nazi party in 1919. Hitler, knowing how Germans loved military display, staged all kinds of parades and his followers wore a brown uniform with a swastika badge on the sleeve.

Things did not go well for Hitler at first and in 1923 he was imprisoned. In prison he wrote 'Mein Kampf' (which means 'My Struggle') in which he set down what the Nazis wanted to do to make Germany great again. First, Hitler said that the 'punishment' Treaty of Versailles must be overthrown and Germany allowed to have her own army and navy again. Next, he said that the Germans were a great race but had been spoiled by Jews, who should be 'removed' from everyday life. Another part of Nazi teaching was that the Germans needed 'lebensraum', 'living-space', which must be gained by war if necessary.

The Nazi party grew only very slowly, for German trade began to recover. Soon after the end of the war, German money had become practically valueless. It cost hundreds of thousands of marks (the Germany money unit) to buy a loaf of bread! People had to go shopping with their bags stuffed with banknotes. Those of you who collect stamps may have seen German stamps of this time costing more than a million marks each! The Americans stepped in to help. By 1926 things were much better and few were prepared to listen to the violent speeches of Hitler. It seemed that he would never come to power.

But events in the United States changed things.

The USA and Europe

After the war, as we have read, millions of dollars of American money was invested or lent to European countries. America was prepared to aid Europe with money but it was not prepared to help keep the peace. Although President Wilson had helped to create the League of Nations, the American Congress decided to have nothing to do with it. America did not want to have to fight again to sort out other countries' problems.

These were exciting days in America. The country was very wealthy and most people had money to spend enjoying themselves. One thing they were not allowed to buy, however, was alcohol. In 1920 the American government introduced Prohibition. Americans were prohibited (not allowed) from making, selling and

211

Al Capone

drinking alcohol. People still wanted to drink, however, and gangsters such as Al Capone made fortunes selling drink. Often these gangsters fought among themselves for control of this money-making 'racket'.

Americans read in their papers about the exploits of these gangsters. They also read of the chances to make money by buying *shares* in business companies. As America became wealthier so these shares increased in value and it seemed impossible to lose. So Americans invested millions of dollars in these companies. The bubble burst on October 29th 1929. People started to sell their shares to make a profit. What had started as a trickle became a flood. In that one day 19 million shares were sold as the prices tumbled. This was known as 'The Wall Street Crash' as the Stock Exchange in New York (where shares were bought and sold) was in Wall Street. Thousands were ruined and even banks ran out of money.

With so much American money in Europe (and European money invested in America) this collapse had terrible effects on countries such as Britain and Germany. Thousands were thrown out of work. Indeed many men never found work again. All this misery, though, gave one man his great chance—Adolf Hitler.

THINGS TO DO

1 What problems faced all countries at the end of the First World War?
What particular problems did Germany have?

2 How did the Communists win control of Russia?

3 Why do you think the Allies sent soldiers to Russia in 1918?

4 How did Britain settle the Irish problem? Did this satisfy everybody?

5 How did Mussolini come to power in Italy?

6 Why did the Wall Street Crash of 1929 take place and why did this have such an effect on European countries?

7 'The Russian Royal Family Murdered!'
'The Criminal Nicholas Romanov has been executed!'

Write a newspaper story for each of these headlines. As you can see they both relate to the same event but are written from a different point of view. Make sure that your stories show this difference.

8 Write an obituary for Lenin (using the information in Chapter 24 as well).

9 Many of you will keep diaries. Perhaps you note down interesting events as well as the day-to-day things that have happened to you. These extracts are taken from the diary of a fourteen year–old boy who was living in Edinburgh in 1926. Read them carefully then answer the questions below in sentences:

3rd May General Strike at midnight of all vital services by Trade Union Congress. State of emergency proclaimed.

4th May Students man trams and Corporation buses: volunteers all over the country: Post Office staff will not strike.

5th May Students maintain electrical power: schoolboys acted as dockers.

6th May Attacks on trams, buses and shops in Edinburgh: Policemen and civilians injured. Lord Provost advised citizens to stay at home. 6 arrests. Trains stoned. Fire engine attacked.

7th May Mounted police busy in Edinburgh: many arrests.

8th May Public Houses closed at 3 p.m. Quieter. No trams or trains for tomorrow. Convoys of food passed through London guarded by armoured cars. Stanley Baldwin made a fine speech over wireless.

9th May Country calm. Peace day or lull before storm.

10th May Country very much quieter. Many strikers returning. Many railway lines tampered with. 'Flying Scotsman' [a famous steam train] derailed.

11th May Two disturbances only.

12th May General strike finished.

(*a*) What was the General Strike and why did it take place?

(*b*) What evidence is there in the extracts to show that some people were prepared to keep vital services going?

(*c*) What evidence is there in the extracts to show that not all workers joined the strike?

(*d*) What evidence is there in the extracts to show that there was violence during the General Strike?

(*e*) What evidence is there in the extracts to show that the army was used during the General Strike?

(*f*) Who was Stanley Baldwin?

(*g*) What recent invention did he use and why do you think this was important?

(*h*) From the evidence in the extracts when do you think the General Strike started to collapse?

(*i*) Do you think the writer supported the strikers or the government?

26 The Troubled Thirties

During the 1920s, the possibility of another war was far from people's minds. The horrors of the Great War—'the war to end all wars'—were still too fresh to be easily forgotten. After all, where could another war start? Germany had been so reduced in strength by the Treaty of Versailles that she could never threaten Europe again. The League of Nations had been set up to keep the peace. Countries would in future discuss their problems sensibly there instead of fighting each other. Few imagined that the 1930s would see these hopes for peace shattered.

The sad fact, however, was that in some countries men were prepared to risk war in order to increase their strength. Sadder still was the fact that peace-loving people seemed powerless to stop them. Where did things go wrong?

In 1928, the Nazi Party in Germany was still very small. In the Reichstag (the German Parliament) the Nazis had only twelve representatives. As Germany recovered from the effects of the war it seemed that few were prepared to listen to the outbursts of Adolf Hitler. Then came the Wall Street Crash. We saw in the last chapter how this affected Europe: factories closed, businesses went bankrupt, the unemployment queues grew longer.

Look at these figures. They show the number of people in Germany who were out of work: 1929—1 320 000; 1930—2 000 000; 1933—6 000 000. You can see what was happening. As unemployment rose, so, too, did the membership of the Nazi Party. In 1930 it was 210 000; by 1931 it had grown to 800 000. Why was this?

Hitler seemed to have something to offer to everyone. To the unemployed he offered jobs. To the owners of factories and businesses he offered prosperity and profits. To those looking for people to blame for Germany's defeat he attacked the Jews and the Communists. To all Germans he offered an end to the hated Treaty of Versailles and the promise of a greater, stronger, Germany. He recruited into the ranks of the Nazi Party thousands of ex-soldiers as members of the brown-shirted S.A. or the black-shirted S.S. who made an impressive show as they paraded with their swastika flags through the streets. But there was a darker side to their work. They set out to terrorise Hitler's opponents and thought nothing of breaking up meetings, beating people up and even committing murder.

How did Hitler get his message across? You have read already about his book 'Mein Kampf' ('My Struggle'). This became a best-seller in Germany. Indeed later, after he had come to power, it was to replace the Bible in many German churches. Hitler also made use of newspapers and posters. He was probably the first politician to see the value of the recently-invented radio to get his message into the homes of the people. Above all, however, he was a masterful public speaker. In halls and open-air meetings up and down Germany he screamed out his message of hate.

In 1933 Hitler had so much support that old Field-Marshal Hindenburg, the President of Germany, had to ask Hitler to be Chancellor (Prime Minister). A few weeks later a great fire broke out in the Reichstag building and it was destroyed. Hitler immediately said the Communists were to blame and he persuaded President Hindenburg to give him special powers to arrest and imprison people without trial. Thousands of Germans were seized by the Nazis and sent to special prisons. You have probably heard the names of some of these prison-camps or 'concentration camps'— Belsen, Buchenwald and Dachau. Here prisoners whose only crime was disagreement with Hitler's ideas were horribly punished—or killed. We should remember that concentration camps were first set up to punish the many Germans who opposed Hitler.

Hitler speaking at a
torchlight rally

The first Volkswagen

In 1934 Hindenburg died and Hitler made himself President as well as Chancellor. He called himself the 'Führer', the Leader, of Germany. In June of that year he ordered the killing of many of his old comrades in the Nazi Party whom he did not trust. Nearly one thousand were murdered and Hitler himself took part in these crimes.

Now he was in complete control and he gathered round him a group of men who remained the leaders of Germany till the end of the war. Goering, who loved to cover his big chest with medals, was the head of the 'Luftwaffe', the Air Force. Ribbentrop, who was the German Ambassador to Britain for a time, later became the Minister for Foreign Affairs. Goebbels was in charge of propaganda—the publishing of 'news', much of it twisted or invented to make Germans support the Nazi leaders. A ruthless man named Himmler controlled the Secret State Police, the 'Geheime Staatspolizei' or 'Gestapo'.

At first, people outside Germany admired much of what Hitler was doing. They liked the way he tackled unemployment. For example, thousands of Germans were given work building the new motorways—'autobahns'—the first in Europe. Thousands more were found jobs in factories making the 'people's car', the 'Volkswagen'. Cheap holidays were provided for German workers.

There was the other side to Nazi Germany, however. All political opposition was declared illegal; so, too, were trade unions. Workers had to belong to the Nazi-controlled German Labour Front. Groups such as teachers had to swear an oath of loyalty to the Führer. Their lessons had to follow the teachings of the Nazi Party. All school text books were censored by the Nazis and books that disagreed with them were publicly burned, Children were encouraged to betray anyone who criticised the Nazis: even friends and parents were at risk. No-one was safe from the Gestapo.

Here is how one young German described those years: 'Gradually one after the other the old schoolmasters were weeded out. The new masters who replaced them were young men loyal to the Führer. The new spirit had come to stay. We obeyed orders and we acknowledged the leadership principle because we wanted to and because we liked it.'

Millions of young Germans were *brainwashed* into the Nazi ways. Organisations such as the Hitler Youth made sure that the teachings of Adolf Hitler were not forgotten.

The Jews were singled out for special treatment. Hitler had a real hatred for these unfortunate people. This hatred went back to his early years. As a young man Hitler had failed to make anything of his life. Indeed, at one time he had lived the life of a tramp in Vienna. There he saw many rich Jews who had worked hard and had been successful. He was filled with jealousy. He never

Himmler

forgot or forgave the Jews for having done better than himself. In the end this hatred was to lead to the dreadful deaths of six million Jews in his concentration camps.

Jewish shops had 'Jude'—'Jew'—scrawled over the windows. Jewish people were banned from holding important jobs. Often their homes and property were attacked by Nazi thugs. Jews were quite openly attacked and beaten up or murdered and the police did not lift a finger to protect them.

In 1938 a particularly vicious attack was made on the Jews by the Nazis. 'In Berlin wrecking squads tore through the town at 2 a.m. setting fire to synagogues [Jewish churches] and to Jewish shops. Other squads under the supervision of men in Storm Troopers' (S.S.) uniform, and armed with hammers and axes, broke open the homes of Jews and smashed furniture and everything else they could lay their hands on. The number of victims who suffered death will probably never be known. Whole families took their own lives in order to escape the attacks of the hooligans. Those who remained were hunted like animals, arrested and taken to concentration camps.'

Britain and other countries looked on, horrified but helpless—for what the ruler of Germany did to the people of Germany seemed to be their business, not ours. Britain was also too busy wrestling with the problem of unemployment. From Scotland and elsewhere, long columns of the out-of-work marched on London demanding jobs. But the government did little to help them.

The outlook was gloomy; other events abroad made things gloomier still.

In 1931, the powerful country of Japan, a member of the League of Nations, attacked China and the League did not stop her. Japan conquered the Chinese state of Manchuria and set up a government controlled from Japan. In 1937 Japan attacked China again and this Sino-Japanese War dragged on for eight years.

From 1931 onwards Mussolini had been watching what was happening. He saw how powerless the League was to stop an aggressor-nation and his ideas of a new Roman Empire began to take shape. His eye had fallen on the kingdom of Abyssinia in East Africa, which lay between Italian Eritrea and Italian Somaliland. In 1935 he sent his armies into Abyssinia and they won easy victories over the poorly-armed Abyssinians. The Emperor of Abyssinia, Haile Selassie, went into exile and appealed to the League of Nations for help. The member-countries of the League decided to stop trading with Italy but this had little effect, and Abyssinia became part of the new 'Roman Empire'. So for a second time the League showed that it was too weak to stop a bully, and trade with Italy soon began again.

Mussolini and Hitler

This 'punishment' of Italy by the League made the dictators of Italy and Germany work more closely together and their friendship came to be called the 'Rome-Berlin Axis'. Now Hitler had seen how weak the League of Nations really was and he felt that he could be more daring. He showed this first in Spain.

King Alfonso XIII had given up the throne of Spain in 1931, and a republican government had been set up. Later a group of rebels led by General Franco were trying to defeat the government. Both Germany and Italy sent men and arms to General Franco. Russia sent help to the Spanish government. Other countries such as Britain were not eager to help either side because they feared that this might be the beginning of another world war. But men of many nationalities fought against Franco's armies in the International Brigade. Franco did not win the quick victory he hoped for, but after three years' struggle he found himself the leader of a poor, broken, country.

Hitler had helped Franco to victory but he was not really very interested in Spain. He wanted to make a Greater Reich, a Greater German Empire. He had taken the first step in 1935 when he built up the strength of the German army. The next year he began to build a large fleet and a new air force. The German navy was equipped with U-boats and a new type of battleship—the 'pocket battleship'. It was smaller than other battleships but extremely powerful with very heavy guns and thick armour plating. All of this had been forbidden by the Treaty of Versailles but who was going to stop him? Certainly not the League of Nations which

218

had shown itself to be so weak.

In 1936, Hitler sent his troops into the Rhineland, a part of Germany bordering France. The Treaty of Versailles had forbidden this, too. Then in 1938 he moved into Austria and told the world it was now part of Germany. Again, this 'Anschluss' or 'Union' had been forbidden by Versailles.

Worse was to follow. Hitler said he wanted to bring into the 'Reich' those parts of other countries where most of the people were Germans. Soon afterwards he said he wanted the 'Sudetenland' ('the southern land'): that part of Czechoslovakia which bordered on Germany. Here there were Germans living but they had never been part of the old Germany. The Czechs were not going to give up the 'Sudetenland' without a struggle, and they were led by their courageous President, Dr Benes.

The Czechs looked to France and Britain to support them but they were disappointed, for the leaders of these two countries wanted to avoid war at all costs. Anyway, the people of the 'Sudetenland' were of German blood, and many of them did want to be joined to Germany. It looked as if Hitler was ready to go to war, and in September 1938 Neville Chamberlain, the British Prime Minister, flew to meet Hitler to persuade him to keep the peace. At the Munich Conference, Britain, France and Italy agreed that the 'Sudetenland' should be given to Germany. In return, Hitler promised that he was now satisfied and that he did not want any more lands.

Neville Chamberlain on his return from Munich

This policy of 'giving-in' to Hitler was later called 'appeasement'. Why did Britain and others not stand up to his bullying? For one thing, the Allies were divided amongst themselves as to how to deal with Hitler. For another, our armed forces were not ready to fight. Chamberlain and other leaders were very anxious to avoid a new terrible war. They had seen the sufferings caused by the First World War; they did not want to have to ask another generation of young men and women to make such sacrifices. In the end, they were so desperate for peace that they wanted to believe Hitler when he said that he did not want war. 'Germany needs and deserves peace. Germany's problems cannot be solved by war.' Surely then, Hitler could be trusted? Chamberlain thought so: 'In spite of the harshness and ruthlessness I thought I saw in Hitler's face, I got the impression that here was a man who could be relied upon when he had given his word'.

Six months later Hitler showed what his promise was worth. Without warning, his Nazi troops marched into the remainder of Czechoslovakia and added it to Germany. These peoples he now conquered were not Germans, and it was obvious that Hitler was simply out to conquer. No nation was safe. Certainly Poland was not. Part of Poland was the 'Polish Corridor', a narrow strip of land reaching to the Baltic Sea. It divided East Prussia from the rest of Germany. Hitler told the Poles that he wanted a wide 'road' across the Corridor, but they refused—even though they knew what it meant to refuse. By this time France and Britain realised that Hitler must be stopped, even at the risk of war, and they promised to help Poland if Germany attacked her.

The summer of 1939 was a dreadful one, for every day seemed to bring war nearer. Obviously Hitler meant to attack Poland, for he put out false news about the ill-treatment of Germans living in Poland. Britain and France saw that they would need the help of Russia, Poland's neighbour, if Poland was to be saved. So they sent representatives to Moscow to try to persuade Stalin to join them in stopping Hitler. The talks went on and on for weeks. Meanwhile Hitler had sent his Foreign Minister, Ribbentrop, to try to persuade Stalin not to go to the help of Poland. Hitler won, and on August 23rd Stalin and Ribbentrop signed a treaty in which Germany and Russia promised not to attack one another. Together they would attack Poland and divide the country between them. It was astonishing to see the Nazis making friends with their enemies, the Communists.

The world could hardly believe what had happened—for now there was nothing to stop Hitler marching into Poland. There was not long to wait. On September 1st German troops attacked Poland, and Warsaw was bombed from the air. Britain and France demanded the withdrawal of German troops from Poland. Hitler, of couse, refused and we declared war on September 3rd 1939.

On that Sunday the air-raid sirens sounded in Britain and folk went down to their bomb shelters. Another war had begun.

Ready for War—Auxilliary Fire Service man, summer 1939

220

THINGS TO DO

1 In the 1920s, Hitler had few supporters yet in 1933 he was made Chancellor of Germany. Try to explain how this happened.

2 What things happened in Nazi Germany that you would not like to see happening in Scotland?

3 Show how the League of Nations was challenged by Japan and Italy. Why do think the League could not keep the peace?

4 In what ways did Hitler break the Treaty of Versailles?

5 Explain in your own words what you understand by 'appeasement'. Why do you think Britain and others followed this policy?

6 What do you think were the causes of the Second World War?

7 On page 219 you saw a picture of Neville Chamberlain on his return from his meeting with Hitler at Munich. He believed he had brought back 'peace with honour'. Imagine that you are a BBC radio reporter interviewing Mr Chamberlain. Your interview should ask questions about the Munich meeting: what he thinks about Hitler; his thoughts on Nazi Germany and why he believes appeasement will work.

Building an autobahn, 1934

8 Here is part of a description of a visit made to Germany in 1938. It was written by a young Scottish holidaymaker. Read the extract then answer the questions below in sentences.

The small town I stayed in that summer of 1938 was called Swinemünde on the Baltic near the naval base at Stettin. Early one morning huge crowds gathered to await the arrival of the 'Graf Spee'—a pocket battleship—which had been built in contravention [against the terms] of the Versailles Agreement.

On our first morning I was woken by a strange noise. It was made by a strange-looking plane. I found out that every day at breakfast time a Stuka divebomber used to fly up the coast to drop the morning papers from Berlin on the beach.

One beautiful summer evening we went to see a torchlight procession which was quite an occasion in the village. The whole population seemed to be involved. There were swastika flags everywhere. Music was provided by several brass bands. All the children were carrying lanterns and where back home in Scotland these three and four year-olds would have danced along behind the bands, here in Germany these children marched meticulously [carefully] in step!

Jews had to wear a Star of David on their clothing to identify them. This sign was also painted on the front of all shops owned by Jews. I remember visiting a German family one evening. We decided to listen to gramophone records. Before the hostess put on one record 'You Are My Heart's Delight' she made sure that the window was shut and the volume turned right down. The singer, Richard Tauber, was a Jew.

(*a*) What was a 'pocket battleship'?

(*b*) What was the 'Versailles Agreement'?

(*c*) How were the newspapers delivered from Berlin? Why do you think it was done this way?

(*d*) From the evidence in the passage, who organised the village torchlight parade?

(*e*) Why do you think such parades were organised?

(*f*) Why do you think children were taking part in the parade? What evidence in the passage shows that the children had been trained for the parade? What other sorts of training were being given to German children at this time?

(*g*) What evidence is there in the passage to show that the Jews were being persecuted? Why was this done?

(*h*) Why do you think the record was played so softly?

(*i*) From what you have learnt in this chapter what do you think might have happened if the record had been heard?

27 The Second World War

Less than three weeks after Hitler's soldiers marched into Poland, that unhappy country was defeated. The idea behind the treaty between Hitler and Stalin was seen now, because Russian troops marched into east Poland and the two dictators divided the country between them.

The fighting in Poland had shown the world the Nazi idea of 'blitzkrieg', 'lightning war'. At first light, the Stuka dive-bombers would strike. Airfields, artillery positions, barracks, transport, troops, would all be pounded from the air. Before they had a chance to recover from this surprise attack, the shattered defenders would hear the rumble of approaching tanks and the crackle of fire from attacking infantry. And there were not just a few tanks: hundreds of massed Panzers were used to punch huge holes in the enemy's defences. How different from the stalemate of trench warfare!

In the west, however, it looked as if there might be the kind of fighting seen in the First World War: not from trenches this time, but from strongly fortified walls. The French army on the 'Maginot Line' faced the Germans standing ready in the 'Siegfried Line'. There was little fighting, but at home the British people made ready to meet the big air attacks they expected. Policemen, firemen, air raid wardens, ambulance men and women, were all organised

Children being evacuated from Glasgow, 1939

in the 'Civil Defence Service'. Air Raid Precautions (A.R.P.) were made: street lights were not lit and windows were blacked out. Men from 18 to 40 were called up for the Services if they were not in jobs where they were actually helping to win the war. Everyone was given an identity card, a gas mask and a ration book. Thousands of children had to leave their homes and families. They were evacuated to the safety of the countryside, away from the towns and cities which were the likely targets of the German bombers. With their suitcases, gas mask satchels and identity labels they said their sad goodbyes and left under the care of their teachers.

This 'phoney war' (as the Americans called it) ended in April 1940. Then Hitler attacked again. The victims this time were small countries who had not even declared war on him but hoped to remain neutral: Norway and Denmark. Within two months both were beaten. The British army, navy and air force tried to get a foothold in Norway at Narvik but were forced to withdraw. This failure was a real shock to the nation, but worse was to come.

In May 1940 Hitler's forces attacked Holland and Belgium, moving round the north of the strong French defences known as the Maginot Line. The right part of the Allied armies stayed behind the Maginot Line. The left part, which included the British Ex-

On the beaches at Dunkirk

224

peditionary Force, the 'B.E.F.', marched north to meet the German troops. But the Germans pushed on, splitting the opposing armies in two, and the German tanks rumbled on into France. The blitzkrieg tactics swept all before them. Even the Maginot Line was broken by the Panzers.

The B.E.F. and their French allies had only one way of escape, to the north, but this meant that all the troops, nearly 350 000 of them, would have to be taken off by sea. It seemed that only a miracle could save them, but a huge fleet of little ships and boats was hastily gathered together in English harbours and sailed for the port of Dunkirk. There the beaches were packed with men, more were crowding along the roads leading to the town, and the German air force bombed them endlessly. But the little ships and the R.A.F. won and in nine days the men were brought home. The miracle had happened.

Those days of June 1940 were the blackest days of the war for us. In just forty days, Hitler had done what the Kaiser had failed to do in over four years. At a cost of only 27 000 men, the German army had beaten the B.E.F. Our ally France had surrendered. The Germans took over the north and west of France and set up a new government in 'Unoccupied France' under Marshal Pétain, an aged veteran of the First World War. Now, when Britain seemed to be finished, Mussolini entered the war against us.

Churchill

But Britain was not finished—although, admittedly, there did not seem to be much hope for her. The disasters of 1940 brought the end of Neville Chamberlain's government, and a new National Government was formed from men of all parties under Winston Churchill. Churchill proved to be the strong leader needed in time of danger. He did not promise that things would be easy: he promised only 'blood, tears, toil and sweat' before victory was won.

Britain became the headquarters of governments whose countries had been overrun: Holland, Norway, Poland, Czechoslovakia. Many Frenchmen disagreed with Marshal Pétain's government at Vichy and wanted to carry on the fight against Hitler. The leader of these 'Free French' or 'Fighting French' was General de Gaulle, who had his headquarters in Britain, too.

At this time Hitler offered to make peace if we would let him keep all his conquests, but Britain and the Commonwealth countries refused. So Hitler now had to try to conquer Britain, and in August 1940 the 'Battle of Britain' began. This was not a battle between armies but the desperate struggle of a few R.A.F. fighter pilots against the bombers and fighters of Hitler's 'Luftwaffe'. London was the main target for German bombs, but many other places were attacked and horribly damaged: Portsmouth, Plymouth, Coventry, Liverpool and Clydebank. In all about 60 000 civilians

Clydebank bomb damage

Spitfires

were killed and three million homes destroyed by German bombing during the war. It seemed impossible that Britain could survive such attacks, but the fighter pilots went up day after day and many of them gave their lives.

Here is part of an account of one of those battles fought at high speed in the skies above South England. It was written by a Spitfire pilot, Richard Hillary. 'We ran into them at 18 000 feet, twenty yellow-nosed Messerschmitt 109s, about 500 feet above us. Our squadron strength was eight, and as they came down on us we went into line astern and turned head on to them. I saw Brian [his Section leader] let go a burst of fire at the leading plane, saw the pilot put his machine into a half roll, and I knew that he was mine. Automatically I kicked the rudder to the left to get him at right angles, turned the gun-button to 'Fire' and let go in a four-second burst. He came right through my sights and I saw the tracer from all eight guns thud home. For a second he seemed to hang motionless; then a jet of red flame shot upwards and he spun out of sight. It had happened. He was dead and I was alive: it could so easily have been the other way round.' Hillary himself was shot down and killed later in the war.

This Battle of Britain was fought during August and September 1940. During those weeks, 515 German planes were shot down by the R.A.F. But 306 British had been lost, too. However, the job had been done. On September 19th, Hitler postponed his planned invasion of Britain. As Churchill said, 'Never in the field of human conflict was so much owed by so many to so few.'

We held out in the air—and we held out at sea, too. The U-

226

U-boat

Execution of
captured Russian

boats attacked our merchant ships more heavily than in the 1914–1918 War and thirty-two thousand merchant seamen lost their lives. This danger to our food supplies was fought by crews of R.A.F. Coastal Command and the Royal Navy, using new inventions developed by scientists. In particular, radar and Asdic helped locate enemy planes, submarines and ships. Dangerous German battleships such as the 'Bismarck' were hunted down and destroyed.

Britain, however, was still on the defensive. In North Africa, where our armies were defending the Suez Canal, they were pushed back by General Rommel almost to the River Nile. Then the strain on Britain was made a little easier because Hitler now felt strong enough to make war on Russia.

In June 1941 a huge attack was launched on the unsuspecting Russians. The Germans advanced at the rate of 80 kilometres a day. Some four million Russians were killed or captured. At Kiev alone, 650 000 Russians were taken prisoner. Hitler's armies swept on until they reached the outskirts of the great cities of Leningrad (formerly Petrograd), Stalingrad and Moscow. Towards the end of 1941 it looked as if Hitler was just about to deal the death blows to Britain and her new ally, Russia.

Now, just as Italy had joined Hitler in our darkest days of 1940, so Japan joined Germany and Italy in time (so she thought) for the 'kill'. Japan believed that Italy and Germany would conquer Britain and Russia, and she tried to deal a knock-out blow to the U.S. Navy. This, she believed, would enable her to build a new Japanese Empire in the Far East. So, without even declaring war, on December 7th 1941 her bombers attacked the biggest base of the American Pacific Fleet at Pearl Harbour. Eighteen American ships were sunk and 349 planes destroyed—mostly on the ground. The Japanese lost only twenty-nine planes.

This was perhaps the real turning-point of the war, for it brought America in on the Allied side. Japan did enormous damage at Pearl Harbour and her troops swept on through the Philippines, the East Indies, Malaya, Singapore and Burma until they were at the doorstep of Australia and India.

Everywhere our armies were being beaten: in North Africa, in Russia, and in the Far East. But we can look back to this time with pride. It was the time of the gallant defence of Malta, bombed daily but continuing to be a most useful base for ships and aircraft.

Then, in the autumn of 1942, the tide began to turn.

In North Africa, Field-Marshal Alexander and Field-Marshal Montgomery struck at General Rommel's troops at El Alamein. The Eighth Army, including the armoured division called the 'Desert Rats,' chased Rommel's army across the Western Desert, across Libya and Tunisia through the ports of Tobruk and Benghazi.

All the way the German and Italian forces were attacked by the bombers and fighters of the Desert Air Force. Meanwhile, a large British and American army under General Eisenhower had landed in Algeria and Morocco and the retreating Germans found themselves between this First Army and the Eighth Army. They were trapped: they could not escape by sea because of the might of the Allied navy and air force. In May 1943 three hundred thousand Germans and Italians surrendered to our forces.

In the following months the Allies conquered Sicily and prepared to invade the Italian mainland. By now the Italians had tired of Mussolini. He was disgraced, pushed out of power and later executed. But the German armies were now in control of Italy and Allied troops had to fight costly battles such as Salerno and Monte Cassino. Then they had to slog their way northwards in the mud and rain of the winter.

Russian troops in action

In Russia, too, the tide had turned. Stalingrad was almost completely in ruins, but the gallant defenders held out against the invading forces. The Germans were unprepared for the harshness of the Russian winter. Without proper protective clothing, the soldiers suffered terribly.

The Russians reorganised their armies and arms factories and struck back. At Stalingrad a powerful German army was defeated. Seventy thousand Germans died in the fighting. Hitler ordered 'no surrender' but it was useless to continue. Frost-bitten, starving and desperate, the survivors gave in. At Leningrad, the siege had lasted an incredible 890 days. The Russians refused to let the Germans take the city. Two hundred thousand Russians died in the fighting while a further 630 000 died of cold or starvation. At last, in May 1943 help came. The Russians began to push the Germans slowly but surely out of Russia.

228

Just as the wars on land were successful, so the 'Battle of the Atlantic', the battle with the U–boats, was being won, too. And in the air the British and American air forces carried the war into the heart of Germany. The first 'thousand-bomber' raid took place in April 1942 and after that the raids became heavier and heavier. While the German coal mines and factories were being attacked, plans were being laid for a great invasion of German-held France under the command of General Eisenhower.

Most careful preparations were made, for an earlier Canadian raid on Dieppe had shown how strong the coastal defences were. On 'D Day' (D for Deliverance)—June 6th 1944—the British, Canadian and American forces landed on the Normandy beaches under an 'umbrella' of fighter aircraft and fire from naval vessels. Two great artificial 'Mulberry' harbours were towed across, and later an underwater pipeline (with the code-name of 'Pluto') carried fuel oil from England to France.

There was heavy fighting for several weeks. Then, while the British and Canadians held most of the enemy tanks at bay, the Americans on the right broke through and began to encircle thousands of German troops. The Germans tried to retreat across the River Seine and the Allies swept on, freed northern and western France and moved fast into Belgium and Holland. By September 1944 the Allies had reached the Rhine. Paratroopers were sent over the river to land at Arnhem in Holland, but the attempt failed in very bad weather. On the Eastern Front the Russians were pushing on. They had cleared the Germans out of Finland, Bulgaria and Rumania and were moving into Czechoslovakia, Hungary and Yugoslavia.

It seemed that the days of Hitler were almost ended. But he still hoped to break Britain. His 'V' or 'Victory' weapons were flying-bombs, sent towards London from firing-places in the Low Countries. The first type was the 'V1', but even more dangerous was the 'V2', a rocket-weapon which was faster than sound. London and Londoners suffered new wounds from these weapons, but they did not take Hitler any nearer to victory.

The spring of 1945 saw the end of the war in Europe. In the west the British and American forces were ready for the last battles over the Rhine. In the east the Russians were ready to take Berlin. Germany was in a scissors-hold.

The advancing Allies already knew that many Jews had been driven from their homes. Now they discovered the full horror of what the Nazis had been doing in their concentration camps. Battle-hardened soldiers were shocked and sickened by what they found in camps such as Auschwitz, Dachau and Belsen.

Polish Jews being arrested in Warsaw

229

Prisoners in a concentration camp, 1945

Thousands of starving, pathetic creatures were the survivors of a horrifying policy of extermination. Perhaps as many as eight million men, women and children—many of them Jews—died at the hands of the Nazis. Some were beaten to death; others tortured or used in horrible medical experiments.

Most, however, were gassed in what Hitler called his 'final solution' to the problem of the Jews. At Auschwitz the unfortunate people were told to strip for 'showers'. Rudolf Hoess, the Camp Commandant, described at his trial what happened next: 'I used Zyklon B which was a crystallised prussic acid which we dropped into the death chamber from a small opening. It took from three to fifteen minutes to kill all the people in the death chamber. We knew when the people were dead because their screaming stopped.'

230

The Allies pressed on, determined to smash Nazism for ever. In May 1945, the two armies met at Leipzig. The Russians stormed Berlin and Hitler killed himself rather than be captured. May 8th was VE Day—the day of Victory in Europe.

Germany and Italy were both out of the war, Hitler and Mussolini were both dead, but Japan held out. British troops, the Fourteenth Army under General Slim, pushed the Japanese eastwards out of Burma in most difficult jungle fighting. American and Australian troops pushed the Japanese northwards away from Australia. Just before VE Day American troops made a costly landing at Okinawa, about 500 km from Japan. American 'Flying Fortresses' bombed Japanese cities, but the Emperor Hirohito's government held on. Obviously the fighting would have to be taken to Japan: but that might mean the sacrifice of thousands more lives.

The American President Truman was faced with an awful choice. Should he send thousands more troops to their deaths? Or should he make use of a fearsome new weapon which would kill large numbers of civilians and injure many more? The decision was made: the first atomic bomb was dropped on the city of Hiroshima, and three days later another was dropped on Nagasaki. This was on the 6th and 9th of August. The results were devastating. At Hiroshima, 90 000 were killed. Here is how one survivor described the scene: 'Hiroshima was no longer a city, but a burnt-out prairie. To the east and to the west everything was flattened. Hundreds of injured

Hiroshima

231

people who were trying to escape to the hills passed our house. The sight of them was almost unbelievable, their faces and hands were burnt and swollen; and great sheets of skin had peeled away from their bodies to hang like rags on a scarecrow. They moved like a line of ants.'

On August 8th, the Russians declared war on Japan. Japan felt she could not hold out any longer and surrendered on August 15th, 'VJ Day'.

Six years of war were ended. Men and women had now to set about repairing the damage and destruction of these years.

THINGS TO DO

1 What was a 'blitzkrieg' attack? How was this way of fighting different from the tactics of the First World War?

2 'Never in the field of human conflict was so much owed by so many to so few' (page 226). Try to explain in your own words what Winston Churchill meant by this.

3 Churchill made many famous speeches that inspired and encouraged the people of Britain. Here is part of one such speech made on June 4th 1940, the last day of the retreat from Dunkirk. Read it carefully, then design a War Poster to keep up the courage of the nation in their fight against Nazi Germany.

We shall go on to the end. We shall fight in France, we shall fight in the seas and oceans, we shall fight with growing confidence and growing strength in the air; we shall defend our Island, whatever the cost may be. We shall fight on the beaches, we shall fight on the landing-grounds, we shall fight in the fields and in the streets, we shall fight in the hills; we shall never surrender.

4 It should be easy to find somebody who took part in the fighting during the war or who was evacuated. Try to find out part of the story of the war first-hand.

5 Imagine that you are a young person evacuated from Glasgow at the start of the war. You have kept a diary of some of the important events of the war. What entries would there have been in your diary?

6 From the information in the last three chapters, write an obituary for Adolf Hitler.

7 Among the first men ashore on the Normandy beaches on D Day were the British commandos. What was it like to have taken part in the greatest invasion ever attempted? Here is part of an account written by one of these commandos, Jim Pearson from

Edinburgh. Read the passage carefully then answer the questions below in sentences.

Having spent a sleepless night on board the landing craft we were now called up on deck. It was 6 a.m. I looked around me. As far as the eye could see there were ships of every shape and size. Overhead there was the continual drone of planes. All around was the constant din of gunfire and exploding shells put down on the Normandy coast by the huge battleships standing off behind us in the Channel.

We stood there gazing at the approaching French beach which kept erupting with German mortar shell bursts. I thought of the many war films that I had seen in the past only now I was one of the actors with a role to play which I had rehearsed until I was word perfect.

Just then a mortar shell hit us. When the smoke cleared I saw that one of my pals had been killed. There was no time then to think of him because in the next minute the ramps were down. We were wading ashore, a crowd of strange figures in parachute smocks, green berets, with large haversacks and folding bicycles over our shoulders. This is what all the training was for.

We moved up the beach. I stopped to help a wounded friend and then ran on. We all met at the top of the dunes—at least all who managed to get off the beach. We then had to push our bikes over marshland to reach the road. All this time we were under fire. I realised for the first time that I was soaked to the waist from wading ashore and above I was drenched in sweat.

Now we were on the road. We mounted our bikes and, still under fire, pedalled through the French countryside to reach our first objective. This was the bridge over the River Orne which we found still intact. It was now 10 a.m.

From there our orders were to move about twelve miles (20 km) inland to relieve some Canadian paratroops holding a village. So once more the crazy cycle club pedalled on into occupied France. We reached the village and made ourselves comfortable in a German dugout.

By this time it was late afternoon. The weather was hot and humid. To make it warmer, the Germans pounded the village with mortars. In a way this helped us. As darkness fell the village was lit by flames from burning houses. With this light we were able to see and fight off at least two German attacks.

In a moment of calm, I remember watching the flames flickering from the village houses and wondering what tomorrow would bring. So ended what seemed like an eternity instead of only one day—D Day, June 6th 1944.

(a) What evidence is there in the first paragraph to show that the D Day invasion was a combined operation?

(b) What evidence is there in the passage to show that the Germans fought back?

(c) What evidence is there in the passage to show that the invaders had been well-prepared for what lay ahead?

(d) Why do you think the commandos carried bicycles ashore?

(e) What was their first objective and why do you think it was important?

(f) How do you think the paratroops had managed to get ahead of the commandos?

(g) Despite the dangers, Jim Pearson still managed to see the funny side of things. What part of the passage shows this?

(h) What helped the commandos hold the village?

(i) From what you have learnt in the chapter why do you think the French people would welcome the invaders? From the passage, however, what shows you that the cost of liberation could be heavy for the French, too?

(j) 'So ended what seemed like an eternity.' Many of those who survived D Day remember it in this way. Indeed a famous book (and film) about D Day was called 'The Longest Day'. Why do you think it seemed like this to those who took part?

28 Problems of peace

Russian flag above
Berlin, May 1945

After nearly six years of war much of Europe—indeed much of
the world—lay in ruins. The tide of fighting had flowed backwards
and forwards over vast areas of land. Countries had been conquered
and reconquered. Cities, towns, villages, mines, factories and farms
had all been devastated in the most terrible war known to man. The
cost of this destruction was staggering. Russia suffered the worst
losses. According to the Soviet government the fighting destroyed
1700 towns, 70 000 villages, 82 000 schools and colleges, 98 000
collective farms and 71 million farm animals. Altogether this damage
cost £30 000 million. And these were the losses of only one country!

Nobody is really sure just how many people lost their lives in

UNO building

the war. It was certainly more than 25 million; perhaps as many as 40 million—nearly eight times the population of Scotland! Some ten million of these had been civilians caught up in the fighting or victims of the bombs of the air raids. What was left for the survivors?

Millions were in need of food, shelter and medical care. Hundreds of thousands of refugees thronged the roads or crowded together in the many camps. Without homes, without belongings, often without families, they were helpless. What on earth could be done to start repairing the damage and easing the misery?

You will remember from Chapter 23 how the idea for a League of Nations had come from the suffering caused by the First World War. We have seen how that League failed yet it had done much good work. The dream of an international organisation, dedicated to solving quarrels between countries peacefully, had not died. So a new 'League' was begun, the United Nations Organisation or UNO. It was born in 1945 with headquarters at Lake Success near New York. There were fifty member-nations at first, and now there are 151. All these members have signed the Charter of the United Nations, in which they declare that they are 'determined to save succeeding generations from the scourge of war, which twice in our lifetime has brought untold sorrow to mankind'.

The United Nations Organisation has a kind of parliament which meets every year to discuss important matters affecting the peace and happiness of the world. This big Assembly cannot do all the day-to-day work and so there are many committees and organisations inside UNO. You have probably heard of the work of the World Health Organisation (WHO), the Food and Agricultural Organisation (FAO) and the United Nations International Children's Emergency Fund (UNICEF). Perhaps the most important of the committees is the Security Council, which tries to settle any quarrel between nations that might lead to war. Indeed, since 1945 UN soldiers have tried to keep the peace in many parts of the world including Korea, Cyprus and the Middle East.

In the years after 1945 the United Nations came to the rescue of many war-torn countries. Medicines, doctors, nurses, food, tents, clothing, were sent to peoples who needed them. Once this kind of help was given, these countries had to start earning their living again. The factories had to be rebuilt, the farms and mines put in order and struggling industries encouraged.

How did Britain face up to the problems of peace?

The end of the war saw tremendous celebrations. The nation deserved it. After all, until 1941, Britain had stood almost alone against the Nazi threat. Now had come victory—but at a tremendous price. The war had taken nearly 300 000 lives and cost £16

236

million a day to fight. Britain had never recovered fully from the losses of the First World War and now huge new debts mounted up. What could be done? A new government had to face up to the task. In 1945 a General Election was held. Winston Churchill and the Conservatives were defeated. Churchill had been a good war leader but people wanted to see a different approach to the problems of peace. So Clement Attlee became the second Labour Prime Minister.

The years after the war were especially difficult. Industry was depressed; unemployment was high and there were serious shortages of food and fuel. Indeed, rationing of some food items had to be continued until 1952. A slow start was made on rebuilding the shattered cities. The Labour government was keen to push ahead with social reforms but found it difficult in the circumstances. Still, changes were made. More money was spent on schools and in 1948 the National Health Service was set up. Now, it was said, the state looked after you 'from the cradle to the grave'.

Attlee

There were changes affecting the Commonwealth, too. Some countries of the old British Empire—Australia, Canada, New Zealand and South Africa—already looked after their own affairs. This meant that they still had close ties with Britain but they were no longer controlled by Britain.

In South Africa, Field-Marshal Smuts, a Prime Minister who was an old and good friend of Britain, was defeated by the Nationalist party led by Dr Malan in the election of 1949. In 1961 Dr Malan's government voluntarily led South Africa out of the Commonwealth and set up a republic. It believed that the increasing 'coloured' population was a danger to the 'white man', and tried to separate white and 'coloured' people in various ways. This policy, called 'apartheid', took away full voting rights from the coloured folk: it made them live in separate districts, and prevented them from working in certain occupations. South Africa has been heavily criticised for this policy. Many countries have broken off trading and sporting links with the South Africans. At lot of pressure has been brought to bear on South Africa by countries such as the United States and Britain to persuade the South Africans to end apartheid.

So far there has been little change. There is mounting pressure, however, from within South Africa itself. Despite the activities of the secret police who can arrest people and hold them without trial, opponents of apartheid are gaining ground. There have been outbreaks of terrorist violence and demonstrations by black South Africans. In 1960, sixty-nine black people were shot during a protest march at Sharpeville. In 1976 there were serious riots in Soweto, a black township on the outskirts of Johannesburg. Over 600 rioters were killed.

Soweto riot

South Africa is now surrounded by black African countries dedicated to ending apartheid. Tension remains high.

Many Commonwealth countries did not have self-government, however, and increasingly these countries have demanded their independence from Britain.

In India it was clear at the end of the war that the people wanted more than ever to govern themselves. It was just as clear that Muslims and Hindus could never agree to live in one country side by side. So in 1947 two new states were set up: India (mainly Hindu) and Pakistan (mainly Muslim). East and West Pakistan were over 1500 kilometres apart. In 1971 a civil war broke out in East Pakistan, and the new independent state of Bangladesh was set up.

Since 1947 Britain has gradually dismantled what was left of the old Empire. Former colonies in Africa, Asia, the Pacific Islands, the West Indies, South America and in Europe (the Mediterranean islands of Malta and Cyprus) have been granted their independence. In some places, such as Kenya, Cyprus and Malaya, the years leading to independence were marred by violence. In the main, the change-over has been achieved peacefully. Most, but not all, of these countries have chosen to remain members of the Commonwealth. One country, however—Rhodesia—has posed particular problems for Britain and we shall take a closer look at these in Chapter 30.

From this it can be seen that Britain's position as one of the world's leading powers was ended. Britain's place had been taken by the United States of America.

After 1945, Britain and other European countries were helped by the USA in the slow struggle to recover. The American *Secretary*

238

of State George Marshall promised money and raw materials to get Europe back on its feet again.

Why did the USA do this? For one thing, America was extremely rich and could well afford to help those countries that had borne the brunt of the fighting. For another, Americans remembered what had happened after 1918. Then, countries had been unable to solve their economic problems on their own. A terrible depression had thrown millions out of work. In their desperation some had turned to *extremists*, particularly Mussolini and Hitler. Unless world trade improved then the same thing could happen all over again. America clearly did not want this so the Marshall Aid Plan was born.

There was another reason. In March 1946, Winston Churchill made a famous speech in the USA. He warned of an 'Iron Curtain' that had fallen across Europe. What did he mean by this? He meant that there was now a threat from the mighty armed forces of the Soviet Union. Many people believed him. Events after 1945 convinced the Americans that Russia, so recently an ally, was not to be trusted.

Let us see what had happened.

We read in the last chapter how Russia's armies drove the Germans out of Eastern Europe and captured Berlin itself. The Russian leader Stalin had promised to hold free elections in the countries that they had liberated. But what happened? In Poland, Hungary, Czechoslovakia, Estonia, Latvia, Lithuania, Bulgaria, Rumania and Yugoslavia elections were held but without any real opposition to the Communists. These new Communist governments quickly showed that they were under the control of the Russians. Censorship, secret police, state control of education, industry and farming, the outlawing of political opponents—all these became part and parcel of the lives of millions of East Europeans. Only Yugoslavia, under its strong leader Marshal Tito, was prepared in those years to stand up to the Russians.

Tito

Why did the Russians do this? Firstly, because some of the lands overrun by the Red Army had at one time been part of the old Russian Empire—so Russia was just taking back what had once belonged to her. Secondly, Communists had played an important part in the war against the Nazis. Men such as Tito had led secret armies of guerrilla fighters against the Germans. This had won them much popular support. Thirdly, the events after the Russian Revolution had still not been forgotten. Then, remember, the Allies had sent armies to support the Whites—and Russians felt that the Allies were still not to be trusted. The German invasion of 1941 was still fresh in Stalin's memory. Russia wanted control of these border countries as a protection—a buffer—against any future attack from the west. Finally, of course, the Americans held the secret of the

Airlifting sacks of
coal for Berlin

Polaris missile

atomic bomb. Here was another threat to the security of Russia.

The Americans were furious that the Russians had not kept their promise about free elections. They in turn were suspicious of what the Russians might do next and they saw the rapidly-growing Russian armed forces as a threat to peace.

The first real test of strength came in May 1948. Berlin, the old capital of Germany, had been divided up between the Americans, British, French and Russians. But Berlin was deep in the part of Germany controlled by the Russians. The Russians blockaded Berlin and refused to allow their former allies to send in supplies. The Allies took up the challenge. For ten months everything needed by West Berlin—the part controlled by the Allies—had to be flown in. This worked and in March 1949 the Russians lifted their stranglehold on the city.

By this time it was clear that a new war, the 'Cold War', had started—and continues. We talk of a Cold War because although there has been no actual fighting between Russia and America, both sides have kept up their armies, air forces and navies and have continued to challenge each other and test each other's strength.

Both sides have built up alliances to defend their interests in various parts of the world. In Europe, the Americans lead the North Atlantic Treaty Organisation (NATO). Britain is a member of NATO. Today nearly 700 000 NATO troops backed up by tanks, rockets, artillery and aircraft are stationed in Europe. Facing them are a million troops of Russia's alliance—the Warsaw Pact—made up of those East European countries controlled by Russia. The Warsaw Pact not only has more soldiers than NATO but also more tanks, rockets, artillery and aircraft. Both sides are kept in a constant state of readiness for war.

Since 1945 all the major powers have spent thousands of millions of pounds on developing ever-more horrifying weapons. In 1949, Russia built her own atomic bomb. In 1953, both Russia and America produced the hydrogen bomb. These bombs are five thousand times more powerful than the bomb dropped on Hiroshima. That bomb was dropped from an aircraft. Now, rockets launched from underground sites or from submarines can travel up to 9000 kilometres to deliver their nuclear warheads. Thousands of these weapons are in store ready for use. Added together, they could destroy the world many times over. Nor is this all. Both sides have spent millions of pounds trying to develop defences against the bombs and the rockets.

Each side is constantly trying to get one step ahead of the other in this terrifying arms race. The Americans are experimenting with a neutron bomb which can kill living things (like a hydrogen bomb) but which does not destroy buildings or machines. No doubt the

240

Russians are trying to build one, too. Perhaps even more sinister are the experiments that both sides have carried out to develop chemical and germ warfare.

Thankfully, these weapons have not been used. Both sides have been deterred from using them because they know that any attack could lead to destruction for themselves. So this 'balance of terror' has brought an uneasy peace between the Great Powers in the troubled years since the war.

The Cold War though has continued and at times has shown signs of 'hotting up'. In 1961, the Russians built a wall right across Berlin to stop people escaping to West Berlin. Tension mounted. In 1962, the Russian leader Khruschev sent nuclear missiles to the island of Cuba only a short distance from the American coast. The Americans saw this as a threat and as a challenge. President Kennedy demanded that the missiles be withdrawn. With more missiles on their way to Cuba aboard Russian ships, what would Khruschev do? For thirteen days the world held its breath. In the end the Russians backed down and the missiles were withdrawn.

Russian missiles on their way to Cuba

This Cuban crisis showed how easily the Cold War could blow up into a full-scale nuclear war. Since then steps have been taken to try to improve the relations between Russia and the USA. There have been regular meetings between the leaders. Treaties have been signed to stop the testing of nuclear weapons and the development of germ warfare. Since 1969 both sides have taken part in discussions to reduce the numbers of weapons held. These Strategic Arms Limitation Talks (SALT for short) have made slow progress.

It is not just in the arms race that there is competition. Both Russia and America have spent millions of pounds on the 'space race' that we read about in Chapter 24. Millions more are spent on trying to win the support of other countries. Even sporting competitions are seen as ways of fighting the Cold War. A constant propaganda war is carried on to persuade the rest of the world that one side is 'better' than the other.

This, then, is the present state of affairs. There has been an easing of tension (called détente) between America and Russia in recent years. But the 1979 Russian invasion of Afghanistan, followed by the American decision to *boycott* the 1980 Moscow Olympics, shows that the Cold War is far from over.

Both Russia and America have had to pay a heavy price for this. For America the cost has been enormous. Twice since 1945, American soldiers have been in action in far-off Asia. (We shall take a closer look at these wars in the next chapter.) There have been demonstrations by Americans who do not like their country taking on the role of 'policeman of the free world'.

Ordinary Russians do not enjoy the same standard of living as people in the West as so much has had to be spent on fighting the Cold War. In several of the Warsaw Pact countries, such as Poland, there has been criticism of the tight control imposed by Moscow. In 1952 riots in East Germany were crushed by force. In 1956 Soviet tanks smashed an armed uprising in Hungary. In 1968 a new Czech government led by Alexander Dubcek tried to introduce reforms—to give Communism 'a human face'. Censorship was ended and political opposition allowed. Once again the Soviet tanks rolled in. Czechoslovakia was invaded by the armies of the other Warsaw Pact countries and Dubcek's government was overthrown. Every year hundreds of people risk their lives to escape from behind the 'Iron Curtain'. In Russia itself there is little political criticism. Those who do criticise risk arrest and imprisonment in terrible labour camps or detention in mental hospitals. The fate of these *dissidents* has aroused much sympathy in the West.

So there are problems for both America and Russia in fighting the Cold War. What has made things even more complicated for them has been the rise of Communist China.

Russian tanks
in Hungary, 1956

THINGS TO DO

1 On December 10th 1948 the United Nations General Assembly adopted a statement about Human Rights. Here are some of the most important of these 'rights'.

   (i) All human beings are born free and equal in dignity and rights. They are endowed [born] with reason and conscience and should act towards one another in a spirit of brotherhood.

   (ii) Everyone has the right to life, liberty and security of person.

   (iii) No one shall be held in slavery or servitude.

   (iv) No one shall be subjected to torture or to cruel, inhuman or degrading treatment or punishment.

242

(v) No one shall be subject to arbitrary arrest, detention or exile.

(vi) Everyone has the right to seek and to enjoy in other countries asylum [protection] from persecution.

(*a*) Say in your own words why you think these Human Rights are important.

(*b*) Do you think the UN has been successful in encouraging countries to respect these Human Rights?

(*c*) Choose one of these Human Rights and design a poster for the UN to let people see why it is important.

2 'From the cradle to the grave' is a phrase which describes our Welfare State. What do you understand by this? Find out as many examples as you can to show how the State helps its citizens.

3 What do you understand by the term 'apartheid'? Do you agree or disagree with this policy?

4 Say in your own words what is meant by the 'Cold War'. Give as many examples as you can of the competition between the USA and Russia.

5 'The balance of terror': organise a class debate on the role of nuclear weapons in keeping the peace between the great powers.

6 Here is part of an eyewitness account of the invasion of Czechoslovakia in 1968. It was written by a Scottish student-teacher, Lynda Napier, who was on holiday at the time. Read it carefully then answer the questions below in sentences:

We had already spent over a week with our Czech friends touring the beautiful Tatra mountains. We were staying for a couple of days in a little town called Piestany. At our hotel there was much talk of Dubcek and his reforms. People seemed to be quite excited by what was going on. It was then that the invasion took place. There was no warning. We came down to breakfast to find everyone listening to transistors. Our friends told us the shattering news. People were stunned and their faces showed disbelief at what was going on. Then someone called out and pointed out of the dining room window. We rushed over to see a large convoy of armoured vehicles and open trucks carrying uniformed troops. They were not Czech soldiers!

It was impossible to leave for two days. All this time we listened for news on the radio station which somehow managed to keep broadcasting in secret. We saw people handing out leaflets in the streets protesting against the invasion. The walls of shops and offices were covered with slogans and signatures criticising what was going on.

We got back to Bratislava to find tanks positioned at all the main crossroads and thirteen where a main road crossed the River Danube. We saw people talking to the tank crews. It seems that they were Polish and had no idea where they were or why they were in Czechoslovakia. The Czechs could not understand why the invasion had taken place.

Russian tanks in
Czechoslovakia, 1968

They bitterly resented the presence of the Warsaw Pact troops. We
were told that Brezhnev, the Russian leader, had visited the country
only a few weeks before and agreed to allow the Czechs to work out
their own type of Communism. Now this had been betrayed.

It had not been a peaceful invasion. In Bratislava at least two people
had been shot by the soldiers. On the pavements lay wreaths and burning
candles as memorials to these victims. The bullet holes could be seen
on the walls. We heard later that many more had been killed in Prague,
the capital city.

We were lucky to get on a train bound for Vienna that took us out
of a very unhappy country.

(a) Who was Dubcek?
(b) What sort of changes did he make in Czechoslovakia?
(c) What evidence is there in the passage to show that these reforms
were popular?
(d) How was news of the invasion received at Piestany?
(e) What evidence is there in the passage to show that Czechs did
not support the invasion?
(f) What evidence is there in the passage to show that it was the
Warsaw Pact forces—not just the Russians—who carried out
the invasion?
(g) What evidence is there in the passage to show that the invasion
had not been peaceful?
(h) Why do you think the Russians decided on an invasion of
Czechoslovakia?
(i) Do you think Lynda Napier supported the Czechs or the
invasion?

244

29 The rise of Communist China

Mao announcing the People's Republic of China

On October 1st 1949, the creation of the People's Republic of China was announced to the world. Twenty years of bloody civil war had ended with victory for the Chinese Communist Party (CCP). The man who made the announcement was Mao Tse-tung the leader of the CCP.

This new government faced tremendous problems. The country had been ravaged by years of fighting; much of the land had been recently occupied by hostile Japanese troops. Most of the people were desperately poor peasants. Few had had any education; indeed, eight out of ten were illiterate. These peasants followed the primitive farming methods of their forefathers, haunted by the constant fear of bad harvests and famine. With practically no industry to speak of, the Chinese economy was in ruins. China was weak in other ways, too. The Chinese army was no match for opponents. For many years, other countries had taken advantage of this. Britain, France, Germany, Russia and Japan had all at one time or another helped themselves to parts of China. Given all this, could the young People's Republic survive?

Consider what has happened since 1949. China is now one of the world's strongest nations. There are now over 970 million Chinese. This means that one person in every four in the world is Chinese! The country itself is the third largest in the world after Russia and Canada. Like neighbouring Russia, much of the land is not fit for agriculture. Deserts, marshlands and mountains, including part of the famous Himalayas, cannot produce food for China's huge, growing population. Despite this, since 1949 China has managed to improve agriculture, conquer famine and build up her industries. With nuclear weapons of their own and an army of 3.5 million China is a force to be reckoned with. The country is no longer at the mercy of other nations. Many *Third World* countries in Asia and Africa look to China for leadership and help. As we shall see, both America and Russia have had to accept China as a super-power.

To understand the importance of these changes we must look at events in China before the Communist takeover.

Mandarin

Chiang Kai-shek

In 1908 the old Empress of China died and the heir to the throne was a young child. In 1911 a revolution broke out and a republic was set up. The first President of China was Dr Sun Yat-sen. He was an educated man who had travelled widely and been impressed by what he learned about the government of other countries.

His task was a heavy one. His chief enemies were Imperial generals and rich landowners known as 'mandarins' who did not like the ideas of democracy. Nor did they like the thought of handing over the land to the peasants. In the north of China bandit leaders set themselves up as local warlords and terrorised the poor peasants. To help him Sun started a party, the Kuomintang (KMT). The KMT was helped by the new Soviet government in Russia anxious for friends. Communist ideas had already reached China and Chinese Communists were encouraged to help the KMT in the struggle to save the revolution.

Amongst these Communists was young Mao Tse-tung. Mao came from a peasant family but had been one of the lucky few who had received an education. He studied the ideas of Karl Marx and in 1921 started the Chinese Communist Party (CCP). For the next few years he worked amongst the peasants trying to convert them to his Communist ideas. Because there were so few factory workers in China, Mao saw clearly that any Communist revolution would have to be led by the peasants. Notice how different this was from what had happened in Russia. There Lenin's revolution had looked to the factory workers.

Meanwhile, Sun had died in 1923. He was succeeded by a young army officer, Chiang Kai-shek. With the help of the Communists an attack was launched on the warlords of the north. In 1927 the stronghold of Shanghai was captured. Then the order was given by Chiang for the KMT to turn on their Communist allies. Many hundreds were killed at this time. Why was this done? It seems that Chiang wanted the support of wealthy Chinese and foreigners who had no time for Communists. So the killings went on.

This really marked the start of a long, drawn-out civil war that was to last on and off for twenty years. As the leader of the CCP, Mao was prepared to fight back. He set up his headquarters in Kiangsi province. He got rid of the landlords, gave the land to the peasants and recruited the young men into his Red Army. In 1933 Mao found himself surrounded by Chiang's KMT armies. Five times they had tried to capture his stronghold; five times they were beaten back. With 100 000 of his followers—men, women and children—Mao fought his way out of the trap and headed for safety. This was the famous Long March.

Here is how Mao described those times of struggle. 'For twelve months we were under daily reconnaissance and bombing from the

Mao at Yenan

air by scores of planes. We were encircled, pursued, obstructed and intercepted on the ground by big forces of several hundred thousand men, we encountered untold difficulties and great obstacles on the way, but by keeping our two feet going we swept across a distance of more than twenty thousand li [10000 km] through the length and breadth of eleven provinces. Has there ever been in history a long march like ours?' The cost had been heavy, however. Only 20000 survived. During the march, Mao himself had had to leave his children with a peasant family for safety. He never saw them again.

In October 1935, what was left of the Communists reached Yenan. Here, protected by high mountains, they were safe from attack. Mao at once set about controlling the surrounding country-side and winning the peasants to his cause. As before, the landlords were removed, often by violence, and the land given to the peasants. The young men were recruited into the Red Army while the children were trained in the Communist ways.

By now Mao had the support of twelve million people. Soon he would be ready to renew the struggle with the KMT.

The breathing-space was short, however. In 1937 the Japanese invaded China. Their victorious armies swept all before them. What was to be done?

Mao persuaded Chiang that it was best for them to fight together against the common enemy. So an uneasy peace was made between them. For eight years the Communists and the KMT battled to defeat the Japanese. Meanwhile the Second World War had begun and in 1941 the Allies were also at war with Japan. So they poured money and supplies into China—but all their aid went to the KMT. Can you guess why? But most of the fighting was being done by the Red Army and Mao's guerrilla tactics hit the Japanese hard.

When peace came in 1945, Mao's reputation had spread throughout China. He was now strong enough to challenge Chiang for the control of the country. The civil war started again. Although Chiang received help from America it was quite clear that the KMT were no match for the Red Army. Not only were the Red Army soldiers better in battle but they had the support of the people tired of the cruelties of the KMT and the corruption of the government.

With this support, the Communists swept to victory. In January 1949 Peking was surrendered without a fight. Chiang and his KMT supporters retreated to the island of Taiwan. There he set up a rival Nationalist government.

As we read at the start of the chapter, Mao proclaimed his Communist government on October 1st 1949. 'Henceforth our nation will enter the large family of peace-loving and freedom-loving

247

nations of the world. It will work bravely and industriously to create its own civilisation and happiness, and will, at the same time promote world peace and freedom. Our nation will never again be an insulted nation. We have stood up.'

Brave words—but Mao was faced by desperate problems. With the help of Soviet Russia, however, a start was made. The Communist government took control of all industries. The land was taken from the landlords and given to the peasants. This was often done with great cruelty as old scores were settled. Many thousands were killed at this time.

The first problem was to produce enough food to feed the people. So the land was organised into huge collective farms. In these farms hundreds of families worked together in the fields. Later even larger farms known as communes were set up. Here thousands of Chinese were grouped together by the government. Life on a commune is very different from life on one of our farms. The commune is run like a little welfare state. The commune builds homes for the people, educates their children and cares for them when they are old or sick. Many communes have their own small factories producing the goods needed by the commune members. Every effort is made to make the communes self-sufficient.

There were changes in the cities, too. New homes, hospitals and schools were built. Roads and railways stretched outwards across the countryside, linking the farthest corners of the land. Like Russia, China had her own Five-Year Plan to speed up the growth of industry. Great progress was made but Mao was not satisfied. In 1958 he called for a 'Great Leap Forward' to try to catch up with other countries. Millions of peasants were ordered to leave their

'Blue ants' at work

fields to work in factories or in the building of roads and dams. The armies of 'blue ants' (for all the peasants wore the same blue tunics) toiled with great enthusiasm—but not much else. Projects failed; three bad harvests threatened famine.

Mao realised that he had made a mistake. To make matters worse, the Russians withdrew their aid to China in 1960. They disagreed with what Mao was doing. Also they realised that Mao was not going to be a 'puppet', doing what the Russians told him. The Russians refused to share the secrets of the atomic bomb with China, for they saw that a strong China would challenge them for the leadership of the Communist world. Since then relations between the two Communist giants have not improved. There have been several incidents along the 11 000 kilometre frontier that separates Russia and China.

The failure of the 'Great Leap Forward' was a bitter disappointment to Mao. By now he was sixty-seven, no longer able to be an active leader—or so it seemed. He was replaced as Chairman of the Republic but remained Chairman of the CCP. It seemed that his influence was over.

In 1965, however, he staged a remarkable comeback. Mao was worried that the Chinese Revolution—his revolution—had 'gone soft'. People were no longer prepared to make sacrifices. There was a danger that China might return to the old ways where power and influence lay in the hands of a few people.

Mao appealed to the young people of China to fight against this. Millions of Chinese answered his call and took to the streets. These 'Red Guards' took over factories and schools. People in positions of importance such as university professors were ordered to work as peasants in the fields. Huge demonstrations were held. Mao's portrait was everywhere. He was worshipped almost as a god. Everyone was expected to have a copy of 'The Thoughts of Chairman Mao'. This famous 'Little Red Book', as it was called, became the bible of the Red Guards.

Soldiers of the Red Guard waving their 'little red books'

This 'Cultural Revolution' threw China into turmoil and confusion. For many months it seemed that civil war was about to break out again. There were reports of fights between peasants and Red Guards. Food production and industrial output both fell. The country was facing disaster. So China's other leaders took control. The Cultural Revolution was ended in 1969. Mao went into retirement but still remained Chairman of the CCP.

Events outside China were causing concern. We have seen already the breakdown in friendship between China and Russia. Relations with America had never been good but during the 1950s and 1960s they got steadily worse. America had never trusted the Communists and refused to allow China the chance to join the United Nations. Instead they supported Chiang's Nationalist government in Taiwan.

In 1950 a war started in Korea. The Communist North invaded the South. The Americans were sure that the Chinese were to blame. The UN was persuaded to intervene. An army (90 per cent American) was sent to Korea. The UN forces cleared the North Korean troops from the South. But the American General McArthur decided to invade the North to teach them a lesson. Look at the map on the next page. China felt threatened, so thousands of Chinese 'volunteers' fought against the UN troops. The war dragged on until 1953 with neither side making any real gains. America and China looked on each other with suspicion.

More trouble was to come in South-East Asia. Before the Second World War, France controlled Laos, Kampuchea and Vietnam. Then these lands were seized by the Japanese. In Vietnam, the peasants fought back. They were led by a Communist Ho Chi Minh. His guerrillas fought a savage war against the Japanese. At the end of the war the Vietnamese expected their independence. Instead the French returned. Now the guerrilla war was against them. By 1954 the French were beaten. It was agreed that Vietnam should be made into two countries—a Communist North and a 'democratic' South. (In fact, the South quickly became corrupt with power lying in the hands of a rich few.) Ho Chi Minh was determined to make all of Vietnam Communist. War broke out again.

As in Korea, the Americans saw this as a Communist threat and sent help. At first they sent money and advisers. But as the war continued, American troops entered the fighting to defend South Vietnam. It was a sickening, bloody, war. Both sides were guilty of dreadful cruelty. The Americans were fighting some 200 000 guerrillas in the South—the Vietcong—backed up by 55 000 North Vietnamese regular soldiers. The Communists received massive help from both China and Russia. For all their strength, the Americans were at a loss to know what to do with a lightly armed enemy who struck hard, then melted back into the cover of the

Ho Chi Minh

250

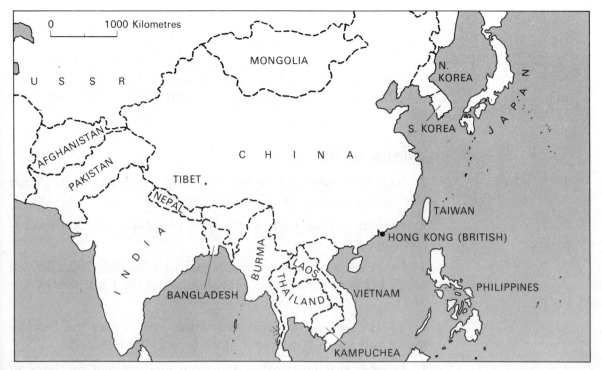

American casualties
in Vietnam

jungle. By 1968, 500 000 Americans were in South Vietnam. An attempt was made to bomb North Vietnam into surrender. More bombs were dropped on Vietnam than in the whole of the Second World War! This only made the North Vietnamese more determined. Now once again there was the threat that China might send more 'volunteers'. In the West many voices were raised against the war. By 1971, 48 000 Americans and 200 000 Vietnamese had been killed. In 1973 a peace was signed in Paris between the Americans and the North Vietnamese. Despite their promises, however, the North Vietnamese quickly invaded the South and conquered the whole country.

This time the Americans did nothing. Why was this?

Both America and China saw the advantages of closer friendship. Both mistrusted the Russians; both wanted to avoid a major war. Talks between the two countries began. In 1971 the Americans withdrew their support from Taiwan and agreed that Communist China should become a member of the UN. In February 1972 the American President Nixon made an historic visit to China. Since then there have been regular meetings between Western leaders and the Chinese. Important trade links are being developed. In 1980, the Chinese joined the Americans in boycotting the Moscow Olympics in protest against the Russian invasion of Afghanistan.

And Mao himself? Although he had lost power after the Cultural

251

Revolution he remained a much-respected figure. In September 1976 he died. In his lifetime—seventy-nine years—he had seen tremendous changes both inside and outside China. One thing was certain. The words he had spoken in 1949 had come true. 'Our nation will never again be an insulted nation. We have stood up.'

THINGS TO DO

1 'Has there ever been in history a long march like ours?' What was the 'long march' and why was it so important?

2 Explain in your own words why you think the Communists won the civil war.

3 From what you learned in Chapter 24 what differences do you notice between the Russian Revolution and the Chinese Revolution?

4 Try to explain in your own words why China has become less friendly with Russia and more friendly with America.

5 Imagine that you are an American reporter sent to China in 1972. Your job is to describe your first impressions of China and to tell your readers something about the life of Mao Tse-tung.

Chinese soldiers guarding the Great Wall, 1943

30 Today's headlines are tomorrow's history

WORLD OIL CRISIS WORSENS

EEC MINISTERS NEAR AGREEMENT

PROGRESS MADE IN MIDDLE EAST PEACE TALKS

HOSTAGES HELD BY TERRORISTS

THE COLD WAR HOTS UP

IRA terror campaign continues in Ulster

'And here again are the main points of the news. . . .'

You have heard these words often: as you know, you can hear them several times each day on radio and TV. Thanks to developments in communications, you can see and hear each evening reports on the day's events all over the world. In fact, with TV pictures being 'bounced' off satellites from one part of the world to another we can often see and hear events as they are taking place! Other programmes such as 'Panorama' or 'This Week' bring us background information and comments about these events. Thousands of people are employed—reporters, editors, TV crewmen, sound recordists, technicians, secretaries—to keep us informed about what is happening worldwide. Thousands more work for the newspapers and magazines that bring us more information about each day's happenings.

There is plenty for them to do! In every country important decisions are being taken by politicians, civil servants, businessmen, trade unionists, military leaders—and ordinary individuals. Of course very few of these actions will hit the world's headlines. Our news tends to be dominated by the activities of the leaders of the Great Powers or by disasters such as air crashes, earthquakes or famines—the great problems.

But all the time other things are happening and information about them is being preserved. In local newspapers, radio stations, books, documents, photographs, ciné film, diaries, eyewitness accounts, today's events are being recorded. At every level— individual, family, neighbourhood, place of work, district, region —the day-to-day happenings are being remembered in some way. And, just as we have tried to reconstruct the events and the ways of life of people in the past, future historians will try to do the same for our own times. What is news for us today will be the evidence they will use tomorrow.

Newsmen at work at an EEC meeting

What are some of the great problems facing Britain today? Quite clearly our country has never really recovered from the cost of fighting two world wars. Our older industries—iron and steel, textiles, shipbuilding—have had to face challenges from competitors abroad. Many overseas markets have been lost to challengers such as the highly efficient Japanese. Britain is no longer 'the workshop of the world'. With every country seeking to build up its industries, Britain faces a hard struggle in the competition for markets.

Our governments have tried to deal with this problem. In 1973, after two years' negotiations, Britain became a member of the European Economic Community, the EEC. The EEC had been set up in 1957 by France, West Germany, Italy, Belgium, Holland and Luxemburg. The idea was to create a huge 'common market' where the goods of member nations could be moved and sold without payment of expensive tariffs and duties. The Common Market would protect itself from outside competition by tariffs.

254

But the EEC aims to do much more than protect the trade of its members. Workers of member countries should be free to move anywhere in the Common Market in search of employment. Help should be given to those member countries with serious economic problems—and to poorer countries of the Third World.

It is intended that member countries will be brought closer together and will eventually be joined under one government. (Many people see this as an important aim for, remember, these same countries have twice gone to war with each other this century.) The first step was taken in June 1979, when the first elections for a European Parliament were held. Four hundred and ten Euro-MPs, including eighty-one from Britain, were elected. We shall have to wait, however, to see if EEC members join together under one government.

At first most people in Britain were very much in favour of our joining the EEC. In 1975 the Labour government of Harold Wilson agreed to Britain's first ever *referendum* to find out what voters felt. The result was a clear one. 17 378 581 (67.2 per cent) voted in favour of membership; 8 470 073 (32.8 per cent) voted against.

Since then, perhaps, the mood has changed. Certainly not everyone who voted in favour in 1975 is convinced that membership has benefited Britain. Running the EEC is a costly business—and there is much inefficiency and waste. Particular trades and industries, such as farming and deep-sea fishing, feel unfairly treated under EEC laws. Many people argue that Britain is paying far more into EEC funds than we are getting back in benefits. On the other hand, many others believe that Britain needs the protection and help of the EEC—particularly when member countries have to deal with great problems in world trade.

What do you think? As voters of tomorrow, you may well have to decide for yourselves.

One great problem facing all EEC members is the need to have supplies of oil. This precious mineral powers our factories, drives our transport and heats our homes. Many oil products, such as plastics, are now essential for our everyday lives. Quite simply, we have come to depend on oil as never before.

Until the 1960s, Britain and other countries of Europe could count on plentiful supplies of cheap oil. Since then, however, these supplies have been threatened and the price of oil has risen alarmingly. The trade and industries of Britain and other countries have been severely shaken; the cost of living has risen and the jobs of countless men and women have been threatened. Events in the Middle East, where most of the world's oil comes from, have at times even threatened the peace of the world.

What has happened?

Israeli tanks

For part of the answer we have to look at events in the Middle East nearly two thousand years ago when the 'Holy Land' was part of the Roman Empire. About AD 70 the Jews rebelled against their Roman rulers but, after fierce fighting, were totally defeated. Their great temple in Jerusalem was destroyed and the surviving Jews moved out of their homeland. For centuries Jews lived uneasily in many Christian countries of Europe and were persecuted, more or less, in every one. (Later, thousands moved to new homes in the USA.) One hope bound them together: the dream of returning one day to that same Holy Land—to a new Israel.

But the Holy Land—like other countries of the Middle East—had been conquered by the Arab followers of Mohammed, who were in turn conquered by the Turks. This was still the state of affairs at the beginning of the First World War. Britain, struggling to survive, sought help from both the Arabs and the Jews. Promises were given to both that they should be given their independence.

Can you see the problems raised by these promises? Clearly a Jewish homeland in the Holy Land, Palestine, could be created only at the expense of the Palestinian Arabs already living there. At the end of the war, several Arab states were established—but not a new Israel. During the 1920s and 1930s, however, some Jewish settlements were built and there were violent clashes with the Palestinian Arabs who had been moved out of their homes.

After the Second World War what had been a trickle became

a flood. Thousands of Jews, many of them survivors of Hitler's 'final solution', came to settle in what they called 'their' homeland. Britain tried to keep the peace but British troops were attacked by both Jewish and Palestinian terrorists. In 1947 the problem was passed to the United Nations and in 1948 the new state of Israel was created.

The Jews were delighted—but not, of course, the Arabs. About three million Palestinians had become refugees. They now lived in overcrowded camps in Jordan and other countries. Here the young men trained as terrorists, determined to win back what they saw as 'their' homeland. Naturally, they looked for help to the Arab states of Egypt, Jordan, Syria and Lebanon. The new citizens of Israel, for their part, were equally determined to defend themselves from any attacks.

They soon came and since 1948 four wars have been fought. Each time the Israelis have been able to beat off the attacks. In the last war, from October 1973 to May 1974, the Israelis even managed to cross the Suez Canal, advancing several hundred kilometres into Egypt. Then the United Nations moved in and separated the rival armies.

Since then there has been an uneasy peace. Palestinian terrorist attacks have continued, however: in 1972, for example, eleven Israeli athletes were killed at the Olympic Games in Munich. The Israelis, for their part, have launched several attacks against the camps of the Palestinians in neighbouring countries. In 1977 President Sadat of Egypt made an historic visit to Israel in search of peace. Then President Carter of the USA persuaded President Sadat and Mr Begin, Prime Minister of Israel, to meet in America. The following year they signed a peace treaty but other Arab states refuse to recognise Israel and remain determined to destroy her. The terrorist attacks have continued.

President Sadat, President Carter and Mr Begin

How does all this affect Britain today? Throughout we have supported the idea of an independent Israel. The Arabs, however, have brought a lot of pressure to bear on Britain by increasing the price of oil and, indeed, by threatening to cut off oil supplies altogether to any country that supports Israel.

Fortunately, this threat has not been carried out—but the situation in the Middle East is still explosive. The revolution in Iran in 1979 added to the tension. There the Shah—a friend of the USA and European countries—was overthrown and forced into exile, where he died the next year.

Meanwhile there had been one surprising development nearer home.

In the 1960s oil and natural gas were discovered under the North Sea, off the coasts of Britain. In 1975 the first oil was brought ashore and since then millions of barrels of precious oil have reached Britain by pipeline or tanker. Incredibly, Britain is now able to export oil to other countries. This has brought much more than money to Britain. Many jobs have been created by the North Sea bonanza. Huge oil-rigs and production platforms have had to be built; about ten thousand oil-rig workers have been recruited; thousands more work on pipe-laying operations or supply services.

North Sea oil rig

North Sea oil and gas have not solved our country's economic problems but they have certainly eased them.

One problem which still seems as far from a solution as ever, however, is Northern Ireland.

We have seen already, in Chapter 25, the background to the present troubles. The nationalist hopes for independence from Britain are still fiercely resisted by the Protestant people of Ulster, determined to remain part of the United Kingdom. On page 208 you read how Lloyd George's division of Ireland failed to work— and throughout the 1930s and 1940s the troubles continued.

Matters came to a head in 1968, when demonstrations turned to violence. Extremists on both sides took advantage of the situation. Since then the Provisional IRA has carried out a campaign of shootings and bombings, often against innocent civilians. Protestant terrorist groups have also killed and maimed. Between these two, British soldiers have tried to maintain law and order. Sadly, we have become accustomed to news of another bomb incident, another death to add to the list of more than a thousand. It is tragic to think there are young people of your age in Northern Ireland who have been witnesses of violence all their lives.

Elsewhere, what was left of the old British Empire moved rapidly to independence after the Second World War. In Africa, Asia, South America, the West Indies, the Pacific Islands, new names appeared on the maps as British rule was ended.

In almost all cases this was done by agreement. Certainly in countries such as Kenya and Cyprus there had been violence before independence but the actual handover of power was made peacefully. Indeed, so successful was this approach that almost all these newly-independent countries chose to become members of the Commonwealth. Today, with more than thirty members and one-quarter of the world's population, the Commonwealth is a huge family of nations—each with its own government, but recognising the Queen as 'Head of the Commonwealth'.

A meeting of leaders of the Commonwealth

One country, however, refused to agree to the independence offered by Britain. In Rhodesia, 250 000 white people controlled a land with a population of six million black people. All power was held by the whites: government, industry, commerce, farming, police, armed forces—were controlled by them. Independence would mean handing this power to black control. The whites were determined to resist.

In 1965 Prime Minister Ian Smith declared Rhodesia to be independent of Britain. This Unilateral Declaration of Independence

260

(UDI) was condemned by Britain and the other members of the United Nations. Trade sanctions were introduced—which meant that countries were forbidden to sell goods to Rhodesia or buy goods from her. But these steps failed, because some countries took advantage of the large profits to be made from this illegal trade. Meanwhile the Smith government began to copy the policy of apartheid from their neighbour South Africa.

Many black Rhodesians decided to fight for an independence that gave them power. With the help of neighbouring black African states, such as Tanzania, these people were trained to fight for their freedom. A bitter guerrilla war began under the leadership of Joshua Nkomo and Robert Mugabe—both of whom had been imprisoned in Rhodesia for their beliefs. The guerrillas struck again and again and twenty thousand men, women and children died in the fighting. Ian Smith had to give way: he tried to share power with black Rhodesians but this was not enough.

In 1979 a peace conference was held in London and after weeks of negotiations an agreement was signed. Britain played a leading part in the conference and in the preparations for the first proper elections in Rhodesia—now renamed Zimbabwe. In February 1980 Robert Mugabe swept to power with an overwhelming majority.

Today Britain is no longer the head of a mighty Empire, capable of looking after her own affairs. Times have changed. As a member of such organisations as the Commonwealth, the EEC and the UN we have a part to play in coping with the problems of the world.

Mugabe

THINGS TO DO

1 What do you think are the main problems facing Britain today?

2 Organise a class discussion on the future of Northern Ireland. The information in Chapter 22 should be of some help.

3 'Should Britain have joined the EEC?' Try to find out more information about the work of the EEC then organise a class referendum on this question. How do your results compare with those of 1975?

4 Select one of the problems discussed in the chapter and start a collection of newspaper cuttings dealing with it.

5 Imagine that the class are a TV news production team with the job of putting on a weekly programme about world events. Divide into groups, select your 'stories', research them and present them as part of the 'broadcast'. One or two members of the class should act as news readers linking the stories together.

Our global village

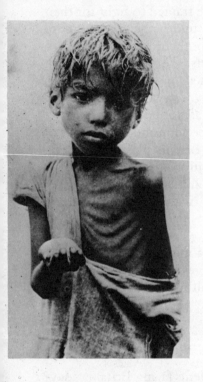

It has been said that the people of the world now live in a 'global village'. What is meant by this?

All countries have been brought closer together. We have seen already how quickly news can travel—but so can people. Journeys that once took months can now be made in a matter of hours. But there is more to the global village than speedy communication. Economic problems, such as the supply and price of oil, affect us all. And, as you know already, if ever a nuclear war breaks out we are all at risk.

Our 'village' is faced with other problems, too.

One is that its population is growing at a fantastic rate. Today there are about 4000 million people in the world. At the present rate of growth there may be 6500 million by the year 2000! How are all these people to be fed, housed and clothed? Already it is estimated that half the world's population do not have enough to eat to keep healthy and that many millions are close to starvation—or are already starving. Can the global village cope with this problem?

The number of people in our 'village' is creating other problems, too. Our Earth's stocks of fuel—not only oil, but also coal and gas—are being used up in vast quantities and cannot last for ever. Can we find other sources of power in time? And as men cut down forests to plough up the land for food, rare animals and birds are being driven out. Already more than a thousand species face extinction. Can people survive only by killing off the wildlife of the world?

Only now are people waking up to the damage they are doing to the global village by pollution. We must find ways to avoid being swamped and poisoned by the waste materials of our lives. Already our towns and countryside are often choked with carelessly-dropped litter; our air is poisoned by the fumes that pour from factory chimneys and motor car exhaust pipes; our fields are contaminated by the chemicals used by farmers to protect

Wreck of the tanker 'Torrey Canyon'

The American, Neil Armstrong on the surface of the moon, 1969

crops and animals from insect pests and diseases; our rivers are fouled with sewage and our seas and beaches with oil spilt from damaged tankers. Moreover, it is not only today's 'village' that is at risk. The waste material from our nuclear power stations will remain dangerous for hundreds of years! What is to be done with it? Is it right just to bury it in a remote part of the Highlands or dump it in the sea?

We global villagers must cope with all these—and other—challenges.

What about Scotland?

We have not said much about our own country in the last few chapters. Quite obviously, Scotland as a country—with its own people, its own history and traditions, its pride in its achievements—still exists! Our story as a nation continues but, increasingly, it has been influenced by events elsewhere. The Agricultural and Industrial Revolutions, the drive for an Empire, the ravages of world wars, have all left their mark. We cannot ignore the Cold War nor shut our eyes to the problems of the global village—for we, too, are part of it. We must play our part on the world's stage—as Scots always have done.

You are growing up as the twentieth century draws to a close. It has been a century of remarkable change. There have been tremendous developments in science, medicine, communications, education. Man has walked on the surface of the Moon and sent rockets to explore the secrets of outer space. Wars and revolutions have redrawn the map of the world. There has been social change, too. In Britain much has been done to improve the lives of ordinary people and to give women a fairer place in society.

But there has been great suffering, too. Terrible wars have devastated large parts of the world; millions of people have been violently killed; cruel dictatorships have trampled on the rights of ordinary folk to live their lives freely and in peace. Today, racial and religious prejudice still divide communities and, while the rich nations enjoy a high standard of living, millions go hungry.

History can help to explain the present, but it cannot predict the future. The hope for mankind is that—with the spirit of co-operation shown in the Commonwealth, the EEC and the United Nations—the people of the global village will cope with, and solve, these problems.

One thing is certain, however. You will be the eyewitnesses of the challenging and exciting times that lie ahead.

Glossary

(A list of words printed in *italics* in this book, with their meanings)

abdicate to give up the position of being a king or queen

ambassador a government official sent to look after the interests of one country in another country

apartheid the policy (in South Africa) of keeping people of different races apart by making them live in different places etc.

apprentice a young person who is learning a trade

archbishop a chief *bishop*; the highest ranking churchman in the Roman Catholic Church, the Scottish Episcopal Church, or the Church of England

assassination the murder of an important person, especially someone concerned with politics

ballot the way of voting in secret by marking a paper and putting it into a special closed box, called a ballot box

bayonet a steel stabbing blade, like a short sword, fixed to the muzzle of a soldier's rifle

bias the favouring of (for example) one person, one side of an argument, one football team, instead of being neutral

bishop a churchman of high rank (next to an *archbishop*) in the Roman Catholic Church, the Scottish Episcopal Church, or the Church of England

blockade to surround a fort or a country so that food and other supplies cannot reach it; the act of doing this

Bolshevik a follower of Lenin who helped him to seize power by *revolutionary* ways in 1917 (Now our slang word 'bolshy' describes anyone who is a rebel or who tries to be as uncooperative as possible.)

boycott to refuse to do business or trade with a person, group of people or country

brainwash to force a person to change his view, often by affecting his state of mind

bred (people) brought up in a certain way or a particular place; (animals) reared in a certain way to produce particular results, e.g. sheep to produce more wool

buccaneer a pirate

Budget the plan for a government's spending and taxation put before *Parliament* each year by the *Chancellor of the Exchequer*

burgess (in earlier times) a Member of Parliament for a burgh, usually a merchant or businessman

candidate someone who enters for a competition or examination for a job or qualification (A parliamentary candidate is someone who enters for election as MP.)

censorship the removal from books, films, newspapers etc. of anything which might be offensive or which a government does not wish to be known

census a counting of the people in a country (The first census in Great Britain was taken in 1801.)

Chancellor of the Exchequer the leading minister of a government who is responsible for taxation and government spending

charitable An organisation set up to collect money to help those in need is a 'charity' or 'charitable organisation'.

cholera an infectious and very deadly disease, now commonest in hot countries, caused by drinking *polluted* water or eating *polluted* food

city state a city which is independent; where the people look after their own affairs (especially in Ancient Greece, where 'cities' were very small by our standards)

civil war a war between groups of people belonging to the same country

clan chief The chief of a clan owned the land, was responsible for defending it against raiders, punished wrongdoers and looked after the sick and needy. His chief tenants, called tacksmen, let out part of the land they rented from the chief to the ordinary clansmen. The clansmen paid rent with things they made or grew and had to be ready to fight for the chief when ordered to do so.

collective farm a large farm, controlled by a government, but run by the workers themselves for the good of them all

Commons the House of Commons, the elected House of *Parliament* (Its members are called Members of Parliament or MPs.)

confiscate to take away something, perhaps land, as a punishment

contemporary living at, belonging to, or happening at, the same time So a contemporary document was written at the time of the event being described. (The word can also mean 'happening in our own time'.)

corruption evil, moral badness, especially dishonesty or bribery; giving a gift, usually money, to persuade a person to do something dishonest

croft a small farm with a cottage, usually in the Scottish Highlands

demobilise to free a soldier, sailor or airman from service after a war is over

depression (in a country) a period when trading conditions are very discouraging and many people are out of work ('The Depression' in Britain usually means the period of the early 1930s.)

dictatorship the government of an all-powerful ruler, called a 'dictator'

diplomat someone engaged in the business of looking after the affairs of his own country in another country

discrimination the act of treating people differently—because of their race, religion, age, sex or any other reason

dissident someone who disagrees, especially with those in power in some countries

dragoon a heavily-armed mounted soldier

drover someone who drives cattle to market

economist an expert in economics, the study of the ways in which people and nations produce and distribute money and goods

emigrate to leave one's own country to settle in another

enclosed In the late 18th century the old run-rig farming disappeared as landowners 'enclosed' land with dykes or hedges. These enclosed fields made it possible to use the new methods of farming.

episcopacy the way of ruling a church by *bishops*

evict to put someone out of his or her house

exile to banish, to drive a person away from his own country 'An exile' means (1) a long stay in a foreign land, in earlier times usually as a punishment; (2) a person who lives outside his own country either because he is forced to do so, or from choice.

exploit to make use of someone or something, often selfishly

extremist someone who carries ideas further than most people consider wise

ferm toun a group of perhaps eight to ten cottages surrounded by farmland The men of a ferm toun divided the surrounding land between them so that each had a share of the 'infield' (the better land) and the 'outfield' (the poorer land).

food rationing See *rationing*

foreign policy The plans of a government or ruler of a country for its dealings with other governments or rulers

galleon a large Spanish warship

general strike When members of all *trade unions* strike or stop work at the same time, this is a *general strike*. (When people talk of 'The General Strike' in Britain, they mean the one in 1926.)

hieroglyphics the picture signs used in writing in Ancient Egypt

Home Secretary a leading minister of a government who is responsible for matters concerned with law and order: for example, the police, fire service, immigration

illegal not lawful, against the law

income tax a tax paid to the government by individual persons according to the amount of income they receive

inefficient not working as well as possible: for example, wasteful in time or energy

invest to put money into a company or other organisation, usually in the form of a *share* or number of shares, with the aim of making a profit

kirk session in the Church of Scotland, a

committee of the minister and elders of a church which looks after its affairs

Liberty, Equality, Fraternity the slogan or motto of the French Revolution: meaning that all men should be free, equal and act in a brotherly way towards each other

Local Authority A Community Council, a District Council or a Regional Council is a local authority, in which men and women called Councillors are elected by the voters in the area to look after its affairs.

Lords the House of Lords, the non-elected House of *Parliament*

luckenbooth a stall or shop which could be locked up at night

magistrate a person who has the power to act as a judge and sentence those found guilty of lesser crimes

man o' war a warship

mercenary a soldier paid by a foreign country for serving in its army

mobilise to gather troops together for war service

nationalise to make an industry (the railways, for example) the property of the nation

nationalist someone who believes strongly about the need for a nation to be united, independent and self-governing

negotiate to bargain, to discuss a subject with someone in order to reach an agreement

nuclear warhead the explosive part of a missile, using nuclear ('atomic') energy, which can cause immense damage and destruction

obituary an article (usually in a newspaper) about the life and career of someone who has just died

organisation a group of people working together for a purpose they all believe in

Parliament the chief law-making group of a nation; in Britain, the House of Commons and the House of Lords

peasant a person, usually a poor one who does not own land, who lives and works on the land

pension a sum of money paid regularly to a retired person, a widow or someone who has been injured in war

pollution the making of land, rivers or sea harmful to people, animals or plants (The sea and rivers may be polluted by oil or sewage; land by chemicals used to spray crops.)

post mortem an examination of a dead person to find out the cause of death

Presbyterian In a Presbyterian Church, like the Church of Scotland, the affairs of a particular church are looked after by the *kirk session*. The affairs of the churches in a district are looked after by a presbytery, made up of ministers and elders from those churches.

President a person chosen by the people to be the head of government of a country which is a *republic* (that is, does not have a king or queen)

press gang a group of sailors who had the right to carry off men by force to serve in the navy

privateer a privately owned ship used by a government or ruler to capture or rob the ships of an enemy

proclamation an official announcement made publicly: for example, the announcement of the death of a king or queen

propaganda the spread of particular ideas and opinions, usually highly organised and often exaggerated or very one-sided

rationing sharing fairly anything in short supply, giving each person a *ration* (especially of food in wartime)

raw materials materials, often in their natural state, from which other things are manufactured

referendum the way of giving people of a country a chance to give their opinion about an important matter by voting for or against it

reformed changed, improved

reformer a person who tries to bring about changes and improvements

regent a person who governs in place of a king or queen

repeal to do away with, to cancel (especially a law)

republic a form of government in which power is in the hands of the elected representatives of the people, with a *president* instead of a king; a country which is governed in this way

reveille a bugle call at daybreak to waken soldiers

revolutionary someone who is in favour of bringing about a revolution (that is, a complete change—especially in the government of a country—quickly instead of gradually)

Riot Act   a law passed by *Parliament* to prevent the gathering of crowds which might lead to disturbances and trouble   (After the Riot Act had been read publicly by a *magistrate*, soldiers could fire on those who continued to make a disturbance.)

sanction   permission, approval, a penalty for not keeping a law

sanctions   measures taken to separate a nation from other nations (e.g. by stopping trade with it) with the aim of forcing it to stop a certain course of action

satellite   a smaller body moving round a larger, like the moon round the earth; a man-made object fired into space to travel round a planet; a smaller country controlled by a more powerful neighbouring one

seat   A 'parliamentary seat' means a constituency (the area which on MP represents) or the position held by an MP.

secretary   a person employed to write letters, keep records and make business arrangements

Secretary of State   (in Britain) a government minister in charge of a department; (in USA) the person in a government responsible for foreign affairs

share   (in a company or business) one of the parts into which the money, or capital, of the company is divided

sheriff   the title of the judge in the main local lawcourts in Scotland   (Originally the sheriff was the 'shire reeve' or 'shire officer', the representative of the king in a country.)

smuggler   someone who takes goods in or out of a country without paying the taxes fixed by law

sniper   a soldier who shoots very accurately and fires on an enemy from a hidden position

Socialist   a person who believes in socialism: the idea that a country's wealth (its land, mines, industries, railways etc.) should belong to the people as a whole and not to private owners

statistics   facts and figures set out in order to show information as clearly as possible

superpower   one of the most powerful countries in the world: China, the USA and the USSR

Third World   the developing countries of the world—especially those which are not allied to the USA or the USSR

toll   a tax charged for using a bridge or road (or for selling goods in a market)

Tory   a member of one of the two main political parties in Britain, especially in the 18th and early 19th centuries   (See also *Whig*.)

trade union   a group of workers in a certain trade or number of trades who join together to bargain with employers about wages, hours and conditions of work

transported   taken as a prisoner to a prison in another country to serve a sentence

try   (in a court of law) to judge the case of a person accused of breaking a law

tryst   an arrangement (often secret) to meet someone at a certain place at a certain time; a cattle fair or market where *drovers* met

typhus   a very dangerous fever carried by body lice

vaccination   the method of giving a person protection against a disease: by injecting into the skin a substance made from the germs that cause the disease

Whig   a member of one of the two main political parties in Britain, especially in the 18th century (The Whigs stood for the rights of ordinary people, the *Tories* for the power of the king. After about 1830 the name 'Whig' was used less than the new name 'Liberal'.)

winnow   to separate chaff from the grain of cereal crops by throwing in the air and allowing the wind to blow the lighter chaff away

workhouse   a house of shelter for poor, especially old or disabled, people where they were fed and clothed and worked for their keep

working classes   In this book you read about 'working classes' in the 19th century in particular. Then, and long afterwards, the meaning was very clear: it meant all those men and women who worked with their hands for the owners of factories, mines or farms.   (Today some people would say it still means only these 'manual workers'. Some would say that it means all those who work for the owner or manager of a company or *organisation*. Others would say it means—or should mean—everyone who works to support himself or herself and, perhaps, a family. What do you think?)

wright   a carpenter or joiner

Index

Aberdeen 103, 105, 110
Aberfeldy 54, 69
Adam, Robert 110
Afghanistan 242, 251
Africa 37, 40, 41, 150, 179, 180, 184, 227, 228, 237, 238, 245, 260, 261
Agricultural Revolution 64, 65, 72–7, 82, 141, 147, 198, 263
Air raids 191, 192, 220, 225–7, 231, 232
Albert, Prince 68, 69, 169, 178
America 12, 37, 39, 40, 59, 64, 84, 96, 106, 107, 114–7, 119–30, 133, 182, 183, 192–4, 197, 206, 207, 211, 212, 224, 227–9, 231, 238–43, 245, 247, 250–2, 257
Anne 46, 48, 52
Apartheid 237, 238, 243, 261
Appeasement 219, 220
Architecture 62, 71, 76, 106, 107, 109, 110, 111, 113, 115, 166–8, 171
Argyll, Duke of 52, 53
Armada, Spanish 13, 38
Arms race 184, 198, 240, 241
Armstrong, Neil 96, 263
Attlee, Clement 237
Austerlitz, Battle of 136
Australia 133, 179, 192, 227, 237
Austria 133–6, 183, 187, 188, 194, 201, 206, 219

Baird, John Logie 210
Baldwin, Stanley 209, 213
Begin, Premier 257
Belgium 133, 136, 187, 188, 224, 254
Bell, Henry 103
Berlin 205, 217, 229, 231, 235, 239, 240
Bishops' War 23
Bismarck 183
Blantyre 179, 180
Blitzkrieg 223, 225
Bolshevik 201, 203, 204, 206
Boston Massacre 124, 128
Bothwell Brig, Battle of 32
Brest-Litovsk, Treaty of 207
British Army 32, 53, 56–61, 64, 67, 114, 115, 119–27, 133–7, 139, 143, 144, 150, 171, 184, 185, 187–90, 192, 193, 196, 207, 209, 224–9, 231–4, 259
British Empire and Commonwealth 179, 180, 184, 186, 225, 237, 238, 260, 261
Brougham, Henry 140, 143
Burns, Robert 68, 109
Burt, Captain 62, 63

Cameron of Lochiel 56, 60
Cameronians 32, 45
Canada 70, 117, 119–23, 125, 127, 128, 229, 237
Canals 96, 99–102
Carnegie, Andrew 182, 183

Carron Ironworks 85, 138
Carter, President 257
Chamberlain, Neville 219–21, 225
Charles I 19–28, 33, 130
Charles II 28–30, 33, 39
Charles Edward Stuart, Prince 54–9, 62
Chartists 149–52, 155
Chiang Kai-shek 246, 247
China 218, 242, 245–52
Church of England 9, 12, 20–2
Church of Scotland 9, 12, 20–2, 28, 30
Churchill, Winston 173, 225, 226, 232, 237, 239
Civil War 24–7
Clan system 45, 51, 53, 54, 62–5, 70, 72
Clive, Robert 117, 118
Coal mining 85, 86, 91–5, 138, 144, 163, 164, 183, 209, 210
Coatbridge 85, 105
Cockburn, Lord 104, 143, 148, 160
Cold War 239–44, 253
Colonies 30, 32, 37–43, 114–29
Communism 200, 201, 206–8, 212, 215, 220, 239, 242, 245–52
Concentration camps 215, 217, 229, 230
Conservative Party 163, 209, 237
Cook, Captain 119, 179
Cope, General 56
Cotton industry 83, 84, 89, 93, 160
Covenanters 22–5, 28, 30, 32, 33, 37
Craig, James 109
Crieff 54, 62
Crime and Punishment 11, 12, 16, 19, 21, 25–8, 32, 35, 39, 48, 50, 53, 59, 63, 64, 67, 107, 108, 131–3, 143–5, 150, 153, 154, 156, 160, 161, 198, 200, 201, 211, 215–7, 261
Cromwell, Oliver 24, 25, 29, 30
Culloden, Battle of 58–63, 65, 119
Cumberland, Duke of 57–60
Czechoslovakia 195, 219, 220, 225, 229, 239, 242–4

D Day 229, 232–4
Dale, David 84, 94
Dalrymple, Sir John 45, 46
Dalyell, General 32
Darby, Abraham 85
Darien Scheme 41–4, 48
Defoe, Daniel 43, 49, 50, 106
Divine Right of Kings 9, 10, 19, 20, 44
Domestic System 81–3, 87
Drake, Sir Francis 13, 37
Drovers 54, 62
Duma 201, 203
Dunbar 56, 75
Dunbar, Battle of 29
Dundee 101, 105, 110
Dunfermline 21, 49
Dunkeld 45

Dunkirk 225

East India Company 39, 118
Edinburgh 7, 8, 11, 22, 28–30, 32, 44, 49, 50, 53, 56, 57, 63, 68, 75, 81, 87, 91, 97–101, 105, 106, 108, 109, 112, 113, 126, 131, 133, 140, 143, 147–9, 154, 166–70, 175, 191, 213
Education 8–10, 89, 94, 132, 168, 169, 173, 179, 216, 237
Edward VII 180, 184
Egypt 257
Eisenhower, General 228, 229
El Alamein, Battle of 227
Elizabeth I 8, 9, 13, 19, 37, 39
Elizabeth II 260
European Economic Community 254, 255, 261, 263
Evelyn, John 27, 35, 36

Factory system 84–95, 105, 107, 141, 143, 160, 166, 198
Falkirk 58, 62, 144
Farming 62, 64, 65, 68, 70, 72–8, 80, 138, 141, 198, 202, 203, 245, 248, 249
Fascism 210, 211
Fawkes, Guy 12
Ferdinand, Archduke Franz 188
Fire of London 33, 35, 36
First World War 164, 174, 186–96, 201–3, 206, 208, 210, 211, 214, 220, 223, 225, 236, 237, 254, 256, 263
Five-Year Plans 208, 248
Fletcher, Andrew 41, 49
Fort William 45, 53
France 20, 33, 40, 45, 48, 53–5, 59, 67, 81, 114–23, 125–8, 130–40, 142, 181, 183, 185, 187, 188, 193, 194, 206, 207, 219, 220, 223–5, 229, 250, 254
Franco, General 218
Franco-Prussian War 181, 183, 187
French Revolution 130–40, 159

Gallipoli 192
Gargarin, Yuri 197
General Strike 209, 210, 213
George I 52
George II 57
George III 112, 124, 125, 127, 128, 137, 141
George IV 68, 112, 141
George V 187, 209
Germany 170, 181, 183–94, 196, 199, 201, 203, 205, 206, 210–2, 214–34, 239, 240, 242, 245, 246
Gestapo 216
Glasgow 24, 49, 58, 83, 84, 86, 87, 97, 99, 101, 105–7, 110–3, 133, 143, 146–9, 151, 160, 170, 171, 179, 195
Glencoe massacre 45, 46, 51
Glenfinnan 55

268

Glenshiel, Battle of 53
Glorious Revolution 44
Government and Law 9, 12, 14–26, 29, 30, 33, 35, 44, 48–50, 53, 63, 64, 94, 95, 97, 104, 112, 123, 124, 127, 128, 130–3, 140–5, 147–56, 159–61, 163, 164, 169, 173, 174, 190, 208–10, 223–5, 237, 254, 255, 259–61
Graham, John of Claverhouse 32, 45
Great Exhibition 178
Great Plague 33, 34
Greenock 103, 149
Gunpowder Plot 12, 13
Guthrie, Thomas 168, 169, 175

Haig, Sir Douglas 188
Hampton Court Conference 12
Hardie, Keir 154, 163, 164
Health and Medicine 10, 14, 33, 34, 42, 82, 89, 91–5, 109–12, 166–76, 190, 199, 236, 237, 262
Heriot, George 11, 14
Highland clearances 64–7, 70
Hiroshima 231, 232, 240
Hitler, Adolf 206, 210–2, 214–6, 218–21, 223–5, 228–31, 239, 257
Ho Chi Minh 250
Holland 12, 35, 40, 74, 81, 126, 133, 193, 224, 229, 254
Holyrood Palace 8, 56, 107
Home Front 190, 191, 223–6, 229
Hume, David 109
Hungary 194, 229, 239, 242

India 37, 39, 48, 115, 117, 118, 124, 227, 238
Industrial Revolution 80–95, 99, 104, 107, 116, 117, 133, 141, 147, 178, 198, 263
Inglis, Dr Elsie 154
Inverness 58, 64
Iran 258
Ireland 13, 29, 45, 102, 111, 151, 185, 186, 190, 208, 209, 253, 259, 260
Iron and steel 84, 85, 91, 101, 103, 138, 142, 254
Ironsides 24, 29, 30
Israel 256, 257
Italy 134, 206, 210, 218, 219, 225, 227, 228, 254

Jacobites 44, 45, 52–9, 62
James VI and I 6, 8–14, 19–21, 48
James II 33, 35, 44, 45, 52
Japan 201, 207, 218, 227, 231, 232, 245, 247, 254
Jenner, Edward 82, 171
Jones, Paul 126
Jutland, Battle of 192

Kennedy, President 241
Killiecrankie, Battle of 45, 51
Korea 236, 250

Labour Party 164, 173, 209, 237, 255
Laud, Archbishop William 20, 21
League of Nations 195, 211, 218, 236
Lenin 200, 201, 203, 204, 207, 246
Liberal Party 163, 164, 173, 175, 185, 209
Lincoln, President 182, 183
Linlithgow 8, 101
Lister, Joseph 170, 171
Liverpool, Lord 140, 146
Livingstone, Dr David 179, 180
Lloyd George, David 173, 174, 193, 208
London 8–11, 14, 19, 24, 33, 35, 48, 57, 62, 74, 97, 98, 102, 106, 123, 140, 144, 150,
153, 162, 163, 171, 178, 191, 213, 217, 225, 229, 261
Long Parliament 23
Louis XVI 130–2, 138, 181
Luddites 143, 160

Macadam, John 98
Macdonald, Flora 59, 127
Macdonald, Ramsay 164, 209
Manchester 57, 99, 144, 146, 147
Mao Tse-tung 246–52
Mar, Earl of 52, 53
Marlborough, Duke of 114
Marne, Battle of the 188
Marston Moor, Battle of 24
Marx, Karl 200, 246
Mary, Queen of Scots 2, 4, 8, 26
'Mein Kampf' 211, 215
Melville, Andrew 3, 9
Middle East 192, 194, 236, 256, 257
Monck, General 30
Mons, Battle of 188
Montcalm, General 119, 121
Montgomery, General 227
Montrose, Marquis of 24, 25, 28
Moore, Sir John 137
Moray, Regent 8
Moscow 136, 198, 206, 220, 227, 242
Mugabe, Robert 261
Muir, Thomas 133
Mull, Isle of 65, 68, 70
Munich Conference 219–21
Murray, Lord George 58
Mussolini, Benito 210, 218, 225, 228, 231, 239

Napier, John 10
Napoleon 133, 134, 136–40, 181
Napoleon III 181
National Covenant 22, 23, 28
NATO 240
Navvies 101, 102
Nazism 210, 211, 214–21, 223–32, 239
Nelson 134, 135
New Lanark 84, 93, 94, 161
New Zealand 179, 192
Nicholas II 198, 199, 201–4, 207
Nightingale, Florence 171
Nixon, President 251
Nuclear weapons 198, 231, 232, 240, 241, 249

Oil 255–8, 262
Old Pretender 52, 53
Owen, Robert 84, 93, 94, 161

Paisley 105, 149
Pankhurst, Mrs Emmeline 152, 156
Paris 130, 132, 181, 188, 251
Park, Mungo 179
Parliament of England 12, 14, 17, 19–21, 23–6, 28, 30, 33, 34, 44, 48
Parliament of Scotland (The Three Estates) 9, 12, 18–20, 22, 41, 44, 48–50, 97
Parliament of the United Kingdom 94, 95, 97, 104, 124, 128, 131, 140, 143, 147–56, 163, 164, 169, 173–5
Passchendaele, Battle of 192
Pasteur, Louis 170, 171
Paterson, William 41, 43
Pearl Harbour 227
Peel, Sir Robert 148, 151
Pepys, Samuel 3
Perth 52, 105, 110

Peterloo 144–6, 148
Petrograd 202–4, 206
Philiphaugh, Battle of 25
Pilgrim Fathers 39, 40
Pitt, William the Elder 119
Plassey, Battle of 118
Poland 194, 220, 223, 239, 242
Porteous, Captain 107, 108
Portugal 40, 136
Prestonpans, Battle of 56, 57
Princip, Gavrilo 188
Prussia 115, 133, 135–7, 181, 183, 220
Puritans 12, 21, 24, 30, 39, 128

Quebec 119–22, 135, 179

Radical 133, 140, 144–6
Raeburn, Henry 109
Railways 96, 97, 100–2, 104
Rasputin, Gregory 199, 202
Renfrew 84, 147
Restoration 30, 41
Rhodesia 238, 260, 261
Roman Catholic 9, 12, 21, 22, 24, 29, 33, 35, 39, 44, 48, 53, 128, 185
Rosetta Stone 4
Rowntree, Seebohm 171, 172, 175
Royal Air Force 225–9, 233
Royal Navy 21, 33, 67, 119, 120, 127, 134, 135, 137, 138, 184, 186, 192, 225, 227, 229
Rullion Green, Battle of 32
Russia 32, 135, 136, 185, 187, 188, 192–4, 197–204, 206–8, 220, 227–9, 231, 232, 235, 239–46, 248, 249, 251, 252

Sadat, President 257
Sarajevo 188
Saratoga 126
Second World War 220, 223–37, 239, 247, 254, 256, 260, 263
Selkirk 25, 97, 179
Selkirk, Alexander 43
Seven Years' War 114, 117–23
Shaftesbury, Lord 94, 95
Shakespeare, William 11
Sharp, Archbishop 32
Sheriffmuir, Battle of 53
Simpson, Dr James 170
Sinclair, Sir John 77, 80
Skye, Isle of 59, 65, 68
Slavery 40, 150, 182
Smith, Adam 109
Smith, Ian 260, 261
Smith, Captain John 39
Solemn League and Covenant 24
Somme, Battle of the 188, 189, 206
South Africa 237, 238, 261
Spain 13, 14, 19, 20, 30, 37, 40, 42, 43, 53, 114, 115, 126, 135, 136, 182, 218
St Helena 137, 181
Stalin 201, 208, 220, 239
Stalingrad, Battle of 227, 228
Statistical Accounts 77, 87
Stephenson, George 101
SALT 241
Strathnaver 67, 70
Suffragettes 152–6, 190
Symington, William 103

Tanks 189, 190, 196, 223, 225, 227, 240
Telford, Thomas 68, 98, 99
Thatcher, Mrs Margaret 155
Third World 245, 255
Tito, Marshal 239

Tobacco Lords   83, 107
Tobermory   13, 67
Tolpuddle Martyrs   161
Tories   33, 140, 148, 163
Trade   11, 17, 37, 39–43, 46, 48, 50, 52, 81,
   83, 84, 105–7, 114–7, 122, 124, 136, 138,
   142, 178–80, 184, 208, 226, 227, 239, 251,
   254, 255
Trade unions   91, 141, 157–65, 190, 198,
   209, 210, 213, 216, 253
Trafalgar, Battle of   135
Tranent   100, 143, 144
Transport and Travel   10, 37, 39–43, 53, 54,
   67–9, 74, 75, 96–104, 117, 119, 120, 179,
   180, 182, 188, 197, 216, 225, 229, 233, 234,
   241, 246, 247, 252, 253, 262, 263
Trench warfare   188–90, 192, 193, 196, 223
Trotsky   201, 207, 208
Turnpike Trust   97, 98

U-boats   192, 218, 226, 227, 229
Union, Act of   44–52, 63, 74, 81, 83–5,
   105–7
United Nations   236, 242, 243, 251, 257,
   261, 263

Versailles, Treaty of   193–6, 206, 207, 211,
   214, 219
Victoria   68, 69, 141, 169, 178, 179, 183,
   199, 209
Vietnam   250, 251

Wade, General   53, 54, 57, 58, 62, 97
Wall Street Crash   212, 214
Warsaw Pact   240, 244
Washington, George   119, 125–8
Waterloo, Battle of   115, 136, 137, 139, 140,
   144, 181
Watt, James   84

Welfare State   111, 143, 159, 164, 173–5,
   237
Wellington, Duke of   136, 137, 139, 140,
   150
Whigs   33, 140, 141, 149, 163
Wilberforce, William   150
William II, Kaiser   183, 184, 187, 193, 206
William IV   141
William of Orange   35, 44–6
Wilson, Harold   255
Wilson, President   193, 195, 211
Witchcraft   10
Wolfe, General James   119–21, 126, 135
Worcester, Battle of   29
Wright, Orville   97

Yorktown, Battle of   127
Yugoslavia   194, 229, 239